Seeing Things
Their Way

Seeing Things Their Way

INTELLECTUAL HISTORY AND THE RETURN OF RELIGION

EDITED BY
Alister Chapman, John Coffey,
and Brad S. Gregory

UNIVERSITY OF NOTRE DAME PRESS NOTRE DAME, INDIANA

Copyright © 2009 by University of Notre Dame
Notre Dame, Indiana 46556
www.undpress.nd.edu
All Rights Reserved

Manufactured in the United States of America

Library of Congress Cataloging-in-Publication Data

Seeing things their way : intellectual history and the return of religion /
edited by Alister Chapman, John Coffey, and Brad S. Gregory.
    p.   cm.
Includes index.
ISBN-13: 978-0-268-02298-3 (pbk. : alk. paper)
ISBN-10: 0-268-02298-4 (pbk. : alk. paper)
1. Religion—History. 2. Intellectual life—History.   I. Chapman, Alister.
II. Coffey, John, 1969–   III. Gregory, Brad S. (Brad Stephan), 1963–
BL237.S44   2009
200.9—dc22

                                                    2009027700

∞ *The paper in this book meets the guidelines for permanence and durability of the Committee on Production Guidelines for Book Longevity of the Council on Library Resources.*

Contents

Acknowledgments vii

1 Introduction: Intellectual History and the Return of Religion   1
JOHN COFFEY AND ALISTER CHAPMAN

2 Can We "See Things Their Way"? Should We Try?   24
BRAD S. GREGORY

3 Quentin Skinner and the Religious Dimension of Early Modern Political Thought   46
JOHN COFFEY

4 "Sie Stinken Beide," or How to Use Medieval Christian-Jewish Disputational Material   75
ANNA SAPIR ABULAFIA

5 Anti-Semitism, Philo-Semitism, Apocalypticism, and Millenarianism in Early Modern Europe: A Case Study and Some Methodological Reflections   91
HOWARD HOTSON

6 Reflections on Persistent Whiggism and Its Antidotes in the Study of Sixteenth- and Seventeenth-century Intellectual History   134
RICHARD A. MULLER

7   Scholasticism Revisited: Methodological Reflections on
    the Study of Seventeenth-century Reformed Thought   154
    WILLEM J. VAN ASSELT

8   The Changing Shape of Religious Ideas in
    Enlightened England   175
    JAMES E. BRADLEY

9   British Methodological Pointers for Writing a History
    of Theology in America   202
    MARK A. NOLL

10 Intellectual History and Religion in Modern Britain   226
    ALISTER CHAPMAN

11 Response: The History of Ideas and the Study
    of Religion   240
    DAVID W. BEBBINGTON

    Contributors   258

    Index   261

Acknowledgments

The editors would like to thank the managers of the George Macaulay Trevelyan Fund of Cambridge University for their financial support of this project; Eugenio Biagini, Richard Rex, Johathan Riley-Smith, Reiner Smolinski, and Carl Trueman for their critical and constructive feedback on earlier versions of these chapters; Barbara Hanrahan at the University of Notre Dame Press for patiently steering this book to publication; and Grace Sollé for her editorial assistance.

Alister Chapman, *Westmont College*
John Coffey, *University of Leicester*
Brad S. Gregory, *University of Notre Dame*

Introduction: Intellectual History and the Return of Religion

JOHN COFFEY AND ALISTER CHAPMAN

Religious history and intellectual history are two of the most dynamic fields of contemporary historical inquiry. Yet historians of ideas and historians of religion often plough separate furrows, paying little attention to each other's work. This book calls for a more fruitful interaction between the two fields. It urges intellectual historians to explore the religious dimension of ideas and commends the methods of intellectual history to historians of religion. It also seeks to model good practice and encourage further research. The introduction locates our project in relation to contemporary historiography, and outlines the opportunities and pitfalls that lie before students of religious thought.

THE PRIORITIES OF INTELLECTUAL HISTORY

Seeing Things Their Way is a title taken from Quentin Skinner, one of the leading figures in the "Cambridge School" of intellectual historians.[1] Alongside J. G. A. Pocock and John Dunn, Skinner carved out his own methodology in opposition to dominant rival schools in the 1960s.[2] On the one hand, there was the materialist reductionism of Marxist and Namierite historians, who saw politics in terms of a struggle for power between different classes or interests, and reduced ideas to "ideology."

On the other hand, there were the rather ahistorical accounts of philosophers such as Leo Strauss and Arthur Lovejoy, who wrote the history of abstract "ideas," and discussed leading political theorists with little reference to their contexts, placing them in conversation with other "great thinkers" across the centuries.

The Cambridge School aimed to plot a course between the materialists and the idealists. Drawing on the speech-act theory of J. L. Austin and John Searle, Skinner argued that we should identify the precise intellectual and political contexts of the texts we are studying, in order to ascertain what their authors *meant* and what they were *doing*. His advice to his fellow intellectual historians is neatly summarized in the following quotation.

> [W]e need to make it one of our principal tasks to situate the texts we study within such intellectual contexts as enable us to make sense of what their authors were doing in writing them. My aspiration is not of course to enter into the thought-processes of long-dead thinkers; it is simply to use the ordinary techniques of historical enquiry to grasp their concepts, to follow their distinctions, to appreciate their beliefs and, so far as possible, to see things their way.[3]

The attraction of this method is that it offers "a more historically-minded approach to the history of ideas," encouraging us to take our subjects seriously on their own terms.[4] Instead of imposing modern (or postmodern) categories upon past agents, we attend carefully to the concepts and language(s) that were available to them. Instead of dismissing the beliefs of our subjects as "irrational," "we must begin by trying to make the agents who accepted [those beliefs] appear as rational as possible," however bizarre their beliefs may seem to us.[5] Instead of setting out to write a normative history of ideas as philosophers or theologians might do, we will concentrate on trying to understand our subjects' points of view.

Skinner's approach has proved highly successful and influential in rejuvenating the history of political thought. Yet in one important respect, it perhaps fails to apply its own agenda consistently. As John Coffey observes in his chapter on Skinner, the Cambridge historian has developed a distinctly secular vision of early modern political thought. Skinner is acutely sensitive to the classical sources of sixteenth- and seventeenth-century political ideas, but often overlooks the biblical citations and religious presuppositions in early modern texts. Although his *Foundations of Modern Political Thought* (1978) undermined one aspect of Whig history by highlighting the medieval (and hence Catholic) roots of early modern ideas, it still equated the "modern" with the "secular," and told a somewhat Whiggish story of how the first "modern" theories emerged.[6] His subsequent work, for all its brilliance, displays little interest in the religious dimension of early modern political thought, and it is significant that he has focussed his energies on Machiavelli and Hobbes, two notoriously "irreligious" thinkers.

Many intellectual historians who came of age in the middle of the twentieth century were influenced by a sociological tradition which assumed—following Marx, Durkheim, and Weber—a sharp division between traditional and modern societies. One of the key features of modernization, according to such theorists, was the decline of religion, magic, and superstition, and the rise of reason, science, and skepticism. Modernization and secularization marched hand in hand. Historians who bought into this secularizing teleology were inclined to write history as a story of progress in which reason and science inexorably displaced faith and dogma. Two of the main tasks of intellectual historians were to trace the development of "the modern mind" and to identify the origins of (for example) "the modern idea of the state." Such a present-centered approach tended to downgrade religious beliefs, for there seemed little point in studying ideas that were doomed to decline and of little relevance to the modern world. Modernization theory (and the classic secularization thesis that arose with it) enjoyed its heyday in the 1950s and 1960s, and its impact can still be detected.

One consequence of its influence is that intellectual historians have traditionally assigned a relatively low priority to the history of theology and religious ideas. A survey of the writing of early modern intellectual history from 1945 to 1995 has sections on the history of science, the history of political thought, the history of the book, the history of scholarship, and the new cultural history, but no equivalent section on the history of religious ideas.[7] Donald Kelley has calculated that of eight hundred submitted and tabulated papers for the *Journal of the History of Ideas,* 25 percent were devoted to philosophy, 18 percent to political thought, 16 percent to literature, 12 percent to science, and a mere 8 percent to religion. No doubt this is partly because 46 percent of those papers were on the (relatively) secularized nineteenth and twentieth centuries, and partly because historians of religious ideas often submit their work to journals of religious history or theology.[8] But the fact that philosophy, political thought, literature, and science all ranked higher than religion reveals much about the priorities of twentieth-century intellectual historians. Even in the twenty-first century, the history of religious thought can still be marginalized. A recent guide to the discipline of intellectual history has essays on its relationship to the history of art, political thought, science, social and cultural history, and feminism, but none specifically devoted to religion. The introduction—by a distinguished historian of eighteenth-century Anglican thought—explains that "a separate chapter on theology" was not required because the book includes a chapter on medieval studies. As a rationale, this is problematic. For by omitting a broader thematic treatment of religious ideas, the book lends support to the lingering assumption that getting to grips with theology is essential for medievalists but optional for historians of other periods.[9]

This book sets out to reorder the priorities of intellectual historians by demonstrating the importance and the fruitfulness of the study of religious ideas. Our point is not that religious ideas be granted special status as the primary category of intellectual history (though in the concluding essay to this volume, David Bebbington does make a case for their priority). Rather, we argue that religious thought be afforded the same respect, and be studied in the same manner, as scientific or political thought. We see no reason why the methodology that Skinner and others have applied to political ideas should not be applied to religious ideas too.

Yet we also want to stress that "religious ideas" are not simply a separate area of intellectual history, one that can be bracketed off and left to a specialist subgroup. Because religion often plays such an important role in the construction of meaning, it is anything but a hermetically sealed compartment—its influence tends to leak into other areas of intellectual life, coloring other realms of discourse. The study of religious ideas does not stop with the study of "religious texts." The *Short-Title Catalogue* of British books published between 1475 and 1640 identifies "religious books" as "the single most important component of the publishing trade, comprising around half the total output of the industry." But as Patrick Collinson observes, identifying a category of "religious books" can be rather misleading: "For the modern world, the term 'religion' marks off a more or less discrete area of life, but this is anachronistic for the [early modern] period under review, in which the commodity which we might want to distinguish as 'religion' permeated much, if not all, of what is now secularized." Thus lists of "religious" titles do not include almanacs, medical treatises, and cookbooks, even though "all [were] saturated with pious vocabulary."[10] For this reason, religious ideas should be on the radar of all historians, not merely dedicated specialists. If historians of political thought, for example, can explore the biblical and theological dimensions of political argument, they will produce more rounded expositions of their key texts. Only when religion is reinserted into our accounts will we be able to deliver a richer and more complete intellectual history.

THE RETURN OF RELIGION

In making this case, we are conscious of reinforcing a growing trend, for there are many signs of a resurgence of interest in religion among historians. As long ago as 1964 the *American Historical Review* published an article by Henry F. May which began: "For the study and understanding of American culture, the recovery of American religious history may well be the most important achievement of the last thirty years. A vast and crucial area of American experience has been rescued from neglect and misunderstanding."[11] May was writing in the wake of the great Harvard historian, Perry Miller, who did so much to rehabilitate the New England Puritans of the colonial period through a meticulous reconstruction of their religious beliefs.[12]

Yet despite the Millers and the Mays, many historians in the 1960s were inclined to leave religion to ecclesiastical historians. When the *Times Literary Supplement* produced three issues on "new ways in history" in 1966, none of the essays (by such luminaries as Keith Thomas,

Eric Hobsbawm, and E. P. Thompson) had anything to say about religious history.[13] This was a self-confidently secular age, and as the sea of faith receded, historians seemed likely to be less and less preoccupied with religion. Since Western man was in the final stages of a longstanding process of secularization, historians needed to explain religion in terms of some more fundamental and enduring aspect of human society. The eminent sociologist Peter Berger predicted in 1968 that "by the twenty-first century, religious believers are likely to be found only in small sects, huddled together to resist a worldwide secular culture."[14]

Like so many others in the 1960s, Berger failed to foresee the dramatic developments of the late twentieth century: the Iranian Revolution and the rise of political Islam, the emergence of the religious right in the United States, the explosive global growth of Pentecostalism, the role of John Paul II and the churches in the collapse of Eastern Bloc Communism, and the events of 9/11. These developments have proved fatal to the belief that religion was doomed to die a lingering death. In 1999, Berger himself edited a volume entitled *The Desecularization of the World*, in which he recanted his earlier opinion: "the assumption that we live in a secularized world is false: the world today, with some exceptions . . . is as furiously religious as it ever was, and in some places more so than ever."[15] Historians, whose work so often reflects contemporary preoccupations, increasingly recognized religious belief as a potent independent variable, an enduring factor in human affairs that needs to be understood in its own right. As a result, the drive to recover the religious dimension of the past has gathered momentum.

The resurgence of religion in the contemporary world was not the only factor leading to a revival of interest in the history of religious belief. Whilst historians of the 1960s had confidently predicted the rise of "cliometrics" and the triumph of social and economic history, the 1970s saw the emergence of the new cultural history. Under the influence of anthropologists like Clifford Geertz, historians became more alert to the role of religion in constructing meaning. Studies of ritual and the history of mentalities proliferated. As Keith Thomas has recently observed, social and cultural anthropology taught historians to conceive of their subject as a "kind of retrospective ethnography" and encouraged them to understand "the native point of view":

Instead of trying to classify and order human experience from the outside, as if historical actors were butterflies, and historians entomologists, much imaginative effort has gone into the re-creation of the way things appeared to people at the time. This shift from the etic to the emic, as the linguists would call it, involves an enhanced concern with the meaning of events for those who participated in them, and a new respect for what people in the past thought and felt. Back in the 1950s, it was common to disparage ideas as mere rationalizations of self-interest. Today, even the hardest-nosed historians seek to recapture the vocabulary, categories and subjective experience of the historical actors, rather than anachronistically viewing their behaviour through modern spectacles.[16]

A prime example of this shift can be seen in the historiography of the French Wars of Religion. In the heyday of Marxian socioeconomic explanation, historians often discounted the religious factor, claiming that the "ideology" of the Huguenots and the Catholic League was a cloak for material or political interests, and that the causes of the conflict were fundamentally secular. But the work of cultural and intellectual historians like Natalie Davis and Denis Crouzet has transformed the historiography, "putting religion back into the wars of religion."[17]

The same trend can be seen in many other fields. In the history of political thought, the methodology of the Cambridge School has fostered a serious exploration of the religious elements in early modern political argument. The concern to avoid anachronism, and to situate thinkers within their own intellectual contexts, has led to studies of their religious environment and of the religious concepts available to them. By promoting a sharper sense of the sheer difference of the past, Skinner's methodological prescriptions have encouraged a desecularization of the history of political thought. As early as 1969, John Dunn's influential study of John Locke's political thought challenged anachronistic secular interpretations of the philosopher by arguing that the *Two Treatises of Government* was "saturated with Christian assumptions."[18] John Pocock too has been noticeably alive to the significance of religious ideas, most recently in his multivolume work on Edward Gibbon.[19] Some of Skinner's own students have contributed to the recovery of the religious dimension of early modern political thought. Richard Tuck has examined the "Christian atheism" and civil religion of Thomas Hobbes, and Mark Goldie has illuminated the connections between religious and political ideas in a series of groundbreaking essays.[20] Scholars increasingly recognize that political ideas were often inextricably bound up with religious ones.

The return of religion can also be seen in the field of Enlightenment studies. As James Bradley's essay in this volume demonstrates, historians have become increasingly dissatisfied with the assumption that the Enlightenment was (by definition) aggressively secularist. England's "moderate Enlightenment" was not hostile to religious belief, and was partly shaped by Anglican clergy and Nonconformist divines. Bradley argues that much that counted as "enlightened" in eighteenth-century England was not particularly heterodox either. Latitudinarian clergy and leading literary figures were more orthodox than has traditionally been recognized, while Evangelicals, Roman Catholics, and high-church Anglicans were more "enlightened." Studies of the Scottish Enlightenment and the American Enlightenment paint a broadly similar picture.[21]

In parts of continental Europe, there is a stronger case for seeing the Enlightenment (in Peter Gay's phrase) as "the rise of modern paganism,"[22] but even here recent scholarship has undermined old certainties, emphasising the varieties of Enlightenment. The French Enlightenment no longer dominates the stage in the way it once did, and we have become used to thinking of "the Enlightenment in national context."[23] As Dorinda Outram explains, "the Enlightenment produced a wide variety of responses to organised religion, ranging all the way from violent Voltairean hostility to religion, through to attempts to bolster orthodox belief by demonstrating its rationality and accordance with natural law."[24] Jonathan Israel has recently excavated a secular(ist) "Radical Enlightenment," originating in the Netherlands with Benedict Spinoza and reaching its apogee with Denis Diderot and other participants in the French High Enlightenment. But Israel's grand survey actually underlines the tenacity of religious belief in the Age of Reason, for his Radical Enlightenment is battling against two much larger movements—the Counter-Enlightenment and the Moderate Enlightenment. The moderate mainstream of Enlightenment thought is depicted as hopelessly compromised, and a host of major Enlightenment figures—including Locke and Voltaire—are chided for being too friendly towards religion (whether Christian or Deist).[25] The Enlightenment is not what it used to be.[26]

The history of science has experienced a similar reversal. Late nineteenth-century histories of the purported conflict between science and religion have now been largely discredited, and replaced by far more subtle studies of the complex and often fertile interplay between theology and science.[27] The "warfare model" still has considerable popular appeal, but it flies in the face of a generation of scholarship. Nowhere is the renewed interest in the relationship between science and religion more evident than in studies of Isaac Newton. The fact that one of the greatest early modern "scientists" penned over a million words on alchemy and around two and a half million on theology hardly fits with the picture of a running battle between heroic rationalists and obscurantist believers.[28] Historians of the Scientific Revolution, irrespective of their own beliefs, have seen the need to get religion.

The same reassessment of the role of religion can be seen in the historiography of the nineteenth century. Secularization was occurring, but it was battling against powerful currents of religious revitalization.[29] In his masterly survey of Britain in the mid-nineteenth century, Theodore Hoppen declares that "never was Britain more religious than in the Victorian age."[30] Historians of the period are increasingly convinced that they must reckon with the force of religious belief more seriously than has been their custom. Chris Bayly summarizes the emerging consensus in his compelling revisionist study of *The Birth of the Modern World*:

> Historians of ideas have come to realize in the last generation how deeply religion influenced the supposedly secular ideologies and sciences of the nineteenth century. For instance, early nineteenth-century economics and demography in Protestant nations were influenced by the idea that periodic economic downfalls were a sign of God's punishment, for which the peoples had to atone. Much liberal, and even socialist, thought continued to reflect deep-rooted ideas about justice and community which were of Christian origin.

When Hindus, Muslims and Buddhists adapted such ideas to their own circumstances, they also tinctured them with religious sensibilities. The social thought of non-Western elites was everywhere suffused with religious ideas about good governance and divine justice. So it was with science. Christian missionaries were pioneers of scientific collection and categorization, especially in Africa and the Pacific, as they sought to display God's bounty to humankind through his creation. The Christian squabble with Darwin has obscured the modus vivendi to which religious people and scientists generally subscribed.[31]

The twentieth century, of course, may be a different matter—at least for Europe and North America. In the United States, for example, the early twentieth century witnessed a dramatic secularization of public life and higher education.[32] By the 1970s, religious titles accounted for just over 5 percent of books published in the United States, a far cry from the days when they dominated the market.[33] In Western Europe, secularization went further still. Alister Chapman's essay in this volume explores the challenges this presents to the historian of twentieth-century religious ideas, who is likely to feel far more marginalized than her early modern or medieval counterparts. He argues that the "dominant master narrative" of secularization leads historians to overlook "the ongoing importance of religion in the United Kingdom," from "the confessional dimension of Northern Irish politics, to the inspiration provided by Christian belief for politicians such as Clement Attlee and Tony Blair." Although "organized religion is less influential in Britain today than it was a century ago," "diminished importance does not mean no importance; marginality does not equal irrelevance."[34]

There are strong reasons to think that the influence of religious belief may be waxing rather than waning in the twenty-first century. Even in secularized Europe, the rise of Islam has forced religious beliefs back onto the intellectual agenda. The philosopher John Gray, a secular thinker himself, argues that the brief era when religious ideas were eclipsed is drawing to a close:

> The return of religion as a pivotal factor in politics and war is one of the defining features of the age, and it is time Paine, Marx and other

secular prophets were gently shelved in the stacks. The writings of these Enlightenment savants have stirred events for a very brief period in history, now clearly coming to an end. . . . [T]he books that have most formed the past, and which are sure also to shape the future, are the central texts of the world religions.[35]

Gray underestimates the resilience of secular Enlightenment thought, a resilience highlighted by the rise of "the new atheists." But there is good reason to think that the history of religious ideas is likely to acquire an increasingly high profile within the academy. Indeed, there are already clear signs that intellectual historians are waking up to the realization that religious belief is a powerful (and persistent) feature of human societies, and that studying the history of religious ideas is of greater importance than was once assumed to be the case. In 2005, the International Society of Intellectual Historians held a conference entitled "Rethinking Secularization."[36] The days when the history of religious ideas could be quietly downgraded are drawing to a close.

THE PROBLEM OF REDUCTIONISM

If the prospects for the history of religious ideas look good, there are still some pitfalls in the road ahead. Historians of religious ideas face a dilemma similar to that first confronted by Skinner and his colleagues. Like the Cambridge School, we need to find a middle way between two forms of reductionism: materialist and idealist.

The challenge of *materialist* reductionism is well known. Following in the footsteps of Feuerbach, Marx, Freud, and Durkheim, many historians have assumed that one can (and should) explain religious belief in terms of something more permanent and fundamental—economic interests, repressed sexuality, the need for communal integration. A famous example is provided by E. P. Thompson's classic work, *The Making of the English Working Class,* which subjected Methodist religion to an aggressive Marxist-Freudian critique.[37] If confidence in such reductionist theories has declined, some historians are still inclined to explain religious beliefs as a mask for more fundamental social, economic, or political interests, or as a reflection of psychological needs. Such approaches are deeply problematic because they allow historians to ignore what their subjects actually say. People in the past are portrayed in ways that they would have found seriously deficient or even unrecognizable. Confident in the assumption that he understands his subjects better than they do themselves, the historian feels no need to do the hard work of learning their language, grasping their concepts, and describing their worldview—their religion, after all, is epiphenomenal. As Durkheim once put it: "[Religion] does not know itself. It neither knows what it is made of, nor what need it satisfies."[38]

The challenge presented by reductionist accounts of religious belief is explored in Brad Gregory's study in this volume of the sixteenth-century Mennonite Jacob de Roore. Gregory takes aim at historians who rely on the "grand, explanatory theories of religion" developed by the founding fathers of modern social theory. According to these thinkers (and later reductionists) "precisely the point of studying religion is to show that it is not what its protagonists claim that it is." Religion may well be worthy of close attention, but it must be explained in secular, nonreligious terms. Gregory argues that reductionist theories cannot adequately account for the beliefs or behavior of someone like Jacob de Roore, who was executed for refusing to recant his Mennonite convictions. Rather than resorting to problematic social, psychological, or anthropological theories of religion, our objective as historians should be "to understand and present something of Jacob de Roore's ideas in such a manner that he would recognize them as his own." Gregory recognizes the enormous cultural distance that separates the historian from people like de Roore but maintains the worthiness of this goal. The challenges we face do not justify recourse to reductionist theories.

In a similar fashion, Anna Sapir Abulafia's study of medieval Christian-Jewish disputational material argues against "imposing a modern secular paradigm on medieval religious thinking." She takes issue with Gavin Langmuir's influential work on anti-Semitism, which identifies certain elements of medieval thought as "nonrational" or "irrational." In her view, Langmuir's approach "robs twelfth-century theological activity of one of its main hallmarks, that of *ratio* or reason." What contemporaries regarded as highly rational explorations of the virgin birth or the incarnation "would have to be classified as the suppression of rational doubt by nonrational conclusions." Abulafia, by contrast, wants to take the arguments of medieval scholars seriously according to "their own terms of reference," rather than pronouncing on their rational status from the perspective of modern secularism. She shares Quentin Skinner's belief that historians of ideas should try as far as possible "to vindicate the rationality of our ancestors," even when their ideas seem alien or bizarre.

Howard Hotson's major essay explains how Protestant millenarianism undermined theological anti-Semitism of the kind discussed by Abulafia. Additionally, Hotson critiques secular reductionism. As he points out, historians have often worked with a decidedly nontheological definition of millenarianism, one that would not have been recognized by their subjects. Norman Cohn's *Pursuit of the Millennium* was particularly influential in defining millenarianism in sociological terms as the creed of "rootless and desperate men" who anticipated an apocalyptic revolution and were characterized by genocidal fervor and anti-Semitism.[39] As Hotson points out, a more precise theological definition of millenarianism leads to a radically different view. If millenarianism is strictly defined (in theological terms) as the expectation of an extended future period of greatly enhanced felicity for the church on earth, its great age is not the medieval but the early modern era, and it is strongly associated not with anti-Semitism but with philo-Semitism. The dominant sociological model has obscured these realities and distorted our understanding of the history of millenarianism in quite fundamental ways.

If the phenomenon of materialist reductionism is well known, the danger of *idealist* reductionism may be less familiar. The idealists typically ignore all material considerations, reducing their problem to abstract intellectual terms and (in practice) generally assessing their subjects from an anachronistic perspective. In the field of religious ideas, most of the idealists are not old-fashioned "historians of ideas" like Lovejoy or Strauss, nor are they the "internalists" who once dominated the history of science: they are the even more old-fashioned confessional theologians and church historians. In the past, scholars working within jealously guarded confessional traditions have often failed to engage fully with previous religious beliefs, not because they do not take theology seriously but because they take *their own* theology so seriously that they judge all other theologies in the light of it.

This form of reductionism can usefully be divided into two camps. In the one group are those historians of theology who fail to engage historically even with the fountainheads of their own tradition because they view them from the perspective of more recent theology. The flaws of this approach as it has been applied to the Reformed tradition are ably exposed in the essays in this volume by Richard Muller and Willem van Asselt. As they point out, historians of theological ideas have often imposed the categories of modern theology onto early modern theologians, especially in viewing Calvin and others through a grid devised by Karl Barth. Muller critiques this "wildly anachronistic" approach to the history of theology, which involves "the consistent importation of twentieth-century theological jargon to the task of analysis." Moreover, he observes that historians of the Reformed tradition who have interpreted Calvin in Barthian terms (rather than sixteenth-century terms) have gone on to condemn later "Calvinists" for departing from his doctrine. As van Asselt shows, that approach has been challenged in recent years by a far more historically minded methodology, one that is much more subtle and complex in its treatment of scholasticism and humanism, continuity and change. The new scholarship examines the Reformed scholastics on their own terms and explains them by reference to their own theological context, rather than chiding them for failing to parrot Calvin. The older scholarship was more theological (and prescriptive) than historical (or descriptive). Whilst it took theological content seriously, it tended to assimilate early modern theology to modern categories, and was as keen to censure as to explain. The result was a severely reductionist paradigm ("Calvin versus the Calvinists") that failed to do justice to complex phenomena.

A rather different form of theological reductionism is evident, for instance, in much Lutheran historiography. Between the wars, Lutheran scholarship removed the Kantian lenses which had distorted previous accounts of Luther in much the same way that Barthian preconceptions still distort Calvin. The result was a "Lutheran renaissance" that (after some fateful deviations under National Socialism) has applied the most scrupulous historical study to every aspect of Luther himself, including the most problematic ones.[40] But this singular revival of appreciation for Luther has threatened to replace one form of anachronism with an equal and opposite one. The attention lavished upon Luther has distracted generations of German historians of theology from broader aspects of their subject while strongly inclining them to judge all subsequent theological developments within German Protestantism from the privileged standpoint of this one individual: to deplore all meaningful developments within the Lutheran tradition as debasements of the great Reformer's message, and to recoil from the more radical views that proliferated outside confessional Lutheranism with the same repugnance that Luther reserved for the "Schwärmer" of his own day. Here too, however, there are signs of change. Luther's lieutenant, Philipp Melanchthon—long reviled as a virtual traitor to the cause of true Lutheranism—has experienced a remarkable renaissance of his own in recent years.[41] The religious revival in the decades around 1700 known as "Pietism" has likewise attracted a fresh wave of systematic and sympathetic study from within the Lutheran theological community.[42] In German historical faculties as well, the "confessionalization thesis" has directed unprecedented attention to the roles of religion in society and politics in the post-Reformation period.[43] Yet in many respects the theological reductionists have done more damage to a balanced appreciation of the religious thought of this period than their materialist opponents. The richest survey of nonconfessional religious thought in post-Reformation Germany, in any case, has been written, not by a west German historian of theology, but by an east German historian of philosophy—one of the few Marxist professors to survive the collapse of the Berlin Wall with his academic reputation intact.[44]

Against these varieties of materialist and idealist reductionism, this volume advocates and exemplifies a middle way. It insists that religious ideas are not more or less intrinsically intelligible than political or philosophical ideas; that religious ideas are at least as important in understanding the general course of history and the texture of past societies as political or philosophical ideas; and that religious ideas (like political, philosophical, or scientific ideas) need to be understood first and foremost in their owns terms—not in terms of some competing set of religious ideas, nor in terms of some anachronistic standpoint.

In short, we share Skinner's conviction that the historian's principal obligation is to do everything possible to see things their way—to understand past agents on their own terms in their own contexts, rather than framing the ideas of the past in familiar modern (or postmodern) categories. Instead of determining what is "rational" or "nonrational" about the discourse of medieval theologians, we should examine their own concepts of reason. Rather than defining "millenarianism" sociologically, we should work with early modern theological definitions. We should depend less on Marx and Freud (or Barth) and rely more on the contemporary sources and authorities available to our subjects. As Muller and van Asselt advise, we should make far more use of contemporary dictionaries in order to understand the conceptual world of early modern philosophers and theologians. In short, intellectual historians should try to be less "present-minded" and work harder to master the languages and vocabulary of the past.

Neither Skinner nor any of the contributors here are suggesting that it is ever possible to get inside another person's head and think precisely as he or she did, but this does not absolve historians from the hard work of seeking to understand others on their own terms. As it relates to religion and intellectual history, seeking to see things their way demands attention to the religious dimensions of people's thought and a refusal to explain away what is religious by reference to what is supposedly more fundamental. And these demands can only be pursued through laborious attention both to the texts themselves and to the variety of intellectual, social, and political contexts in which they were written.

To some, of course, this may savor of naïveté. Much recent methodological work on intellectual history has challenged the very endeavor of attempting to see things their way. Inspired by the work of thinkers such as Jacques Derrida and Roland Barthes, skepticism about the reader's ability to recover authorial intention is now commonplace and has been vigorously articulated by historians such as Dominick LaCapra and David Harlan.[45] But if the challenges of radical epistemological skepticism have had an appropriately chastening effect, they have failed to convince most practising historians.[46] As Brad Gregory observes in the following chapter, "To claim that the ideas of past people cannot in principle be understood is, to understate the matter, a less than promising guideline for historical research." Gregory argues that although by definition "we cannot experience life and think the thoughts of our subjects exactly as they did," we can, given adequate sources and the proper scholarly willingness, acquire an understanding of their beliefs.

It is precisely because of its explanatory power that the contextualist approach to intellectual history deserves serious consideration. By encouraging us to recover the original contexts of our subjects, it enables us to provide convincing historical accounts of their authorial intentions. This approach has proved its value in both the history of political thought and the history of science, and our proposal is that it be consistently applied to another field of human thought. As the essays in this collection show, the new intellectual history can open exciting new perspectives on religious history. Contrary to what its critics allege, it does more than contribute to our knowledge of elite discourse. Brad Gregory's essay on Jacob de Roore reminds us that given adequate sources it is possible to reconstruct the beliefs of relatively modest figures in considerable detail, just as Carlo Ginzburg recovered the unique mental world of the Italian miller Menochio.[47] Richard Muller reminds us that the historian of Reformed theology might draw on the writings of John Bunyan, "a largely untrained, popular writer." Moreover, as this collection illustrates, there is no reason why intellectual historians should restrict themselves to the study of weighty tomes. In the essays that follow, reference is made to sermons, disputations, pamphlets, letters, petitions, committee minutes, devotional writings, and other sources. The tools of intellectual history can be applied to a wide range of texts and a great variety of thinkers.

For some historical purposes, this richly contextualized intellectual history of religious ideas may be an end in itself. In other cases, it will also provide the foundation of a sounder social history of religion and religious ideas (or even provide raw material for philosophers and historical theologians). Whilst most of the essays in this collection focus on the philosophers and intellectual context of ideas, we also recognize the value of exploring the social context. Muller observes that some traditional historians of ideas seemed to assume that "as thoughts emanate from the decontextualized minds of great thinkers, they take on a life of their own and inhabit a realm that subsists independently like a Platonic realm of ideas, dipping down at significant moments to 'influence' actors in the human drama." He believes that intellectual historians should learn from the critique of social history as they study "the statements of living, breathing, eating, drinking, buying, selling, religiously expressive, *thinking* people in a past era." Van Asselt also calls for "fruitful dialogue . . . between students of the history of theology and practitioners of social history." While Howard Hotson insists on the priority of "seeing things their way" by "understanding early modern religious thinkers on their own terms," he rejects the claim that "social-scientific perspectives have no place whatever in a holistic account of millenarianism." The historian of eschatological ideas should *begin* with theological definitions, but she does not need to *end* there.

Two of the essays in this volume place particular emphasis on the need to look beyond the purely intellectual context. James Bradley's study of the anti-subscriptionist movement among eighteenth-century Nonconformists challenges the received wisdom that opposition to signing orthodox creeds was largely driven by heterodox ideas. Instead, he emphasizes the "social location and the self-interest of minority groups," showing that many orthodox ministers opposed subscription because it was yet another imposition on them from secular authorities who (in their eyes) were usurping the role of Christ. Ideas, on this view, "became embedded in congregational practice," and it was "the idea-laden practice" that fed into the anti-subscriptionist campaign.

Mark Noll's history of theology in the United States, *America's God*, provides another example of an "externalist" history of ideas that attends carefully to intellectual, social, and political contexts.[48] In his contribution to this volume, Noll theorizes his approach to the history of ideas, drawing on the work of Skinner and Pocock. He sees theologians—such as the New Englander Nathaniel W. Taylor—"tailoring" or promoting their projects by employing "languages" or "vocabularies enjoying power in the culture at large," such as the language of republicanism and common sense realism. In this way, Noll argues, theology gets "incarnated" in particular times and places. To understand it we need to familiarize ourselves with the relevant contexts, and write "*an intellectual and social history* of theology" (our italics). Just as Skinner and Pocock positioned themselves between Marxist materialists and political philosophers in search of "perennial ideas," so Noll finds a *via media* between secular reductionists and historical theologians.

Readers will have to make their own judgements about the viability and value of this middle way. But we believe that a contextualist approach to intellectual history has much to offer the student of religion, and that the study of religious belief has a serious claim on the attention of intellectual historians.

NOTES

The authors would like to thank Brad Gregory and Howard Hotson for their help on this introduction. Hotson's help was particularly invaluable for the section on recent Lutheran historiography.

1. See Quentin Skinner, "Introduction: Seeing Things Their Way," in *Visions of Politics,* vol. 1, *Regarding Method* (Cambridge: Cambridge University Press, 2002), 1–8, and 47.

2. Skinner's influential methodological essays have been revised and reissued as *Visions of Politics,* vol. 1, *Regarding Method*. For critical assessments of his method see J. Tully, ed., *Meaning and Context: Quentin Skinner and his Critics* (Cambridge: Polity Press, 1988); K. Palonen, *Quentin Skinner: History, Politics, Rhetoric* (Cambridge: Polity Press, 2003); A. Brett, J. Tully, and H. Hamilton-Bleakley, eds., *Rethinking the Foundations of Modern Political Thought* (Cambridge: Cambridge University Press, 2006). See also the following essays by other major figures in the Cambridge School: J. G. A. Pocock, "The History of Political Thought: A Methodological Enquiry," in *Philosophy, Politics and Society,* series 2, ed. P. Laslett and W. G. Runciman, 183–202 (Oxford: Blackwell, 1962); J. Dunn, "The Identity of the History of Ideas," in *Philosophy, Politics and Society,* series 4, ed. P. Laslett, W. G. Runciman, and Q. Skinner, 13–28 (Oxford: Blackwell, 1972); J. G. A. Pocock, "Introduction: The State of the Art," in his *Virtue, Commerce and History,* 1–34 (Cambridge: Cambridge University Press, 1985); and R. F. Tuck, "History of Political Thought," in *New Perspectives on Historical Writing,* ed. P. Burke, 2nd ed., 218–32 (Cambridge: Polity Press, 2001).

3. Skinner, *Visions of Politics,* vol. 1, 3.

4. Ibid.

5. Ibid., 40.

6. More recently, Skinner has confessed that the "teleology" of *Foundations* with its concentration on the emergence of "a secularizing and purportedly neutralist and universalistic idea of the state" is something that "troubles me now." See M. L. G. Pallares-Burke, *The New History* (Cambridge: Polity Press, 2002), 236.

7. D. R. Woolf, "The Writing of Early Modern Intellectual History, 1945–1995," in *Companion to Historiography*, ed. M. Bentley, 307–35 (London: Routledge, 1997).

8. D. Kelley, "What is Happening to the History of Ideas," *Intellectual News: Newsletter for the International Society for Intellectual History* 1 (1996): 43n.28.

9. R. Whatmore and B. Young, eds., *Palgrave Advances in Intellectual History* (Basingstoke: Palgrave Macmillan, 2006), 6.

10. P. Collinson, A. Hunt, and A. Walsham, "Religious Publishing in England, 1557–1640," in *The Cambridge History of the Book in Britain*, vol. 4, *1557–1695*, eds. J. Barnard and D. F. McKensie, 29–66 (Cambridge: Cambridge University Press, 2002), 29.

11. Henry F. May, "The Recovery of American Religious History," *The American Historical Review* 70, no. 1 (1964): 79–92.

12. See P. Miller, *The New England Mind*, vol. 1, *The Seventeenth Century* (New York: Macmillan, 1939), and vol. 2, *From Colony to Province* (Cambridge, Mass.: Harvard University Press, 1953). But note the following critique of Miller's secular priorities: G. Marsden, "Perry Miller's Rehabilitation of the Puritans: A Critique," *Church History* 39, no. 1 (1970): 91–105.

13. See L. Sanneh, "Religion's Return," *Times Literary Supplement*, October 13, 2006, 13.

14. P. Berger, "A Bleak Outlook is Seen for Religion," *New York Times*, April 25, 1968, 3. See also Berger's influential work *The Sacred Canopy* (New York: Doubleday, 1969).

15. P. Berger, *The Desecularization of the World: Resurgent Religion and World Politics* (Grand Rapids, Mich.: Eerdmans, 1999), 2.

16. K. Thomas, "New Ways Revisited: How History's Borders Have Expanded in the Past Forty Years," *Times Literary Supplement*, October 13, 2006, 3.

17. See Mack P. Holt, "Putting Religion Back into the Wars of Religion," *French Historical Studies* 18, no. 2 (1993): 524–51.

18. J. Dunn, *The Political Thought of John Locke* (Cambridge: Cambridge University Press, 1969).

19. See J. G. A. Pocock, *Barbarism and Religion*, 4 vols. (Cambridge: Cambridge University Press, 1999–2005).

20. See R. Tuck, "The 'Christian Atheism' of Thomas Hobbes," in *Atheism from the Reformation to the Enlightenment*, ed. M. Hunter and D. Wootton, 111–30 (Oxford: Clarendon Press, 1992); R. Tuck, "The Civil Religion of Thomas Hobbes," in *Political Discourse in Early Modern England*, ed. N. T. Phillipson and Q. Skinner, 120–38 (Cambridge: Cambridge University Press, 1993); M. Goldie, "The Civil Religion of James Harrington," in *The Languages of Political Theory in Early Modern Europe*, ed. A. Pagden, 197–222 (Cambridge: Cambridge University Press, 1987); M. Goldie, "The Theory of Religious Intolerance in Restoration England," in *From Persecution to Toleration*, ed. O. P. Grell, J. I. Israel, and N. Tyacke, 331–68 (Oxford: Oxford University Press, 1991); M. Goldie, "The Scottish Catholic Enlightenment," *Journal of British Studies* 30, no. 1 (1991): 20–62; M. Goldie, "Priestcraft and the Birth of Whiggism," in *Political Discourse in Early Modern Britain*, ed. Phillipson and Skinner, 209–31.

21. See especially R. Sher, *Church and University in the Scottish Enlightenment: The Moderate Literati of Edinburgh* (Princeton, N.J.: Princeton University Press, 2002); and H. F. May, *The Enlightenment in America* (New York: Oxford University Press, 1976).

22. See P. Gay, *The Enlightenment, An Interpretation: The Rise of Modern Paganism* (New York: Knopf, 1966).

23. See R. Porter and M. Teich, eds., *The Enlightenment in National Context* (Cambridge: Cambridge University Press, 1981).

24. See D. Outram, *The Enlightenment* (Cambridge: Cambridge University Press, 1995), 35. See also the essays by Jonathan Sheehan and Dale van Kley in a special review section entitled "God and the Enlightenment," *American Historical Review* 108, no. 4 (2003): 1057–1104; J. Bradley and D. van Kley, eds., *Religion and Politics in Enlightenment Europe* (Notre Dame, Ind.: University of Notre Dame Press, 2001); and, more polemically, S. J. Barnett, *The Enlightenment and Religion: The Myths of Modernity* (Manchester: Manchester University Press, 2003).

25. See J. Israel, *Enlightenment Contested: Philosophy, Modernity and the Emancipation of Man, 1670–1752* (Oxford: Oxford University Press, 2006).

26. See David Sorkin, *The Religious Enlightenment: Protestants, Jews, and Catholics from London to Vienna* (Princeton, N.J.: Princeton University Press, 2008).

27. Compare J. W. Draper, *History of the Conflict between Science and Religion* (New York: Appleton, 1875), and A. D. White, *A History of the Warfare of Science with Theology in Christendom*, 2 vols. (New York: Appleton, 1896), with J. H. Brooke, *Science and Religion: Some Historical Perspectives* (Cambridge:

Cambridge University Press, 1991), and G. Ferngren, ed., *Science and Religion: A Historical Introduction* (Baltimore: Johns Hopkins University Press, 2002).

28. Many of Newton's religious and alchemical writings are now available online through the Newton Project, www.newtonproject.sussex.ac.uk.

29. See H. McLeod, *Secularisation in Western Europe, 1848–1914* (New York: St. Martin's Press, 2000).

30. K. T. Hoppen, *The Mid-Victorian Generation, 1846–1886* (Oxford: Oxford University Press, 1998), 427.

31. C. A. Bayly, *The Birth of the Modern World, 1789–1914* (Oxford: Blackwell, 2004), 363.

32. See G. Marsden, *The Soul of the American University: From Protestant Establishment to Established Unbelief* (New York: Oxford University Press, 1996); C. Smith, ed., *The Secular Revolution* (Berkeley: University of California Press, 2003).

33. S. Bruce, *Religion in the Modern World* (Oxford: Oxford University Press, 1996), 138.

34. For an ambitious attempt to reincorporate the religious factor into an account of modern European political history from 1789 to the present, see Michael Burleigh's two-volume work: *Earthly Powers: Religion and Politics in Europe from the French Revolution to the Great War* (London: HarperCollins, 2005), and *Sacred Causes: Religion and Politics from the European Dictators to Al Qaeda* (London: HarperCollins, 2006).

35. John Gray, "Battle of the Books," *New Statesman,* July 31, 2006, available online at http://www.newstatesman.com/200607310052.

36. See http://www.history.upenn.edu/isih/Davis.html.

37. E. P. Thompson, *The Making of the English Working Class* (Harmondsworth: Penguin, 1968), chaps. 2 and 11. For a recent analysis of Thompson's approach, see J. Walsh and D. Hempton, "E. P. Thompson and Methodism," in *God and Mammon: Protestants, Money and the Market, 1790–1860,* ed. M. A. Noll, 99–120 (New York: Oxford University Press, 2001).

38. Quoted in J. Thrower, *Religion: The Classic Theories* (Edinburgh: Edinburgh University Press, 1999), 183.

39. Norman Cohn, *Pursuit of the Millennium* (London: Secker & Warburg, 1957).

40. On the darker side of this movement cf. Heinrich Assel, *Der Andere Aufbruch: Die Lutherrenaissance—Ursprunge, Aporien und Wege: Karl Holl, Emanuel Hirsch, Rudolf Hermann (1910–1935)* (Göttingen: Vandenhoeck & Ruprecht, 1994); James Stayer, *Martin Luther, German Saviour: German Evangelical Theological Faculties and the Interpretation of Luther, 1917–1933* (Montreal and Kingston: McGill-Queen's University Press, 2000).

41. For the older approach, see for instance Franz Hildebrandt, *Melanchthon: Alien or Ally?* (Cambridge: Cambridge University Press, 1946). Evidence of a renaissance in Melanchthon studies includes the critical edition of his correspondence, the microfiche edition of his works missing from the *Corpus Reformatorum*, the foundation of a monograph series, a journal, and two separate centers devoted to the study of him and his legacy: *Melanchthons Briefwechsel*, ed. Heinz Scheible (Stuttgart: frommann-holzboog, 1977–); Timothy J. Wengert, ed., *Philipp Melanchthon, Theologian and Humanist*, ca. 200 microfiche (Leiden: IDC Publishers, 2001); *Fragmenta Melanchthoniana*, eds. G. Frank and S. Lalla (Ubstadt-Weiher: Verlag Regionalkultur, 2003–); Günter Frank and Johanna Loehr, eds., Melanchthon-Schriften der Stadt Bretten, vols. 1–6 (Sigmaringen: Thorbecke, 1988–2002), vols. 7– (Stuttgart: frommann-holzboog, 2003–); Europäische Melanchthon-Akademie Bretten (www.melanchthonakademie.org); Melanchthonhaus Bretten (http://www.melanchthon.com).

42. Especially apparent in Martin Brecht, ed., *Geschichte des Pietismus*, 4 vols. (Göttingen: Vandenhoeck und Ruprecht, 1993–2004).

43. For an excellent recent introduction see Ute Lotz-Heumann, "Confessionalization," in *Reformation and Early Modern Europe: A Guide to Research*, ed. David M. Whitford, 136–57 (Kirksville, Mo.: Truman State University Press, 2007).

44. Siegfried Wollgast, *Philosophie in Deutschland zwischen Reformation und Aufklärung, 1550–1650* (Berlin: Akademie-Verlag, 1988; repr. 1993).

45. Dominick LaCapra, "Rethinking Intellectual History and Reading Texts," in *Modern European Intellectual History: Reappraisals and New Perspectives*, ed. Dominick LaCapra, 47–85 (Ithaca, N.Y.: Cornell University Press, 1982), esp. 57–60; and David Harlan, "Intellectual History and the Return of Literature," *The American Historical Review* 94, no. 3 (1989): 581–609.

46. For further discussion on the possibility of history in the face of skeptical turns in hermeneutics, see Thomas L. Haskell, *Objectivity Is Not Neutrality: Explanatory Schemes in History* (Baltimore, Md.: The Johns Hopkins University Press, 1998); Joyce Appleby, Lynn Hunt, and Margaret Jacob, *Telling the Truth About History* (New York: Norton, 1994); Richard J. Evans, *In Defence of History* (London: Granta Books, 1997); and the comments of Skinner in *Visions of Politics*, vol. 1, 91–127.

47. Carlo Ginzburg, *The Cheese and the Worms: The Cosmos of a Sixteenth-century Miller*, trans. John and Anne Tedeschi (London: Routledge, 1980).

48. Mark A. Noll, *America's God, from Jonathan Edwards to Abraham Lincoln* (New York: Oxford University Press, 2002).

2 Can We "See Things Their Way"? Should We Try?

BRAD S. GREGORY

I think it worthwhile to reflect on some broad conceptual and methodological issues related to the study of the history of religious ideas. My point of departure will be the phrase in the title to our volume, which is taken from the title of the introduction to the first volume of Quentin Skinner's collected essays, "Seeing Things Their Way."[1] At the same time, it seems to me that such issues are best tested, debated, and refined in conjunction with actual historical research, and so I will combine these general reflections with reference to a relatively simple test case, the religious ideas of an individual. Accordingly, this article shuttles back and forth between the very general and the highly specific: it considers possible objections in principle and practice to "seeing things their way," in which the "things" are religious ideas and "they" are the protagonists of those ideas, and it approaches the particular issues through the religious ideas of a single, sixteenth-century Flemish Anabaptist, Jacob de Roore, who was executed as a heretic in the city of Bruges on June 10, 1569.

It seems important to offer some preliminary remarks about our quarry. What do we mean by "seeing things their way" in the domain of religious ideas? The metaphor of seeing to denote an intellectual grasp of something is at least as ancient as Plato in the Western tradition. The phrase itself is suggestive rather than technical, which seems to me intellectually prudent: it points us in a direction rather than specifying in advance exactly what we seek, which in turn permits the particularities of content to shape the results of the inquiry.[2] Such a stance is important, lest we insist from the outset, for example, on sharp distinctions between "ideas" and "sensibilities," "convictions," or "attitudes," conceptual categorizations that would distort rather than illuminate what we seek. I take "seeing things their way" to be more or less synonymous with understanding religious people on their own terms, or with reconstructing the ways in which they viewed themselves and their world, or with depicting them in a manner in which they would have recognized themselves. Perhaps even more colloquially, we might say that to see things their way is to "get it" from the perspective of religious believer-practitioners, whoever they might be, and to represent them accordingly. Such a stance is less a method per se than it is an approach or even an attitude, one in which, in Skinner's phrase, we "approach the past with a willingness to listen."[3] Such an understanding of religious people on their own terms, past or present, should not be confused with the adoption, approval, or endorsement of the views that we seek to understand. If it is possible to see things as the members of a religious tradition see them, this does not imply that we thereby appropriate or condone their beliefs or ideas. Otherwise, seeing things their way would lead ineluctably either to conversion to or advocacy of the positions that one has grasped, which is certainly not the case. Nor does such an approach imply anything, one way or the other, about the truth or falsity of the views that one seeks to understand.

Applied to the particular instance at hand, then, the objective is to understand and present something of Jacob de Roore's ideas in such a manner that he would recognize them as his own. De Roore (also known as Jacob de Keersmaecker or de Keersgieter, because his father was a chandler) was born at Kortrijk in Flanders around 1533 and became a weaver. He left the Catholic church in 1551, was baptized as a Mennonite Anabaptist in 1554, and became an important traveling preacher among Anabaptist congregations in the Low Countries between then and his apprehension in Bruges in 1569. Like other Anabaptists, who comprised a wide array of geographically and doctrinally distinct groups, Mennonites rejected infant baptism as unbiblical and as the rotten root corrupting the doctrine and morals of magisterial Protestants and Catholics alike. Imprisoned and interrogated, de Roore refused to recant his religious views and was burned at the stake in Bruges under the auspices of civic authorities on June 10, 1569.[4] I have chosen him as an example here for reasons that will help to illustrate some of the broader points that I wish to make (although I might have chosen any number of individuals from the Reformation era who fit similar criteria). Most importantly, we have significant source material that provides evidence for his religious ideas: while he was imprisoned between April 1569 and his death two months later, he wrote numerous letters from prison, nineteen of which were gathered and published, first (apparently) in 1571, then again in 1577, 1579, 1581, 1584, and 1622.[5] In addition, outside a small number of specialists in the history of Anabaptism in the Reformation era, few scholars have heard of Jacob de Roore, and so are less likely to have preconceptions about his ideas in comparison to those of major religious thinkers. Related to both these points, Jacob de Roore was neither a sophisticated intellectual nor illiterate, and so offers an example of a person from the intellectually middling ranks of his day.

I think that to some extent we can, depending upon both the evidence available to us and our willingness to pursue the objective, understand the religious ideas of people in the past on their own terms, and I spend much of my time as a working scholar of the Reformation era seeking to do just this. (Here it is perhaps worthwhile to interject a cautionary note about separating "religious ideas" from religion as a whole, which almost always entails more than ideas.) Yet since the nineteenth century and the heyday of philosophical positivism, the denunciation of revealed religion as superstition, and the creation of grand, explanatory theories of religion à la Feuerbach and Marx, and later Weber, Durkheim, Freud, and others, the secularization of Western intellectual life has led to the widespread view—sometimes explicit, but more often, especially in recent decades, simply assumed—that religion is not something that can or ought to be understood on its own terms. Indeed, according to this view, precisely the point of studying religion is to show that it is not what its protagonists claim that it is; Durkheim, for example, asserted that no religious believers should be consulted for an account of religious ideas, even their own.[6] A wide variety of reductionist theories of religion derived from sociology, anthropology, and other disciplines are today available to scholars, which share in one way or another in this basic assumption. More extreme are challenges that concern the very possibility of understanding religious ideas. Other criticisms can be made about the evidentiary basis for the enterprise, as well as about the biases that scholars bring to their interpretative efforts.

In an attempt to provide a framework for grasping some of the basic objections to the aim of seeing things their way, I have classified these theories and critical perspectives according to whether they reject the goal in principle or in practice, and whether the root of the problem is regarded primarily as epistemological or ideological. This yields a classificatory grid with four quadrants: (1) we *cannot in principle* understand religious ideas on the terms of those who hold them; (2) we *should not* in principle try to understand religious ideas on the terms of those who hold them; (3) we *cannot in practice* understand religious ideas on the terms of those who hold them; (4) we *should not* in practice try to understand religious ideas on the terms of those who hold them. The remainder of this paper explores each of these four objections in conjunction with some of the ideas of Jacob de Roore as expressed in his prison letters. The goal is to shed some light on the different sorts of objections that have been made to the attempt to reconstruct the religious convictions of past people, and to try to discern what is at stake in each case.

Different Sorts of Objections to "Seeing Things Their Way"

Epistemological Objections	*Ideological Objections*
Cannot in principle	Should not in principle
radical skepticism	*reductionist theories of religion*
Cannot in practice	Should not in practice
alterity, insufficient evidence, biases	*antiquarianism, uninteresting*

We cannot in principle understand religious ideas on the terms of those who hold them.

This position constitutes a radical, epistemological claim against the very possibility of understanding religious ideas in the past—and, it would seem, in order to be consistent, against the possibility of understanding any ideas in the past whatsoever. For it is difficult to see what about *religious* ideas would altogether prevent their being understood, whereas other, nonreligious ideas in the past would remain amenable to our grasp—ideas about, say, familial order, human labor, or political authority. Put more bluntly: if in principle we cannot do the history of religious ideas or the history of theology, then neither can we do the history of political, philosophical, or any other kind of ideas. Very little about the mentalities of premodern peoples, for example, is readily intelligible or easily accessible to us, whether or not we are specifically concerned with their religious aspects. I would extend this point to include the nineteenth and most of the twentieth centuries, the similarities of which in comparison to our own times so often prove to be superficial and therefore misleading.

Indeed, a *principled* objection to the possibility of understanding religious ideas in the past, it would seem, must be extended to embrace not only the nonreligious ideas of the past, but also the religious and nonreligious ideas of the present. If there is some fundamental barrier that altogether prevents us from comprehending, for example, the ways in which Anglican vicars of the 1950s in England viewed their relationships to God and their parishioners, then it is unclear how we might come to understand current vicars' ideas about such relationships. At stake in both cases is the use of evidence as such as the basis for knowledge, whether left by past people in bits and pieces or gathered in the present on the basis of interviews, writings, images, and by other means. To reject entirely the possibility of understanding religious (and other) ideas in the past (and present) is tantamount to rejecting the possibility of knowledge as such. Note that such a rejection differs from questions about the possibility of historical knowledge that stem from concerns about evidence or from limitations of scholarly perspective, both of which are discussed separately below.

To claim that the ideas of past people cannot in principle be understood is, to understate the matter, a less than promising guideline for historical research. Indeed, taken seriously, it renders impossible the doing of history in any conventional sense. It is one form of a radical skepticism, associated in recent decades with some expressions of poststructuralist literary criticism. While there is a certain superficial plausibility and apparent intellectual humility in a claim such as "we can never *really* understand someone else," it is worth analyzing precisely what is intended by such an assertion. If it means that we can never ourselves actually *have* the experiences of someone else, that we cannot ourselves *be* another person, then of course it is true, but trivially so. It is patently obvious that the methodologically self-conscious, second-order understanding of someone else on their own terms is different than the unselfconscious, direct experience of that person per se.[7] In this respect, seeing things their way by historians is not and can never be the same as the seeing by the subjects whom one studies. The metaphor of attempting to "get inside the heads" of those whom one studies can therefore be misleading, as can Collingwood's notion that all history is intellectual history, the aim of which is to rethink the thoughts of past people.[8] It is obvious that we cannot experience the life and think the thoughts of our subjects exactly as they did, but this is simply a trivial corollary of the fact that we are not them. If this point, however, is therefore taken to imply that others' ideas and convictions, hopes and sorrows, dreams and disappointments remain intellectually impenetrable regardless of their words or actions, then it is thoroughly mistaken, whether we are talking about the late twentieth or the late sixteenth centuries. Every email message comprehended and answered disproves such a notion, which does not reflect what we mean when we speak of understanding someone or seeing things their way. To embrace this position would entail that one cease to be a historian and to become instead an advocate against the possibility of doing history.

In the case of the letters of Jacob de Roore, it is not apparent what a principled rejection of the possibility of understanding his ideas would even mean. The issue here is not whether certain passages or phrases in his letters are obscure, but whether his letters are of any use at all as evidence for understanding his ideas, as a man who lived and died in the Low Countries more than four hundred years ago. On May 2–3, 1569, in anticipation of his death, de Roore penned a substantial letter of admonition to his children. Among his many instructions, he wrote that "the Lord is a just God, who will not put up with sin, but will punish those who commit it. Therefore we must fear him and not sin, for the fear of God drives out sin, and those who fear God will do good.... Therefore, my children, walk in the fear of the Lord from your youth onwards, so that you will not consent to sin at any time and will not forget the commandments of your Lord and your God."[9] Of course, these few sentences, like analogous sentences from any historical source, cannot be intelligible considered in strict isolation. In this case, they require that we have some knowledge of notions such as sin, fear of God, divine punishment, and divine commandments as understood from a Christian perspective, but given this, de Roore's meaning is plain: he is telling his children that because God will punish sin, they should fear him and avoid it, obeying his commandments and doing good instead. Therefore we can understand this religious idea of his, as far as it goes. As is characteristic of all his letters, de Roore backs up his words with profuse biblical references, which implies that he regards scripture as an authority to be followed, that he considers its authority sufficient to ground his exhortations, and that he thinks he has appropriately interpreted the adduced passages for his children. This much is clear, it seems to me, in ways that cannot meaningfully be challenged from a position of radical epistemological skepticism.

A little over a month after he wrote to his children, and just days before his death, de Roore sent a letter to fellow Anabaptists in the small town of Armentières. In it, among many other ideas, he expressed his views about the way in which God had written his law on the hearts of the ancient Israelites, on early Christians, and on de Roore himself and his fellow Anabaptists, drawing on passages from the biblical books of Isaiah, Jeremiah, Ezekiel, Hebrews, Exodus, and Deuteronomy. "There is no need for me to tell you," he wrote, "everything that you know and have learned from the Lord, who has made his covenant with the house of Israel, saying 'I will set my Law in their hearts, and write it in their souls [*sinnen*].' For just as he wrote on stone tablets the Law of the Old Testament, which he had written in them with his finger, so has he now written on the fleshly tablets of the hearts of the children of the New

Testament, in the Law of the Spirit, by means of the Holy Spirit."[10] Again, such a passage requires some familiarity with notions such as the Old Testament, covenant, New Testament, the Holy Spirit, and the relationship between the Old and New Law in Christianity, but given such familiarity, de Roore's ideas are indeed comprehensible. He is asserting that, because his fellow believers know God's Law in their hearts, they are the heirs of the ancient Israelites as well as of Christians of the apostolic era, and that such knowledge was imparted by God himself to all three groups. Such notions are complex, related to many others, and might prompt any number of questions about de Roore's views, some of which might well be unanswerable, but it seems absurd to say that his ideas are unintelligible, impenetrable, or that we are not "really" understanding them. Literally hundreds of other examples of similarly intelligible passages from his correspondence could be given.

We should not in principle try to understand religious ideas on the terms of those who hold them.

In contrast to the self-marginalizing, epistemological rejection of the very possibility of understanding religious ideas, this second position constitutes an *ideological* rejection of the *desirability* of attempts to see things their way. As such it is much more common. This is the domain of reductionist theories of religion drawn from sociology, psychology, cultural anthropology, cultural studies, or other disciplines. Here it is maintained that the central task of the scholar of religion is to explain its doctrines and ideas, its rituals and practices, its regulations and prohibitions as the product of something ostensibly more fundamental and "real," whether the antirevolutionary ideology that inhibits an oppressed class from rising to revolutionary consciousness (Marx), for example, or the social relations that create and conserve society (Durkheim), or the systems of symbols that *seem* to imbue the cosmos with supernatural significance (Geertz). We are simply not to *try* to see things their way; rather, religion is to be explained in nonreligious, secular categories. To seek to understand religious people on their own terms is not regarded as impossible, as with a radical epistemological skepticism, but rather as a scholar's dereliction of duty or the sign of a deficient critical sense. In recent decades this perspective has been the predominant scholarly approach to the study of religion, and to some extent it probably remains so. One indication of this is the widespread assumption (in U.S. graduate programs, at least) that the preliminary, appropriate training for the historical study of religion consists in "reading theory" (by which is usually meant classic and contemporary sociological, anthropological, and cultural theories of religion), rather than reading the theology, prayers, and other writings of the religious people whom one intends to study. One is fit to tackle the latter only when one has been outfitted with the proper (post)modern, secular intellectual equipment, which will yield the approved results.

Importantly, not all aspects of all explanatory theories of religion are inimical to the goal of trying to understand religious people on their own terms. Indeed, many otherwise reductionist theories have contributed in certain respects to scholars' efforts to see things their way. Durkheim's sociology of religion, for example, helped to transform a rather narrow, traditional type of church history into the history of religion, minimally by pointing out the obvious, namely, that religious groups and institutions are comprised of people linked by social relationships. Such relationships are evident in the case of Jacob de Roore, who addressed his letters not only to his children and to fellow Anabaptist believers, as we have already seen, but also to his wife, his sister, his brother, and to various colleagues, all of which point to a social network mediated by shared religious convictions.[11] Moreover, even those scholars most sympathetically disposed to the nonreductionist reconstruction of religion should acknowledge that religion can be, and often has been, deliberately used and cynically manipulated for various nonreligious ends (although identifying when this is the case is often much more difficult than is frequently implied, and certainly cannot be done by labeling two intellectual boxes "Religious" and "Political," as it were, and distributing the evidence accordingly). Finally, insofar as ideas are expressed and held by people, and people always live in some or other social, political, and cultural context, the emphasis on context in many explanatory theories of religion is important for intellectual historians otherwise disposed to treat ideas as elements in a Platonic stratosphere, floating freely above the messy complexities of human life. (I reiterate the potential danger involved in studying religious *ideas* apart from religion as a whole.)

At the same time, it is far from clear that the necessarily embedded character of religious ideas implies that they *cannot* be more than the product of their historically conditioned contexts, that they *cannot* be more than cultural constructions or political expressions or assertions of social identity. Such claims express not a neutral historicism that justifiably recognizes the distinctive character of different cultures across time and space, but rather an ideological historicism grounded in a post-Enlightenment metaphysical naturalism that in effect denies the possibility that *any* religious beliefs *could* be true. It does not follow that Islam cannot be true because it arose in seventh-century Arabia, any more that it follows that Christianity cannot be true because it originated in first-century Palestine, or that Jacob de Roore's Anabaptist beliefs cannot have been true because they were rooted in multiple contexts in sixteenth-century Flanders. Nor are the foundational assumptions of metaphysical naturalism self-evident. Ironically, this means that reductionist historians of religion who operate as though this were so are secular believers of a sort in their own right—the secular converse, as it were, of traditional confessional historians.[12] Ultimately, the conviction that one should not in principle seek to understand religious ideas on the terms of those who hold them is connected to the dominant, Western, liberal narrative of modernity as secularization, the ideological backbone of which is the claim of the progressive liberation of individuals from traditional ideas and values, which of course were steeped in religion, particularly (for the large majority in the West) Christianity. Here history and theory coalesce: a particular narrative of modernity dovetails with a methodological imperative about how to approach the study of that which is regarded as the principal obstacle to modernization, whether intellectually, politically, culturally, or technologically.

Whatever one's own verdict on this position, it seems clear that its interpretative results, whatever their plausibility, are not to be conflated or confused with an understanding of religious people on their own terms. Seeking to see things their way is from the outset an *entirely different* intellectual endeavor than seeking to explain "what they see" in secular categories.[13] It seems self-evident that no religious people, past or present, would or do accept a reductionist, secular explanation of their religious beliefs; to do so would seem to be synonymous with ceasing to be a religious believer. Could he be present today, Jacob de Roore would certainly not acknowledge a Freudian, Durkheimian, anthropologically functionalist, or any other reductionist interpretation of his convictions, none of which would amount to seeing things his way. In fact, the use of secular categories to explain religious views is analytically equivalent to the use of religious categories to explain secular views: the theoretical converse of religion as a set of cultural constructions used to justify oppressive morality and a traditional social order, for example, is secular liberalism as a set of ideological inventions used to legitimate sinful selfishness and justify individual desires without regard for God's will. Surely the latter claim and its metaphysical presuppositions would be rejected by most secular liberals—but then, so is the former claim and worldview repudiated by most religious believers.

A patient, systematic application of reductionist theories of religion to the case of Jacob de Roore, evaluating each in turn, lies much beyond the scope of this chapter. Suffice it to say that those theories that emphasize some sort of material or worldly self-interest behind religious convictions are bound to be unconvincing when applied to men and women who voluntarily join religious groups in circumstances of severe persecution (doubly so when they are in prison facing execution). Social theories of religion that seek to account for religious affiliation according to categories of status, class, or occupation are unpersuasive for periods such as the Reformation era, when divergent religious convictions often ruptured social ties rooted in family, neighborhood, and occupation. Why did some urban Flemish weavers, such as Jacob de Roore, become Mennonite Anabaptists, others embrace Reformed Protestantism, and still others retain their allegiance to the Roman Church? Why, among people from the same social background, were some deeply devout and others religiously indifferent? Modern psychological theories of religion are problematic for historians for a host of reasons, including intellectual anachronism (unless one can demonstrate that a given theorist has discovered something metahistorically and transculturally true of all human beings) and a frequently speculative (not to say far-fetched and fanciful) use of evidence (think of Richard Marius's studies of Thomas More and Martin Luther, for example).[14]

Jacob de Roore explicitly prioritized his love for Christ above his love for his wife and children, even though he knew that this stance would cost him his life, leave her as a widow, and leave his children as orphans. Rather than assuming that such an attitude must, for example—despite the lack of any supporting evidence—reflect the pathology of a hardhearted man in a family situation from which he sought to escape, we should shave the claims of the would-be methodological reductionist with Occam's razor: de Roore's own scriptural justification not only accounts for his attitude and behavior without the unnecessary invocation of reductionist theories, but also has the advantage of having been written by himself in clear, calm prose, corroborated by the tender tone of multiple letters to his wife and children. As he put it in a letter to his wife written on April 24 of the year in which he was killed, "Christ says 'Whoever loves his father and mother more than me is not worthy of me, and whoever loves sons or daughters more than me is not worthy of me.' . . . Yes, [we must forsake] brothers and sisters, wife and children, including our own life and all that we possess, or we may not be Christ's disciples, although this hatred [of family members] extends no further than the extent to which in clinging to these things, they draw us away from Christ."[15] De Roore's distinction between rejecting family altogether and rejecting them only insofar as they interfere with one's biblically commanded love for Christ reveals a capacity for making precise, directly relevant distinctions. It does not suggest an imbalanced fanatic with a death wish nor a desperate husband and father eager to escape a terrible familial situation, any more than any of his letters do.

We cannot in practice understand religious ideas on the terms of those who hold them.

Rather than denying the possibility of understanding religious ideas as such, this position rejects their comprehensibility in practice. Historians might be committed to understanding the religious ideas of Jews from the second century or Anabaptist Christians from the sixteenth, but, as it turns out, the sheer alterity of their respective worldviews and ideas is so formidable as to resist our best efforts at sympathetic reconstruction, or there is an insufficient evidentiary basis for doing so, or the limitations and biases of all scholars necessarily distort the endeavor.

These are all important considerations that self-conscious, working historians will have encountered in the course of their own research at some time or another (and sometimes on a daily basis). Each of these three positions must be taken seriously, but none of them, in my opinion, constitutes an absolute barrier to understanding, provided that by "understanding" we do not mean a complete, perfect reconstruction of the ideas of the people whom we study.

Evidence is an absolutely critical consideration, both in terms of its quantity and quality. Sources that might help us to answer one question (for example, "What sorts of biblical images do we find in Jacob de Roore's prison letters?") often prove unable to help with another ("Who read these letters in print, and what difference did it make in their lives?"). Without a doubt, the more and better evidence that we possess, the greater our opportunities for understanding someone's religious ideas—although in the case of major figures who generated a huge mass of sources, one might well argue that the pendulum swings the other way, as it were, and we face different challenges of understanding due to the quantity of evidence. If we lack specific evidence about a given person—which is true for the vast majority of men and women in premodern Europe—then we cannot know anything in particular about their religious (or other) ideas, regrettable as this is. We have little more than the names and dates of execution for many sixteenth-century Christians who were killed for their faith, for example, and unless new sources come to light, we will never know as much about them as we can know about Jacob de Roore, because of his nineteen letters. We might make intelligent inferences based on evidence about people of similar background and beliefs, but we cannot reconstruct anything about the particularities of their ideas or the texture of their experiences. To this extent, historians of religion are no different than other historians. They should openly and honestly admit the limitations of their sources (as of course responsible ones have been doing for more than a century). Barring the discovery of new sources, we cannot know much about Jacob de Roore's preaching or travels in the Low Countries prior to his imprisonment in 1569, or about whether his Anabaptist ideas underwent any sort of development between his baptism in 1554 and the weeks just prior to his death. By the same token, it seems obtuse and, indeed, simply mistaken to say about a person for whom we possess sound source material—as with de Roore's nineteen prison letters—that we simply cannot understand his ideas.[16] If we have good evidence about someone and possess the requisite scholarly skills to read and comprehend that evidence in relevant contexts, then at least to some extent it is possible to understand his or her ideas. It is only to be expected that different interpreters will on some points disagree and dispute what the sources mean or permit us to conclude, but such debate presupposes at least some degree of understanding. A sheer opacity in the evidence would generate a consensus of incomprehension, not a debate about interpretation.

The practical objection to seeing things their way that derives from a sense of the radical otherness of the past is valuable as a constant warning against facile presumption and what E. P. Thompson called, in his wonderful phrase, "the enormous condescension of posterity."[17] It reminds us that we are apt to underestimate the difficulty of what we are trying to do and cautions us against the false similarities that we are likely to draw when we compare the past to our own world. Historians should always proceed under the yellow light, as it were, with a sense of cautious tentativeness and humility about what they are trying to do. It would be rash to imagine sixteenth-century Anabaptists as essentially like contemporary Christians, only without the technological trappings of the modern world. At the same time, this objection itself becomes objectionable when elevated to the status of an axiom—because we know from experience that the otherness of the past does not present us with an impenetrable wall. Rather remarkably, we *can* learn to read and understand in context—to some degree, and admittedly almost always less fully than we would like—ancient scriptures, medieval monastic charters, early modern prison letters, and nineteenth-century hymns. Jacob de Roore's ideas about central Christian doctrines, including God the Father, Jesus Christ, the Holy Spirit, baptism, the Lord's Supper, the church, and the ban, are all intelligible and are presented in a letter to his children that in effect constitutes a profession of faith.[18] Paradoxically, those who raise "otherness" objections to our claims of understanding sources from different past worlds almost always do so based on considerable *knowledge,* which grounds their criticism of our (flawed) claims.

A critique of problematic claims about historical knowledge *presupposes* knowledge, without which the critique would be empty. The result is not a resigned ignorance in the face of historical alterity but a *greater* knowledge of the distance between the world that we study and our own, based on a *better* understanding of the former.

The practical objection to understanding past religious ideas due to scholarly biases and shortcomings is similar. Any of us would be rash to claim that we are without such limitations and liabilities as scholars, and as a result we should be open to criticism and correction in our attempts at historical understanding. Yet just as it would be mistaken to think that the otherness of the past is and remains impenetrable, so it is mistaken to think that biases are analogous to an unalterable genetic condition—as though we cannot change our points of view and amend our biases. We can, as again we know from experience. For the purposes of understanding protagonists in the past, mine is a deliberately anti-Gadamerian hermeneutic: to concede that what we are after can only be a "fusion of horizons" between historical interpreter and past people in a common tradition is, it seems to me, tantamount to saying that we cannot understand past people on their own terms but *only* on ours. The fact that we can never attain perfect interpretative purity does not preclude our becoming aware of and improving upon our scholarly shortcomings, provided that this is in fact what they are, and that they are pointed out to us convincingly. Still less does it imply that because we can never be entirely free from biases, we might as well seize upon whatever politically useful theory we can to serve our own desires or the ideologically approved scholarship of the moment—to construct a "usable past." Criticisms of scholarly bias, like criticisms of an inadequate recognition of the otherness of the past, depend upon knowledge, on the basis of which a convincing case that demonstrates the bias can be made. In other words, in the case of religious ideas, it is only *because* understanding religious ideas is possible that distortions in interpretations of them can be pointed out. If one were to criticize, for example, a biased presentation of Jacob de Roore's ideas about adult baptism and infant baptism, one would be obliged to point out the shortcomings in that presentation, awareness of which depends upon understanding his ideas better than the scholar whom one is criticizing. I have never been impressed by the general claim that all interpretations must be flawed because all scholars are biased. This seems facile and the product of intellectual laziness. The issue is rather how *precisely* is *this particular* interpretation inadequate, if at all? This question applies whether we are trying to understand one source, a historical episode, or an entire tradition over a period of centuries. If no serious, substantive, specific arguments are forthcoming, we should conclude not that the interpretation indeed "must be biased" (because all interpretations are) but rather that such an assertion in this particular instance is unfounded until and unless such distortion is demonstrated.

We should not in practice try to understand religious ideas on the terms of those who hold them.

This position raises not epistemological questions about the character of our evidence, the otherness of the past, or scholarly bias, but rather suggests that in practice there is something objectionable about the attempt to understand religious ideas on the terms of those who hold them. The accusation of "mere antiquarianism" might be associated with this position: in short, we could, if we wanted to, reconstruct sympathetically the religious ideas of people in the past, but what would be the point? Would not the result be simply an account of people who believed what they believed and did what they did? What is gained by understanding Jacob de Roore's ideas sympathetically, such that he would recognize himself?

At least two responses might be made to this line of questioning. First, I suspect that someone who denigrates the aim of reconstructing alien ideas in historical contexts, as though it were a simple and straightforward enterprise, probably has not spent much time actually trying to do it. Indeed, going further, it seems that it is typically *easier* to apply to religious ideas one or another (post)modern theory congruent with current secular beliefs of one sort or another than it is to try to understand those ideas on their own terms, apart from one's own preconceptions. To assert that Jacob de Roore's ideas were no more than cultural constructions serving social functions is much easier than to render them as an internalized web of divinely revealed truths, held by a man who regarded himself and his fellow believers as sustained by the Holy Spirit, who rendered them all "God's children, and because children we are also heirs, namely God's heirs, and fellow heirs with Christ, because the children must share in their father's goods."[19]

A second response to the accusation of antiquarianism is that, pursued systematically across different religious individuals and communities, across and within religious traditions, the endeavor to see things their way does not yield an explanatorily sterile antiquarianism. Rather, by disclosing differences and disagreements within the domain of ideas and commitments, the enterprise lays at least part of the foundations for explaining change over time, which is arguably the most difficult and most important challenge that historians face. In and of itself, to be sure, the sympathetic understanding of Jacob de Roore's ideas touches on a quite narrow range of issues, as does an analogous understanding of the ideas of most individuals in the past. But a careful, patient reconstruction of the religious ideas and commitments of many people from among Lutherans, Reformed Protestants, Roman Catholics, and the various sorts of radical Protestants in the Reformation era, embedded in their respective social and political contexts, does not leave us with a mere compilation of lifeless descriptions. Rather, the disagreements and disruptions exposed in such a comparative picture provide essential aspects for the explanation of such fundamental historical processes as the emergence of the confessional state, the growth of religious toleration as a matter of practical political policy, the secularization of knowledge and eventual marginalization of theology, and the gradual divorce of economic activity and consumer acquisitiveness from religious and moral constraints. Jacob de Roore is only a tiny piece in a vast puzzle, but he is a piece nonetheless, and there is no shortcut to assembling the whole without careful attention to the pieces and their reconstructive description as a necessary part of the historian's task, one that precedes historical analysis and the explanation of change over time.

One might also claim that in practice, the project of seeking to see things their way is simply uninteresting. We can try to understand religious people such as Jacob de Roore and other Anabaptists on their own terms, but such an aim is boring or at least not compelling, and therefore we should not pursue it. This type of reaction might greet any sort of historical research, or indeed any type of intellectual undertaking, and seems largely a matter of individual taste and predilection. Just as some people find algebraic geometry or oceanographic research boring, so some historians find detailed diplomatic history boring while others find the nonreductionist reconstruction of religious ideas boring. Such views are not arguments, it seems to me, but rather simply the expression of individual preferences. What might one say in response? Each intellectual enterprise faces different challenges of self-justification. By the quality of one's scholarly work—demonstrating the connections among different aspects of a religious worldview or theological system that do not at first meet the eye, showing what was at stake for those who espoused them, analyzing the implications of discrepant convictions for multiple domains of human life—one can endeavor to convert the bored to the interested. Clearly, no scholars are likely to be entirely successful. Not everyone is going to take intellectual satisfaction in learning about the relationship among the lack of explicit scriptural sanction for infant baptism, the Anabaptist insistence on believers' baptism, and the social and political subversiveness of the Anabaptists' view in sixteenth-century society, in which religious and social identity were so closely intertwined. Nor is everyone going to be intrigued by the intricacies of Reformation-era doctrinal controversies, despite the enormous impact of religious disagreement for historical change in early modern and modern Europe. This suggests another strategy to try to move the unmoved: for those left cold by the intrinsic character of religious ideas, there is always the argument based on extrinsic influence—as Americans, for example, have learned in dramatic fashion regarding radical, militant Islam since September 11, 2001. Regardless of whether a particular person happens to find religious ideas interesting, in their variety they have had a profound influence for millennia and continue to affect the lives of literally billions of people. Indeed, notwithstanding the self-satisfied secularism of many Western scholars, in a global perspective religion continues to be the predominant way in which most human beings make sense of their lives. To say, then, that one is unconcerned with understanding religious ideas on the terms of those who maintain them implies that one does not care to understand most people in the world on their own terms.

■

In conclusion, the classificatory grid that I have proposed provides a way of thinking through different kinds of objections that are made about the attempt to understand the religious ideas of people on their own terms. As such, it might be useful for negotiating the relevant intellectual landscape with respect to issues of theory, evidence, and bias in the study of religion, for meeting different kinds of challenges to the enterprise. A radical denial of the value of evidence as such is different than an argument disputing the relevance of a particular kind of evidence for a certain sort of question. So too the insistence that religion be studied in secular terms is different than an accusation of antiquarianism. Correlatively, responding to an assertion such as "we can never really understand them" requires a different tack than responding to a claim such as "modern people cannot believe in miracles," as such assertions are brought to bear on methodology in the study of religion. We can indeed aspire to see things their way in the realm of religious ideas, no less than in the realm of any sort of ideas, but this is a particular sort of intellectual undertaking with crucial prerequisites. The most important, it seems to me, sounds so deceptively simple that we might be tempted to dismiss it as banal: we must be willing to pursue the objective. This in turn requires that we be sufficiently aware of our own moral and metaphysical convictions to distinguish them from those of the people whom we study; and that we reject, as incompatible with our objective, theories whose embedded moral or metaphysical claims preclude the understanding that is sought. In other words, the endeavor to see things their way is the antithesis of the endeavor that takes a reductionist, (post)modern theory of religion and applies it to the evidence. Certainly, scholars are free to believe whatever they wish about God, religion, faith, religion and politics, and so forth. But if they want to understand other religious people on their own terms, they must as a matter of methodological necessity set their own views aside, which implies the self-awareness just mentioned. Such an admonition to set one's own convictions aside has long been a commonplace (and justifiably so) among scholars of religion in criticizing traditional confessional historians—Catholic scholars, for example, who viewed Protestants through polemical lenses and never sought to understand them on their own terms, or vice versa. Ironically, however, such criticisms of confessional history permitted ostensibly neutral—but in fact no less morally or metaphysically contentious—secular views to dominate the study of religion. It is time to recognize, in a manner analytically identical to the critique of traditional confessional history, that secular ideas and ideologies are just as capable of distorting the study of religion as are particular religious commitments.

NOTES

1. Quentin Skinner, Introduction to *Visions of Politics,* vol. 1, *Regarding Method* (Cambridge: Cambridge University Press, 2002), 1–7.

2. Aristotle's admonition seems apropos: "it is a mark of an educated person to look in each area for only that degree of accuracy that the nature of the subject permits"; Aristotle, *Nicomachean Ethics,* ed. and trans. Roger Crisp (Cambridge: Cambridge University Press, 2000), 1.3, 5.

3. Skinner, "Seeing," in *Visions of Politics,* vol. 1, 6.

4. For this information on Jacob de Roore, see A. L. E. Verheyden, *Het Brugsche martyrologium (12 October 1527–7 Augustus 1573)* (Brussels: "Wilco," [1944]), 58–60; *The Mennonite Encyclopedia,* vol. 3 (Scottdale, Pa.: Mennonite Publishing House, 1957), 62–63; and M.-J. Reimer-Blok, "The Theological Identity of Flemish Anabaptists: A Study of the Letters of Jacob de Roore," *Mennonite Quarterly Review* 62, no. 3 (1988): 318–31, at 318–19.

5. *Bibliographie des martyrologes protestants néerlandais,* ed. Ferdinand Vander Haeghen et al., vol. 1 (The Hague: Martinus Nijhoff, 1890), 307–18, 667–68.

6. Emile Durkheim, *The Elementary Forms of Religious Life,* trans. Karen E. Fields (New York: Free Press, 1995), 21–22: "Well before the science of religions instituted its methodical comparisons, men had to create their own idea of what religion is. . . . But since these notions are formed unmethodically, in the comings and goings of life, they cannot be relied on and must be rigorously kept to one side in the examination that follows. It is not our preconceptions, passions, or habits that must be consulted for the elements of the definition we need; definition is to be sought from reality itself." By definition, according to Durkheim, this reality is strictly naturalistic and material.

7. On this point, see Peter Winch, *The Idea of a Social Science and Its Relationship to Philosophy,* 2nd ed. (Atlantic Highlands, N.J.: Humanities Press, 1990), 132: "But though extinct ways of thinking may, in a sense, be recaptured by the historian, the way in which the historian thinks them will be coloured by

the fact that he has had to employ historiographical methods to recapture them. The medieval knight did not have to use those methods in order to view his lady in terms of the notions of courtly love: he just thought of her in those terms."

8. R. G. Collingwood, *The Idea of History* (Oxford: Oxford University Press, 1946), esp. 282–315.

9. Thieleman Jans van Braght, *Het Bloedig Tooneel, of Martelaers Spiegel der Doops-gesinde of Weereloose Christenen . . .*, vol. 2 (Amsterdam: J. vander Deyster et al., 1685), 456–57. Beginning in 1615, several of de Roore's letters were anthologized in the Dutch Mennonite martyrologies that culminated with van Braght's *Martyrs' Mirror,* the first edition of which appeared in 1660.

10. Jacob de Roore to fellow Anabaptists in Armentières, June 7–8, 1569, in *The Forgotten Writings of the Mennonite Martyrs,* ed. Brad S. Gregory, vol. 8 in Documenta Anabaptistica Neerlandica (Leiden: E. J. Brill, 2002), 114, lines 15–23.

11. In addition to the letters in van Braght's *Martyrs' Mirror,* see the twelve letters, three songs, and final farewell included originally in Jacob de Roore, *In dit teghenwoordighe Boecxken xijn veel schoone ende lieflijcke Brieven . . .* ([Delft: Schinckel-Hendricxsz Press], 1577), but not reprinted in the subsequent Dutch Mennonite martyrologies, and available in *Forgotten Writings,* ed. Gregory, 49–147.

12. For this idea developed more fully, see Brad S. Gregory, "The Other Confessional History: On Secular Bias in the Study of Religion," *History and Theory, Theme Issue* 45, no. 4 (December 2006): 132–49. For a particularly blatant example of such secular convictions regarded as though their truth were unproblematically obvious, see the recent art historical study of sixteenth-century Lutheran images by Joseph Leo Koerner, *The Reformation of the Image* (Chicago: University of Chicago Press, 2004).

13. On this point, see also Brad S. Gregory, *Salvation at Stake: Christian Martyrdom in Early Modern Europe* (Cambridge, Mass.: Harvard University Press, 1999), 10.

14. Richard Marius, *Thomas More: A Biography* (New York: Knopf, 1984), and *Martin Luther: The Christian between God and Death* (Cambridge, Mass.: Belknap Press of Harvard University Press, 1999).

15. Jacob de Roore to his wife, April 24, 1569, in van Braght, *Martelaers Spiegel,* vol. 2, 452.

16. On the reliability of late sixteenth-century Dutch Mennonite printed martyrological sources in general, and the letters of de Roore in particular, see the introduction to *Forgotten Writings,* ed. Gregory, xxvi–xxvii.

17. E. P. Thompson, *The Making of the English Working Class* (orig. pub. New York: Pantheon Books, 1963; New York: Vintage, 1966), 12. Of course, the Marxist Thompson, while extremely careful not to condescend to nineteenth-century English industrial laborers, was enormously condescending to religious believers such as late eighteenth- and early nineteenth-century Methodists, whose religion he referred to as "a ritualised form of psychic masturbation"; ibid., 368.

18. Jacob de Roore to his children, May 1569, in van Braght, *Martelaers Spiegel*, vol. 2, 459–65.

19. Jacob de Roore to his brother, May 24–25, 1569, in *Forgotten Writings*, ed. Gregory, 84, lines 25–29.

3 Quentin Skinner and the Religious Dimension of Early Modern Political Thought

JOHN COFFEY

> *What has Athens to do with Jerusalem?*
> Tertullian, ca. 220

Quentin Skinner is arguably the most influential historian of ideas at work today. He made his reputation with a set of iconoclastic methodological essays in the late 1960s and early 1970s, and consolidated it with a magisterial two-volume work on *The Foundations of Modern Political Thought* (1978), later listed by the *Times Literary Supplement* among "the hundred most influential [academic] books" published since the Second World War. Since 1978, Skinner has produced a steady stream of articles and books, and has become one of the foremost authorities on Machiavelli and Hobbes. He has written two major studies of Hobbes, and in 2002 Cambridge University Press published a three-volume collection of his essays under the title *Visions of Politics*. A fellow of Christ's College, Cambridge, for most of his career, he has been the leading figure (along with John Pocock) in the so-called "Cambridge School" of intellectual historians. Appointed Professor of Political Science in 1979 and Regius Professor of Modern History in 1996, his exhilarating lectures have inspired generations of students. He has also coedited two influential series with Cambridge University Press: "Ideas in Context," in which more than seventy monographs have been published, and "Cambridge Texts in the History of Political Thought," which now includes modern editions of over one hundred key works from the ancient world to the twentieth century. Skinner's influence extends well beyond the world of Anglophone historiography. Fluent in several European languages, he is widely admired around the world, and was a recipient of the prestigious Balzan Prize in 2006. His writings have been translated into numerous languages (including Turkish and Chinese) and have contributed to a variety of academic disciplines. He is routinely billed as one of the world's leading historians. Few (if any) scholars have done so much to elevate the status and shape the profile of intellectual history.[1]

In this essay, I wish to focus on the curious fact that this eminent intellectual historian has largely neglected religious ideas. In doing so, I will be concentrating on Skinner's historical practice rather than on his methodological prescriptions. The two are obviously related, though the degree to which Skinner has followed his own advice is a matter of some debate.[2] In the first half of the paper, I will discuss what some critics have called Skinner's "secularization" of early modern political thought. I will then turn to a case study of his most recent writings on the ideological origins of the English Revolution and suggest ways in which the history of religious ideas might complement Skinner's work.

THE HISTORIAN AS SECULAR EXCAVATOR

In his introductory essay in *Visions of Politics*, "Seeing Things Their Way," Skinner offers a programmatic statement on the task of the intellectual historian:

> If we approach the past with a willingness to listen, with a commitment to trying to see things their way, we can hope to prevent ourselves from becoming too readily bewitched [by our own intellectual traditions]. An understanding of the past can help us to appreciate

how far the values embodied in our present way of life, and our present ways of thinking about those values, reflect a series of choices made at different times between different possible worlds. This awareness can help to liberate us from the grip of any one hegemonal account of those values and how they should be interpreted and understood. Equipped with a broader sense of possibility, we can stand back from the intellectual commitments we have inherited and ask ourselves in a new spirit of enquiry what we should think of them.[3]

This statement depicts the history of ideas as a project of retrieval, in which historians patiently reconstruct "the beliefs of alien cultures or earlier societies" and even employ them as tools of contemporary critique and reform. Indeed, in his inaugural lecture as Regius Professor, Skinner suggested that the historian can act "as a kind of archaeologist, bringing buried intellectual treasure back to the surface, dusting it down and enabling us to reconsider what we think of it."[4] To a naïve historian of religious thought this might suggest an Erasmian programme of Christian scholarship devoted to digging up and dusting down ancient spiritual ideals that can stimulate reform and renewal. But the "buried intellectual treasure" Skinner has in mind is emphatically secular. He has done much to excavate the concept of classical liberty but has displayed little interest in reconstructing early modern religious beliefs.

Skinner has described himself as "a modern unbeliever," and his atheism has clearly had some impact on the shape and the limits of his historical inquiries.[5] In a prickly exchange with the philosopher Charles Taylor, Skinner made it abundantly clear that any project of retrieval which involved the "readoption" of theism would be a "cure for our ills potentially worse than the disease." He took particular exception to Taylor's suggestion (in the final pages of *Sources of the Self*) that the Judeo-Christian tradition offered the best hope for affirming the dignity of humanity. The history of Christianity, insisted Skinner, fatally undermined any such claim. In purple prose reminiscent of Voltaire, he expressed incredulity at Taylor, "the protagonist of theism":

> During the centuries when this [Christian] perspective was imposed on western Europe, however, the outcome in human terms was noth-

ing short of catastrophic. The medieval centuries were marked by unremitting and barbarous persecutions, while the attempt to challenge the powers of the Catholic Church in the sixteenth century led to several generations of savage religious war. . . . It is all too clear . . . that Christianity has often proved an intolerant religion, and that some at least of the wars and persecutions with which it has been associated have actually flowed from its character as a creed.[6]

Given this profoundly derogatory assessment of medieval and early modern Christianity, and Skinner's concern to retrieve "buried intellectual treasure," it is little wonder that he has chosen to focus his energies on secular rather than religious ideas. Although he admires the work of Stuart Clark, whose *Thinking with Demons* offers an extraordinary reconstruction of the discourse of early modern demonologists, it is hard to imagine Skinner himself putting in twenty years of hard labor on rebarbative treatises about witchcraft and evil spirits.[7]

This is not to say that the avoidance of strange religious ideas is required by his methodological prescriptions. He has written sympathetically about the need to "investigate and explain the unfamiliar beliefs we encounter in past societies." His essay on "Interpretation, Rationality and Truth" makes a powerful case for taking the rationality of our subjects seriously even when their beliefs seem to us patently false or even "bizarre."[8] Yet in practice, Skinner has steered clear of working on "bizarre beliefs"—demonology, astrology, and even millenarianism barely feature in his large body of work. Whereas many secular-minded scholars are drawn to the study of religious past simply out of "natural curiosity," Skinner has not been able to escape the feeling that historical research should have some "practical use."[9] In particular, he has displayed an admirable concern to participate (as an historian) in debates in contemporary political theory.[10] But believing that religious traditions have little or nothing to contribute to modern intellectual culture, he has chosen to focus his energies on political traditions that might yield something useful. Although one of his earliest published pieces was a student essay on the sectarian Puritan John Bunyan, he has felt far more at home with two early modern intellectuals who struck their contemporaries as (in some sense) atheistic: Machiavelli and Hobbes.[11]

Having said that, Skinner's magnum opus, *The Foundations of Modern Political Thought*, did engage quite extensively with the political writings of clerics and theologians. *Foundations* remains the finest introduction to early modern political ideas, and continues to generate lively discussion three decades after its publication. It is no exaggeration to say that the book changed the way the history of political thought was written.[12] The second volume, which dealt with "The Age of Reformation," is where we find Skinner's most extended discussion of the religious dimension of political thought. As Mark Goldie has recently noted, Skinner's "exploration of the Middle Ages, and the construction of the second volume around Luther, Calvin and the Counter-Reformation, unavoidably entailed an encounter with theology." It also involved a powerful critique of Whiggish and Weberian modernization narratives that denigrated the Catholic Middle Ages and glorified the Protestant revolt. Although Skinner included a brief discussion of the importance of the Bible in Protestant thought, his central claim was that scholars like Michael Walzer had exaggerated the distinctive contribution of Lutherans and Calvinists to early modern theories of resistance. Like J. N. Figgis before him, Skinner traced the roots of constitutionalism and resistance theory back to medieval theorists. Goldie suggests that he "recovered the Catholic political tradition in order to dispose of Protestant theories of liberal modernity. He did so not of course in order to recommend Catholicism, but rather to clear the ground for a quite different route into the history of concepts of liberty, a subject upon which so much of his more recent work has dwelt."[13]

Despite this engagement with political theology, *Foundations* was still underpinned by a secular teleology.[14] Although Skinner's subjects were often devout Christians, he himself was searching for the first signs of "a recognisably modern, secularised thesis about the natural rights and original sovereignty of the people." The book culminates with the Calvinist George Buchanan, who is credited with a political theory restated "in the language of rights rather than religious duties," "a fully populist as well as a completely secularised theory of the right to resist." Working on the assumption that secularity was one of the chief characteristics of modern thought, Skinner took it for granted that a "fully *political* theory of revolution" would be one shorn of religion—in so far as religion intruded, a political theory was not "genuinely" political.[15]

Skinner's quest for "secularised" nuggets buried in the dark seams of pre-Enlightenment European thought did not cease with *Foundations*. In his work since 1978, he has written almost nothing on Protestant or Catholic thought. Instead, he has continued to work on the concepts of the state and liberty, and on Machiavelli, republicanism, and rhetorical culture, topics he first explored in volume 1 of *Foundations*. He has written about Sir Thomas More, but is attracted to the humanist More of *Utopia*, not the Catholic More who resisted Henry VIII and defended the execution of Protestant heretics. He has also touched on Machiavelli's civil religion, and on republican ideas about religion and civic virtue, but without exploring them in any depth. In writing about Hobbes and Milton, Skinner has managed to bypass the weighty heterodox theology of *Leviathan* parts 3 and 4 and the radical Puritanism of England's great republican poet.

As an historian keen to avoid the charge of antiquarianism, Skinner is determined "to uncover the often neglected riches of our intellectual heritage and display them once more to view."[16] But since the religiosity of pre-Enlightenment Europe was "catastrophic" in its consequences, and since intellectual modernity is (mercifully) secular, he naturally assumes that the intellectual historian who wishes to be of service to his contemporaries will focus on excavating secular ideas, leaving religion to his more antiquarian colleagues.

Of course, this neglect of religion may be entirely defensible. Skinner has given us a uniquely rich body of work, characterized by immense erudition, lucid exposition, and powerful argument. Critics of his work ("a distressingly numerous group" as he observes)[17] are likely to resemble belligerent Lilliputians pestering Gulliver. His writings are an intellectual feast, and carping about what is not on the table seems ungrateful. After all, no one expects historians of theology to do demography or even political thought. Why should anyone expect historians of political thought to do God? Are not historians at liberty to cultivate whatever field they choose, guided by their own interests, passions, and expertise? No one complains when feminist historians study women's history or when socialist historians concentrate on working class radicals. So why should there be a problem when an atheist historian concentrates on secular political theory, or (for that matter) when a Christian historian specialises in ecclesiastical history? Skinner himself recognizes the need for research on the religious aspect of political thought, and recently organized a conference on "Religious Freedom and Civil Liberty" as part of a series entitled "Freedom and the Construction of Europe: New Perspectives on Philosophical, Religious and Political Controversies."[18] But he admits that "there are only a small number of historical topics that truly fascinate me." Since 1978, he observes, "I have always kept off religious themes, and tried to write about themes that won't be skewed by that aversion."[19]

Whether this approach succeeds is a question that we will address below, with particular reference to his recent writings on the ideological origins of the English civil war. But it is worth noting that critics of Skinner's early work on Reformation political thought are not convinced that he did justice to the religious dimension of the subject. They allege that even in *Foundations* his secular orientation distorted his account. In an article on "The Fear of God in Early Modern Political Theory," David Wootton drew attention to the deeply rooted early modern assumption that belief in God was the foundation of morality and society. He pointed out that Skinner's depiction of Althusius and Locke as proponents of a secular political theory is hard to square with the insistence of Althusius that the Decalogue is the bond of civil society and the determination of Locke to exclude atheists from toleration because they could not be trusted to keep their promises. Wootton suggested that Skinner was misled by his own methodology, which searches for specific intentions in particular texts to the neglect of shared and unspoken assumptions, such as the necessity of the fear of God.[20] In "Quentin Skinner and the Secularization of Political Thought," Paul Marshall argued that because Skinner focuses on a narrowly defined set of political texts, he fails to develop a broad picture of Calvinist thought and misses distinctive aspects of the tradition, such as the doctrine of the callings or the idea of sphere sovereignty.[21] In an acclaimed study of Calvinist iconoclasm, Carlos Eire also protested against Skinner's claim that there was nothing distinctive about Calvinist political thought. For Eire, Skinner engages in a "grand secularization of Calvinism" and misses the great shibboleth of the Calvinists, idolatry. "If there is one concept," he writes, "that stands out as some sort of red blinking light in all the Calvinist theories from Calvin to Buchanan, it is precisely this issue of idolatry." "By refusing to consider the full theological dimensions of Calvinist resistance theories, Skinner has failed to take into account the one factor that gives Calvinism its soul."[22]

Most recently, Anne McLaren has taken issue with Skinner's reading of the key work of Huguenot resistance theory, the *Vindiciae, Contra Tyrannos* (1579). Skinner argued that this and other major Huguenot treatises articulated the first "fully *political* theory of revolution," as the French Protestants (aiming to broaden their support base) toned down their religious rationale and increasingly grounded their claims in scholastic and Roman law traditions of radical constitutionalism. But McLaren contends that Skinner's reading of the *Vindiciae* systematically privileges marginal references to classical sources over references to biblical sources, even though the scriptural citations "outweigh all other kinds *combined* in a ratio of roughly 5 to 1." By "pointedly ignoring the overwhelming dominance of scriptural references throughout the text as a whole," McLaren alleges, Skinner "has seriously distorted our understanding of this text." Once we restore the biblical dimension we are reminded of "the absolute centrality of revealed religion to every aspect of early modern culture, including its politics."[23]

Skinner's critics are not beyond criticism themselves. Wootton has displayed a Whiggish preoccupation with the origins of modern atheism.[24] Marshall imports modern neo-Calvinist categories like "sphere sovereignty" into his discussion of sixteenth-century Reformed thought. Eire exaggerates the Calvinism of Buchanan's *De Jure Regni,* missing the fact that unlike Knox, Buchanan's treatise had little to say about idolatry.[25] McLaren is less generous than she might have been about Skinner's achievement in exploring the classical sources and legal arguments employed by the Huguenots, and some of her central claims have been strongly challenged by George Garnett.[26]

Nevertheless, the critics are onto something. Skinner's resolutely secular orientation does become a liability when applied to the Reformation era. For historians of post-Enlightenment political thought, neglect of religion may be less debilitating. But in the sixteenth and seventeenth centuries, the religious dimension is too significant to be sidestepped. When the economic historian Jack Fisher was approached by a student asking for introductory reading on early modern history, he replied: "If you really want to understand the period, go away and read the Bible."[27]

If the Bible is recommended reading for early modern economic historians, it is surely required reading for early modern intellectual historians. Political theorists in the sixteenth and seventeenth centuries were often well versed in theology, and their writings were commonly peppered with biblical citations. It is hardly surprising then that various figures in the so-called Cambridge School have turned to the study of religious ideas in order to understand early modern political thought. John Pocock, for example, has been noticeably alert to the significance of religious ideas, most recently in his multi-volume work on Edward Gibbon. Indeed, Pocock is at the forefront of those arguing that "Enlightenment was a product of religious debate and not merely a rebellion against it."[28] John Dunn, a contemporary and colleague of Skinner, and professor of political theory at Cambridge, made his reputation with a book on Locke that challenged secular interpretations of the philosopher by arguing that the *Two Treatises of Government* was "saturated with Christian assumptions."[29]

Dunn's book prepared the ground for further work on the biblical and theological foundations of Locke's political theory by scholars like Ian Harris, John Marshall, and Jeremy Waldron.[30] Some of Skinner's own students have also written extensively about religious ideas. Mark Goldie, in particular, has illuminated the connections between religious and political ideas in a series of groundbreaking essays.[31]

Indeed, the move towards putting religion back into the history of political thought can be observed even in the case of Skinner's favorite subjects, Hobbes and republicanism. Although the role of God in Hobbes's philosophy was being explored back in the 1960s, there has been a resurgence of interest in the philosopher's religious thought. John Pocock led the way with an essay on the apocalyptic element in Hobbes's politics, Noel Malcolm examined his voluntarist theology and biblical criticism, and Richard Tuck has explored the "Christian atheism" and "civil religion" of parts 3 and 4 of *Leviathan*.[32] With regard to republicanism, a flurry of recent research has uncovered the biblical and rabbinic sources of republican thought.[33] Some of that work has been published in the journal *Hebraic Political Studies* (2005–), whose establishment testifies to the growing recognition of the importance of the Hebrew Bible in the Western political tradition. Meanwhile, historians of Anglophone republicanism have begun to explore its relationship with radical and reformist Protestantism. Jonathan Scott has argued that historians need "to explain why, when classical republicanism came to England, it did so in the moral service of a religious revolution."[34] Mark Noll maintains that after the American Revolution, theologians and other intellectuals forged a synthesis of "evangelical Protestant religion, republican political ideology, and commonsense moral reasoning."[35]

In recovering the religious dimension of political thought, the historians we have just cited are reflecting what we might call "the religious turn" across the humanities. As Jonathan Sheehan recently pointed out in the *American Historical Review*, religion returned "to the scholarly limelight" across a wide range of disciplines in the late twentieth century—a development reflected in the dramatic growth of the religion sections of the major American scholarly associations.[36] In the historical profession, the demise of Marxism and the rise of cultural history have both boosted the study of religion, and political historians have been placing far more emphasis on the religious factor. What makes Quentin Skinner's work so intriguing is that it defies this broader trend by offering a noticeably secularized approach to early modern political thought.

LIBERTY, BIBLICAL NARRATIVE, AND THE ENGLISH CIVIL WAR

Nowhere is Skinner's secularized approach more apparent that in his recent work on the ideological origins of the English Civil War. In his inaugural lecture as Regius Professor in 1997, his Ford Lectures at Oxford University in 2003, and in a series of essays, Skinner has argued that the Parliamentarians went to war with Charles I inspired by a concept of liberty that we have all but forgotten.[37] Drawing on the work of the political philosopher Philip Pettit, Skinner takes issue with Isaiah Berlin's famous essay in which he identified "Two Concepts of Liberty." Berlin distinguished between positive and negative liberty. Advocates of positive liberty assume that human nature has an essence, and that we are only truly free when we fulfil that essence. Thus Aristotelians, who believe that man is a political animal, will teach that true freedom can only be found when we involve ourselves in the life of the polis. And Christians, who assume that man has been created to know God, will maintain with Archbishop Cranmer that service of God is "perfect freedom." Freedom consists in following that way of life in which we finally achieve harmony with our nature. The alternative concept of liberty that Berlin identifies and commends is negative liberty. On this account, liberty consists in the absence of constraint, or noninterference. I am unfree if I am prevented by others from doing what I could otherwise do.

Skinner praises Berlin for clarifying these two concepts of liberty but also faults him for failing to identify "a third concept of liberty." This third concept is also a negative liberty, but it is liberty as *the absence of dependence,* rather than interference. It has its roots in the political theory of the ancient Romans, who defined liberty in opposition to slavery. For the Romans a slave was someone subjected to the dominion of someone else, and a free citizen was someone who was not under the dominion of someone else but capable of acting in his own right. This concept of liberty was popularized by the great Roman historians Sallust, Livy, and Tacitus, codified in the *Digest* of Roman law and in Justinian's *Codex,* and transmitted by the medieval English common-law texts of Bracton and Littleton.

Skinner demonstrates that early Stuart Englishmen were familiar with the classical historians, Roman law, and common law, and that lawyers in the early Stuart Parliaments employed this concept of liberty in their arguments against the royal prerogative. They argued that the English could be deprived of their freedom not merely by direct interference or violation of personal liberties and property rights, but also by any prerogative or discretionary powers that made the freedom of subjects dependent on the good will of the king. After all, what defined a slave was not interference but dependence—a lenient master might grant considerable leeway to a trusted slave, but since this noninterference was dependent on the will of the master, the slave was still a slave. Critics of royal policy alleged that the English people were being reduced to a state of servitude because the king claimed to be able to imprison his subjects without just cause and to impose levies like Ship

Money without consulting their representatives. In 1642, the Parliamentarians used the same argument to deny the king's negative voice. They insisted that if the crown could veto legislation, this would reduce Parliament and the freeborn people it represented to a state of complete dependence on the will of the king. As Skinner puts it, "If there was any one slogan under which the two Houses finally took up arms, it was that the people of England never, never, never shall be slaves."[38]

For those unfamiliar with the period, it is worth underlining the boldness of Skinner's move. The debate over the origins of the English Civil War has been described as the favorite blood sport of English historians, and eminent scholars like R. H. Tawney and Lawrence Stone have limped from the arena carrying severe wounds. Moreover, all major interpretations of the war insist on the centrality of religion in the conflict. The great Whig historian S. R. Gardiner called this "the Puritan Revolution." The Marxist Christopher Hill preferred to speak of the English Revolution, but having been raised a Methodist he had some sympathy for the political traditions of dissent, and throughout his long career he wrote scores of articles and books about militant Protestantism, including *Puritanism and Revolution*, *The English Bible and the Seventeenth-Century Revolution*, and major biographical studies of Milton and Bunyan. For revisionist historians who overturned Whig and Marxist orthodoxies in the 1970s and 1980s, religion was essential to explaining why the English political nation divided in two and why the Parliamentarians took up arms against their king.[39] John Morrill even described the conflict as "the last of the Wars of Religion."[40] Postrevisionists were unwilling to go this far, and wished to rehabilitate social and constitutional factors, but they too emphasized the importance of religion.[41]

Skinner, by contrast, offers an ideological account of the origins of the war that simply bypasses the religious factor and places great weight on classical sources and ideas. In such a contested field, it is hardly surprising that his provocative proposal has already met with some skepticism. Sir Keith Thomas argues that Skinner has greatly exaggerated the impact of "neo-Roman" ideas on Parliamentarians. His key figure, Henry Parker, was not particularly representative; Parliamentary leaders did not oppose the royal veto as such; and there is little evidence of theoretical republicanism among the regicides in 1649. Moreover, intellectual history is inadequate when it comes to explaining political events: "we should not mistake an account of the way in which the war was legitimized for an explanation of why it occurred." Skinner's relatively narrow focus on the history of ideas cannot compete with a broad-based explanation of the causes of the English Civil War, such as that provided by a scholar like Conrad Russell. As Thomas observes:

> [Skinner] does not concern himself with the social, economic, fiscal, administrative, religious and personal contributions to the crisis between 1640 and 1642. Instead, he sees the Parliamentarians as highly cerebral theorists, deeply versed in sophisticated political reasoning, mounting "cases," advancing "claims," making "moves" (frequently "crucial" moves), following "strategies," and developing "lines of attack" in a sort of intellectual chess game. Perhaps this is why G. R. Elton feared that intellectual history was "liable to lose contact with reality."

For our purposes, Thomas's most important point concerns Skinner's failure to deal with religion. He notes that Skinner's interpretation of the ideological origins of the war "is very different from the conventional view, which is that the Parliamentarians typically justified themselves by appealing to the ancient constitution and denouncing the dangers of popery." Although Skinner is openly drawing on Thomas Hobbes's history of the English Civil War, he only concentrates on one half of the philosopher's analysis. Hobbes did emphasize the role of "democraticall gentlemen" like Parker, but he "also regarded the Presbyterian preachers as equally responsible for the Civil War." As Thomas observes, "Skinner ignores the volume of Puritan sentiment and anti-Catholic propaganda which made waverers object to Charles I, not because the King possessed the royal prerogative, but because they felt he could not be trusted."[42]

In the face of such criticism, Skinner acknowledges that the religious dimension is of "great importance," and merits more attention than he has given it. But he stresses that he never claimed "to be offering anything resembling *the explanation* for the outbreak [of the Civil War]." And he continues to insist on the priority of constitutional grievances over religious ones. In his view, the men who were moving towards war were not so much the religious activists who favored root and branch reform of the church, but those who saw arbitrary power as the real threat. In response to Keith Thomas, he points out that his analysis is not merely based on a study of pamphleteers like Henry Parker, but on following through "the whole parliamentary story in 1641–42."[43]

It is, however, hard to see how Skinner's interpretation can prevail without dealing more directly with revisionist arguments about the primacy of the religious factor and integrating religious ideas into his analysis. At present, Skinner and the revisionists seem to be talking about two entirely different events. If revisionists see the English Civil War as a Reformation conflict, Skinner depicts it as a Renaissance phenomenon rooted in a neo-Roman theory of liberty. For John Morrill, the leading Parliamentarian activists are Bible-thumping, Puritan zealots; for Skinner they are classics-loving "democraticall gentlemen."[44]

A more balanced account of the Parliamentarian cause will attend to both the biblical and the classical, the Renaissance and the Reformation.[45] One could argue that Skinner is engaged in rebalancing, since so much of the previous literature neglected the classical in favor of the religious. The Victorians and their successors, being soaked in the Bible themselves, made of the 1640s an emphatically "Puritan" revolution.[46] But by privileging Roman law over Hebrew Scripture, Skinner gives the misleading impression that religion was of negligible importance in 1642. In order to understand Parliamentarianism, one has to go beyond the "democraticall gentlemen" to what Anthony Fletcher has called "the Puritan core of the Parliamentarian party."[47] In order to demonstrate that the Parliamentarians conceived of the civil war as a war of liberation from slavery, we need to turn to the sermons of Puritan preachers and the writings of Puritan activists. These people spearheaded the Parliamentarian cause in 1642 and beyond—no account of Parliamentarian ideology can afford to ignore the godly.[48]

Skinner's reluctance to reckon with Puritanism is hardly surprising, given his habitual avoidance of religious ideas, but it is a missed opportunity. For when we turn to Puritan sermons and writings, the theme of deliverance from slavery looms large. The one scholar to appreciate this is the Jewish political theorist, Michael Walzer, who began his career with a major (and controversial) book on Puritan politics, *Revolution of the Saints* (1965). Walzer's argument, that English Puritans founded modern revolutionary politics, was rejected by Skinner and other historians.[49] Despite the problematic character of its central thesis, *Revolution of the Saints* did contain rich insights into the Puritan political sermon. During his research, Walzer read "many sermons in which the Book of Exodus figured as a central text or a reiterated reference," and two decades later, he published a short study entitled *Exodus and Revolution*. He argued that the biblical Exodus was "crucial . . . to the self-understanding of the English Puritans during the 1640s," and provided "a paradigm of revolutionary politics." For Parliamentarians, as for later political movements, the Exodus was an example of "national liberation," the deliverance of an enslaved people.[50]

Walzer did not document his claims in any detail, but he is quite right about the prominence of the Exodus in the thinking of Puritan Parliamentarians.[51] Indeed, if we turn to the Fast Sermons preached by Puritan divines before Parliament, such as the one preached by Cornelius Burgess at the opening of the Long Parliament in November 1640, we find that the entire history of ancient Israel was interpreted as a story of "deliverance upon deliverance." The Exodus was the foundational narrative of the Jewish nation, and Puritans repeatedly invoked Israel's experience of "Egyptian bondage" under Pharoah and his "cruel taskmasters," and the nation's deliverance through the Red Sea. But the preachers also reminded their hearers that after it reached the Promised Land, Israel fell under the "yoke" of other oppressors and had to be liberated by judges or "deliverers" like Gideon, Deborah, and Samson. Finally, the Jews had endured seventy years of "Babylonish captivity," only to be delivered once again in a second Exodus, when intervention by an army from the north led to Cyrus's "Proclamation of Libertie." England, the preachers declared, had recapitulated the Jewish experience, for England had also enjoyed "a Catalogue" of "many, great, stupendous, and even miraculous deliverances." She had been delivered from popish bondage by Edward VI and by Elizabeth I ("that glorious Deborah"). She had experienced further "deliverances" in 1588, 1605, and now again in 1640–41.[52] Stephen Marshall, the great Puritan demagogue, announced in September 1641 that "this wonderfull yeer" had been a year of "Jubilee," a year of liberation for slaves. "This yeer have we seen broken the yokes which lay upon our estates, Liberties, Religion, and Conscience; the intolerable yokes of Star-Chamber, and terrible High-Commission." Addressing the "Right Honourable and Noble Senators," he declared that they were at the start of their own "Passover."[53] A few months later, the influential London preacher Edmund Calamy pictured the English people as rather further on in their Exodus—he compared the English to the children of Israel, who after being delivered from Egypt through the Red Sea, soon began "to murmur, and to think of making a captain to return to Egypt, never considering the iron bondage they endured in Egypt."[54]

As these examples suggest, the Parliamentarian preachers prompted their congregations to inhabit the biblical narrative. Hearers imagined themselves and their nation enduring Egyptian bondage, sharing the first Passover meal, being pursued by Pharoah's army, crossing the Red Sea, murmuring against their deliverers, wandering in the wilderness, camping at the foot of Mount Sinai, or standing on the verge of the Jordan. In the minds of the godly, England was reenacting Israel's Exodus (and Israel's return from exile), leaving Egyptian bondage (or Babylonian captivity) behind, and marching towards the Promised Land.

Unlike Roman law, biblical narrative did not provide Parliamentarians with legal arguments to justify their rebellion. But it gave them something just as important—a story that legitimized resistance and forced them to choose between the garlic and onions of their Egyptian captivity and the long and arduous trek towards freedom. As early as April 1640, in the first Parliament since 1629, Sir Francis Seymour delivered a speech in which he compared "our affairs to the bondage of the Israelites in Egypt." In a deferential monarchical society, this was an incendiary analogy, and it clearly shocked some contemporaries.[55] But Seymour's belief that the English were being treated like the Hebrew slaves was widely shared. The royalist divine Edward Symmons complained of the Parliamentarians, "How often have they compared [the king] to Pharoah."[56] During the civil wars, zealous Parliamentarians saluted their military commanders for leading them out of slavery—the Earl of Essex, Fairfax, and Cromwell were all described as England's "Moses."[57]

Cromwell himself believed that the "stupendous" events he had witnessed between 1640 and 1653 amounted to England's Exodus. At the opening of the first Protectorate Parliament in September 1653, the Independent divine Thomas Goodwin preached a sermon on the Exodus, tracing Israel's journey "out of Egypt towards the land of Canaan." In his own speech to the Parliament, Cromwell gave his formal stamp of approval to Goodwin's reading of Scripture and Providence: "you had today in the sermon . . . much allusion to a State, and dispensation in respect of discipline and correction, of mercies and deliverances,—the only parallel of God's dealing with us that I know in the world, which was largely and wisely held forth to you this day; Israel's bringing-out of Egypt through a wilderness, by many signs and wonders towards a place of rest: I say, *towards* it."[58] It is no wonder that royalists accused Cromwell of casting himself as England's Moses, called to lead the people through the wilderness and toward the Promised Land.[59]

The biblical narrative of deliverance from slavery had the power to capture imaginations, but for this very reason it was a difficult story to control. The preachers of the Fast Sermons chose not to linger over the emancipatory promise of the Exodus. Although they employed the language of "slavery," "bondage," "yokes," and "deliverance," they mainly used the Exodus narrative to drive home other points—such as the necessity of firm leadership, obedience to divine commandments, and strict adherence to a covenant with God. The divines who preached before Parliament were usually anxious to see a new form of church government and religious uniformity established as soon as possible, and they did not want their hearers to dwell too much on ideas of liberation from slavery.

Yet it was this theme that transfixed many Parliamentarians, especially Independents and radicals. In a key work of Parliamentarian resistance theory, *Anti-Cavalierisme* (1642), the London divine John Goodwin emphasized that this was a war of liberation from "bondage" and "servitude." As Skinner has recently observed, Goodwin's tract provides "perhaps the clearest summary" of the classical distinction between liberty and dependence, and hence between free-men and slaves.[60] Goodwin addressed his audience as "free men and women" who enjoyed "the disposal of your selves and of all your wayes"; but he warned that they could lose their liberty by becoming subject to the "arbitterments and wills" of "domineering" royalists who would "make themselves Lords over you." Goodwin may have imbibed this definition of liberty from classical history, Roman law, or Henry Parker, but his phraseology was derived from scripture. Thus he speaks of "an Iron yoke of bondage" (Deuteronomy 28:48; Jeremiah 28:13–14), "cruell bondage" (Exodus 6:9), "heavy burdens" (Isaiah 58:6), "bands," "chains," and "fetters" (Leviticus 26:13; Jeremiah 39:7; Judges 16:21; 2 Kings 25:7; 2 Chronicles 36:6); and he tells his hearers, "you shall break their cords asunder, and cast their bands from you for ever" (Psalm 2:3). He did not give chapter and verse for any of these phrases, but his biblically literate readers surely recognized their scriptural provenance. Goodwin urged them not to "exchange your Quailes and Manna from Heaven, for the Garlike and Onyons of Egypt."[61] As I have shown elsewhere, deliverance from slavery is one of the key motifs in Goodwin's revolutionary writings from 1642 to 1649 and beyond. For him, the English Civil War was a war of liberation from both civil and ecclesiastical bondage. It was this conception of the conflict and its *telos* that led him to promote liberty of conscience and a free commonwealth.[62]

Goodwin's political trajectory in the 1640s paralleled that of John Milton—both men championed religious liberty against the Presbyterians and then wrote in defence of regicide and republic (indeed, a royal proclamation of 1660 coupled them together and ordered the burning of their treasonous tracts). In his essay, "John Milton and the Politics of Slavery," Skinner shows that Milton was well acquainted with the neoclassical idea of liberty and articulated it with great power in his political treatises. Yet once again, he has nothing to say about the religious dimension of political thought. He ends his essay with a quotation from *Samson Agonistes*, in which the enslaved Samson laments the fact that Judah had failed to fight for her own deliverance and had grown "to love bondage more than liberty." Skinner then adds a final word: "Despite the Biblical setting, it is hard not to feel that Milton is here offering his last and bitterest reflection on the failure of the good old cause."[63] The "despite" here is telling, for it implies that "the Biblical setting" somehow gets in the way of Milton's presentation of a neoclassical idea of liberty. In reality, however, biblical narrative provided the perfect vehicle for articulating a politics of deliverance from slavery in Puritan England. When one studies Milton's references to liberty and bondage, "the Biblical setting" is unmistakeable. In his anti-prelatical tracts, Milton lambasts the bishops as "Egyptian task-masters" and looks forward to the day when the English can take up their harps to celebrate their crossing of the Red Sea. In his defences of the regicide and the republic, he chides the royalists for peddling "Pharoah's divinity" and celebrates deliverance from monarchy, "that yoke of slavery." On the eve of the Restoration, Milton rebukes his fellow countrymen for "choosing them a captain back to Egypt." In *Samson Agonistes*, he turns to the story of a judge who delivered his people from bondage.[64] His language of slavery, whilst indebted to the classics, is shot through with echoes of Scripture. A rounded account of Milton's politics of liberty needs to deal with both the Greco-Roman and the Hebraic, with the neoclassical concept of liberty and the biblical narrative of liberation.[65]

As the quotations from Milton and Goodwin illustrate, Parliamentarians worried about ecclesiastical as much as civil slavery. They were as exercised by tyranny over conscience as they were by royal prerogative powers. Puritans accused the Caroline bishops of binding Christian consciences by enforcing conformity to their "idolatrous" ceremonies. It was the campaign against episcopacy in 1641 that started to divide the political nation down the middle.[66] Skinner's analysis of Parliamentarian argument focuses entirely on secular issues (the king's negative voice, control of the militia, property) and ignores this crucial theme. In expounding a key text like *A Remonstrance in Defence of the Lords and Commons in Parliament* (1642), he underplays the significance of religion. When the Parliamentarians list what they are fighting for, religion is ranked first. They explain: "All true hearted Subjects ought to fight to maintaine the purity and substance thereof, that it may not be changed into the ceremonious formality of Popery, in that their consciences may not be brought into the subjection of Roman slavery." Although this statement mentions "slavery," Skinner does not cite it, perhaps because it illustrates the centrality of antipopery to the Parliamentarian cause. Yet the Parliamentarian fear of slavery was not simply an apprehension of regal bondage, it was also (as the *Remonstrance* makes clear) a fear of "Roman slavery," "the Popes tyrannie," and "loads imposed" by "ambitious Clergy." Parliamentarians worried that "the malignant party" (led by the bishops) would become "masters of our Religion and liberties to makes us slaves."[67]

The attack on prelatical bondage quickly broadened into a general assault on various forms of ecclesiastical tyranny. Radical Parliamentarians contrasted clerical bondage with Christian liberty, the blind obedience of the servile multitude with the willingness of the godly to search the scriptures and think for themselves. The Puritan divine Henry Burton invoked the Exodus in his sermon *England's Bondage and Hope of Deliverance* (1641), and coined the term "Independent" to describe self-governing congregations who were no longer "beslaved under the yoke of Prelaticall tyranny, under Egyptian Task-masters." "Independency" was about liberty from subjection to domineering human authorities.[68] By the mid-1640s, Independents and radicals had turned the language of liberty and slavery against the Presbyterians who sought a crackdown on sects and heresies.[69] The Leveller tolerationist William Walwyn condemned Presbyterian plans for religious uniformity—it was as if "the Israelites, after the Egyptian bondage, had become Task-masters in the Land of Canaan one to another."[70] The Scottish Covenanters, who had been allies of the Parliament, now came to be viewed as the agents of Pharoah. When Cromwell defeated them in battle, John Goodwin wrote a psalm of deliverance, praising God for rescuing England from "the house of slavery" and the "iron yoke" of the Scottish clergy.[71] By portraying the civil war as a war of liberation from servitude, the preachers of the Fast Sermons had inadvertently given opponents of religious uniformity a powerful rhetorical weapon.

As well as being used by tolerationists, Exodus language was appropriated by all the leading radical movements of the 1640s and 1650s. As Skinner himself notes, the Levellers turned the ideas of liberty and bondage against the Lords, the Commons, and the Commonwealth regime in a stream of pamphlets with titles like *Englands Lamentable Slaverie* and *Englands New Chains Discovered*. What he fails to register are the biblical resonances and allusions in Leveller prose. In 1649, for example, Lilburne complained that the "inslaving corruptions" of the day were "as bad in a manner as the old bondage of Egypt." Another Leveller tract urged all who share a "desire of deliverance, or freedome from their worse then Egyptian bondage" to act against the regime, warning those in power that if the opportunity arises their enemies "will swallow and devour them up alive," "like a raging sea on Pharoah and his host."[72] The Digger Gerrard Winstanley praised Cromwell for casting out "an oppressing Pharoah" and gaining "the highest honour of any man since Moses." But he then challenged the Lord General to complete England's Exodus by leading the way to a Promised Land without private property.[73] The Fifth Monarchist, John Spittlehouse, identified numerous parallels between England's Revolution and Israel's Exodus: Egypt represented "our Antichristian slavery"; Pharoah, "our late King"; Moses and Aaron, the Parliament and Assembly of Divines; the Red Sea, "Prelacy"; the death of Moses, the death of General Essex; Joshua, General Fairfax; the River Jordan, "Presbytery." Spittlehouse later argued at length that Cromwell was England's Moses, whose appointed role in history was to overthrow earthly monarchies and replace them with the fifth monarchy of God.[74]

Puritan republicans too believed that England was treading in Israel's footsteps. For them, the abolition of monarchy and the establishment of a free commonwealth was a glorious leap forward towards the Promised Land. Writing in 1651, the republican poet George Wither rejoiced in England's deliverance from "Egyptian thralldome"; like Pharoah in the Red Sea, Charles I had drowned (as it were) in the sea of blood shed in the civil wars.[75] Henry Stubbe also believed that England's story paralleled Israel's Exodus.[76] At the Restoration, as England embraced monarchy and episcopacy once again, disillusioned Puritan republicans joined Milton in complaining that the English had chosen a captain to lead them back to Egypt. As Algernon Sidney put it, "We could never be contented till we returned again into Egypt, the house of our bondage. God had delivered us from slavery and showed us that he would be our king; and we recall from exile one of that detested race."[77] The popularity of this trope is indicated by the young John Locke, who initially welcomed the Restoration and scorned those who lamented that "we are returning to Egypt."[78]

The prominence of the Exodus narrative during the revolutionary decades adds weight to Skinner's claim that the English Civil War was (for Parliamentarians) "a war of national liberation from servitude."

And it helps to explain how the idea of enslavement gripped the Parliamentarian imagination. Familiar biblical stories put narrative flesh on abstract concepts of liberty and slavery, and invested them with intense spiritual significance. It offered a powerful means of dramatizing the contemporary concern about enslavement, mobilizing popular support behind the cause, and reassuring Parliamentarians that God would deliver them. As Walzer observes, "the Exodus isn't a theory of revolution." Instead it is "a story" that has been repeatedly appropriated down the centuries by political actors who have located the events of their own times within its "narrative frame."[79] If we combine Walzer's Hebrew narrative with Skinner's neo-Roman theory, we can build up a picture of the Parliamentarian cause that does justice to both its classical and its biblical sources, its secular and religious dimensions.

Puritan Parliamentarians had no difficulty in weaving these different sources and languages together. In Milton and other classically educated Puritans, appeals to Old Testament narrative sit cheek by jowl with references to Cicero and Roman law. The neoclassical concept of liberty became intertwined with a biblical story of liberation. The Exodus could also be linked to the peculiarly English myth of the Norman Yoke. As Christopher Hill showed in a famous essay, radicals frequently retold the tale of Anglo-Saxon liberties quashed by the Norman conquest.[80] This was England's own story of enslavement, but the parallels with Israel's history were striking. As Henry Stubbe explained in 1659: "I often, communing with my own soul in private, use to parallel our bondage under the Norman yoke, and our deliverance there from, to the continuance of the children of Israell in Egypt, and their escape from that slavish condition."[81]

Historians of political thought are sometimes uncomfortable with this discursive pluralism, wanting to tidy up the arguments of their subjects. But we need to recognize the eclectic, even jumbled, nature of early modern political discourse, and highlight the variety of political languages to be found mingled together within a single text.[82] Early modern writers were intimately versed in the Bible, and by virtue of their grammar school education they were equally soaked in Latin texts. Modern intellectual historians often lack their subjects' intimate familiarity with the Bible or the classics (or both!), and thus we tend to provide rather partial accounts of their writings.

This case study has highlighted the inadequacy of a secularized reading of early modern political texts and the importance of the religious dimension of early modern political thought. The Parliamentarian cause was both a constitutional protest against regal bondage and a religious protest against popish servitude, and it was legitimized by reference to sources both secular and sacred. Parliamentary ideology brought together classical concepts and biblical narratives that we should not put asunder. Of course, few scholars are equally at home in the classics and the scriptures, in political theory and theology. A degree of specialization is inevitable. But the challenge of comprehending early modern ideas forces us to look outside the comfort zones of modern academic compartmentalization. It won't do to define the subject matter of the history of political thought as secular and the subject matter of the history of religious ideas as theological (by which we usually mean nonpolitical). Historians of political thought should be more attentive to theological and biblical argument, while historians of theology would do well to follow Mark Noll's lead by paying more attention to the impact of political context and political ideology on theologians.[83]

The church father Tertullian once asked: What has Athens to do with Jerusalem? The answer, for early modern intellectual culture at least, is that Athens and Rome have a great deal to do with Jerusalem. The history of political thought can only be enriched by the study of its religious dimension.

NOTES

I would like to thank Mark Goldie and an anonymous reviewer for the University of Notre Dame Press for valuable feedback on earlier versions of this chapter. I am especially grateful to Quentin Skinner himself for his generous response.

    1. For a sympathetic assessment of Skinner's career and intellectual project, see K. Palonen, *Quentin Skinner: History, Politics, Rhetoric* (Cambridge: Polity Press, 2003). For Skinner's own view of his development, see the interview in Maria L. G. Pallares-Burke, ed., *The New History* (Cambridge: Polity Press, 2002), chap. 9.

2. For critical engagements with Skinner's methodology see J. Tully, ed., *Meaning and Context: Quentin Skinner and His Critics* (Princeton, N.J.: Princeton University Press, 1988).

3. Q. Skinner, *Visions of Politics,* vol. 1, *Regarding Method* (Cambridge: Cambridge University Press, 2002), 6.

4. Q. Skinner, *Liberty Before Liberalism* (Cambridge: Cambridge University Press, 1998), 112.

5. Q. Skinner, "Who Are 'We'? Ambiguities of the Modern Self," *Inquiry* 34, no. 2 (1991): 133–53, esp. at 148. For further reflections on Skinner's secularism and its relationship to his intellectual project see E. Perreau-Saussine, "Quentin Skinner in Context," *The Review of Politics* 69, no. 1 (2007): 106–22, esp. at 108–10.

6. Q. Skinner, "Who Are 'We'?" 145–50. For Taylor's tart reply see *Inquiry* 34, no. 2 (1991): 237–54, esp. at 240–42.

7. S. Clark, *Thinking with Demons: The Idea of Witchcraft in Early Modern Europe* (Oxford: Oxford University Press, 1997). See Skinner's comments on witchcraft beliefs in *Visions of Politics,* vol. 1, 36.

8. Skinner, *Visions of Politics,* vol. 1, 27–56.

9. See his response to charges of "antiquarianism" in Skinner, *Liberty Before Liberalism,* 106–8.

10. See for example, Skinner, "The Paradoxes of Political Liberty," in *Liberty,* ed. D. Miller, 183–205 (Oxford: Oxford University Press, 1991).

11. Q. Skinner, "John Bunyan," *The House of Whitebread* 21 (1962): 14–17, cited in Palonen, *Quentin Skinner,* 18, 181. Skinner's books on the very un-Bunyanesque figures of Machiavelli and Hobbes are *Machiavelli* (Oxford: Oxford University Press, 1981), *Reason and Rhetoric in the Philosophy of Hobbes* (Cambridge: Cambridge University Press, 1996) and *Hobbes and Republican Liberty* (Cambridge: Cambridge University Press, 2008).

12. See the assessments in A. Brett, J. Tully, and H. Hamilton-Bleakley, eds., *Rethinking the Foundations of Modern Political Thought* (Cambridge: Cambridge University Press, 2006).

13. M. Goldie, "The Context of the *Foundations,*" in *Rethinking the Foundations of Modern Political Thought,* eds. Brett, Tully, and Hamilton-Bleakley, 3–19, quotations at 12, 16–17.

14. Skinner himself admits that the metaphor of foundations virtually committed him to "writing teleologically"; Palonen, *Quentin Skinner,* 71–72.

15. Skinner, *The Foundations of Modern Political Thought,* vol. 2, *The Age of Reformation* (Cambridge: Cambridge University Press, 1978), 338–39.

16. Skinner, *Liberty before Liberalism*, 118–19.
17. Cited in Pallares-Burke, *The New History*, 223.
18. See the project website at http://www.iue.it/Personal/Projects/FreedomProject/.
19. Personal correspondence with Quentin Skinner, July 2007.
20. D. Wootton, "The Fear of God in Early Modern Political Theory," *Historical Papers/Communications Historiques* 18, no. 1 (1983): 56–80.
21. P. Marshall, "Quentin Skinner and the Secularization of Political Thought," *Studies in Political Thought* 2 (1993): 87–104.
22. C. Eire, *War Against the Idols: The Reformation of Worship from Erasmus to Calvin* (Cambridge: Cambridge University Press, 1986), 304–10.
23. A. McLaren, "Rethinking Republicanism: *Vindiciae, contra tyrannos* in Context," *Historical Journal* 49, no. 1 (2006): 23–52, quotations at 32, 52.
24. See for example his *Paolo Sarpi: Between Renaissance and Enlightenment* (Cambridge: Cambridge University Press, 1983), which could be charged with reading modern atheism back into a pre-Enlightenment thinker.
25. Although *De Jure Regni* is hardly a "secular" text, given its obvious theism, it is far from being a characteristically Calvinist work. See the comments of Roger Mason in *A Dialogue on the Law of Kingship Among the Scots: A Critical Edition and Translation of George Buchanan's De Jure Regni apud Scotus Dialogus*, trans. and ed. R. A. Mason and M. S. Smith (Aldershot: Ashgate, 2004), xlvi–xlix.
26. G. Garnett, "Law in the *Vindiciae, contra tyrannos:* A Vindication," *The Historical Journal,* 49 no. 3 (2006): 877–91.
27. Cited in C. Hill, *The English Bible and the Seventeenth-Century Revolution* (London: Penguin, 1993), 4.
28. See J. G. A. Pocock, *Barbarism and Religion,* 4 vols (Cambridge: Cambridge University Press, 1999–2005), vol. 1, 5.
29. J. Dunn, *The Political Thought of John Locke* (Cambridge: Cambridge University Press, 1969). For Dunn, who was a close friend of Skinner and shared his secular outlook, this meant that much of Locke's political theory was dead. On this, see J. Waldron, *God, Locke and Equality* (Cambridge: Cambridge University Press, 2002), 12–13.
30. I. Harris, *The Mind of John Locke: A Study of Political Theory in Its Intellectual Setting* (Cambridge: Cambridge University Press, 1994); J. Marshall, *John Locke: Resistance, Religion and Responsibility* (Cambridge: Cambridge University Press, 1994); Waldron, *God, Locke and Equality*.
31. See for example M. Goldie, "The Civil Religion of James Harrington," in *The Languages of Political Theory in Early Modern Europe,* ed. A. Pagden,

197–222 (Cambridge: Cambridge University Press, 1987); "The Theory of Religious Intolerance in Restoration England," in *From Persecution to Toleration*, ed. O. P. Grell, J. I. Israel, N. Tyacke, 331–68 (Oxford: Oxford University Press, 1991); "The Scottish Catholic Enlightenment," *Journal of British Studies* 30, no. 1 (1991): 20–62; "Priestcraft and the Birth of Whiggism," in *Political Discourse in Early Modern Britain*, ed. N. T. Phillipson and Q. Skinner, 209–31 (Cambridge: Cambridge University Press, 1993).

32. W. B. Glover, "God and Thomas Hobbes," *Church History* 29, no. 3 (1960): 275–97; J. G. A. Pocock, "Time, History, and Eschatology in the Thought of Thomas Hobbes," in *Politics, Language and Time: Essays on Political Thought and History*, J. G. A. Pocock, 148–201 (London: Methuen, 1972); N. Malcolm, "Thomas Hobbes and Voluntarist Theology" (PhD diss., University of Cambridge, 1982); N. Malcolm, "Hobbes, Ezra, and the Bible: The History of a Subversive Idea" in his *Aspects of Hobbes*, chap. 12 (Oxford: Oxford University Press, 2002); R. Tuck, "The 'Christian Atheism' of Thomas Hobbes," in *Atheism from the Reformation to the Enlightenment*, ed. M. Hunter and D. Wootton, chap. 4 (Oxford: Clarendon Press, 1992); R. Tuck, "The Civil Religion of Thomas Hobbes," in *Political Discourse in Early Modern England*, ed. Phillipson and Skinner, 120–38; A. P. Martinich, *The Two Gods of Leviathan: Thomas Hobbes on Religion and Politics* (Cambridge: Cambridge University Press, 1992).

33. See for example, L. C. Boralevi, "Classical Foundational Myths of European Republicanism: The Jewish Commonwealth" in *Republicanism: A Shared European Heritage*, ed. M. van Gelderen and Q. Skinner, 2 vols., 1:247–61 (Cambridge: Cambridge University Press, 2002). See also the works on Milton's "biblical republicanism" cited below in note 65.

34. J. Scott, *Commonwealth Principles: Republican Writing in the English Revolution* (Cambridge: Cambridge University Press, 2004), 6.

35. M. Noll, *America's God, From Jonathan Edwards to Abraham Lincoln* (New York: Oxford University Press, 2002), 9.

36. J. Sheehan, "Enlightenment, Religion, and the Enigma of Secularization: A Review Essay," *American Historical Review* 108, no. 4 (2003): 1061–80.

37. Skinner, *Liberty Before Liberalism;* "John Milton and the Politics of Slavery" and "Classical Liberty, Renaissance Translation and the English Civil War," in Skinner, *Visions of Politics*, vol. 2, *Renaissance Virtues*, 286–343 (Cambridge: Cambridge University Press, 2002); "A Third Concept of Liberty," *Proceedings of the British Academy* 117 (2002): 237–68; "Classical Liberty and the Coming of the English Civil War," in *Republicanism*, ed. van Gelderen and Skinner, vol. 2, 9–28; "Rethinking Political Liberty," *History Workshop Journal* 61 (2006): 156–70; "Freedom, Representation and Revolution, 1603–1651," the Ford

Lectures for 2003, part of which has now been published as *Hobbes and Republican Liberty.*

38. Skinner, "Classical Liberty and the Coming of the English Civil War," 28.

39. See C. Russell, *The Causes of the English Civil War* (Oxford: Oxford University Press, 1990); J. Morrill, *The Nature of the English Revolution* (Harlow: Longman, 1990), part 1, "England's Wars of Religion."

40. See Morrill, *The Nature of the English Revolution,* 68.

41. See Ann Hughes, *The Causes of the English Civil War* (Houndmills: Palgrave, 1998).

42. K. Thomas, "Politics: Looking for Liberty," *New York Review of Books,* May 26, 2005, 47–53, quotations from 52.

43. Personal correspondence with Quentin Skinner, July 2007. See also his latest statement, *Hobbes and Republican Liberty,* chaps. 2–4.

44. See especially Morrill, *The Nature of the English Revolution,* 33–90.

45. The most recent attempt to bring together religious and constitutional considerations is A. Cromartie, *The Constitutional Revolution: An Essay in the History of England, 1450–1642* (Cambridge: Cambridge University Press, 2006).

46. I owe this point to Mark Goldie.

47. A. Fletcher, *The Outbreak of the English Civil War* (New York: New York University Press, 1981), 417.

48. This point is powerfully made in the work of Morrill and other revisionists, but see also Mark Stoyle, *Loyalty and Locality: Popular Allegiance in Devon during the English Civil War* (Exeter: University of Exeter Press, 1994), 178–226, 231–55.

49. See Skinner, *Foundations,* vol. 2, 323; "The Origins of the Calvinist Theory of Revolution," in *After the Reformation,* ed. B. Malament, 309–30 (Manchester: Manchester University Press, 1980).

50. M. Walzer, *Exodus and Revolution* (New York: Basic Books, 1985), 3, 6–7, 32.

51. For earlier Protestant uses of the Exodus story, see S. Schama, *The Embarrassment of Riches: An Interpretation of Dutch Culture in the Golden Age* (London: Fontana Press, 1987), 104–13; Lea Campos Boralevi, "Classical Foundation Myths of European Republicanism: The Jewish Commonwealth," in *Republicanism,* ed. van Gelderen and Skinner, vol. 1, 247–61.

52. Cornelius Burgess, *The First Sermon Preached to the House of Commons . . . Novemb. 17 1640* (1641), passim; quotations at 9, 3, 6, 40, 53.

53. Stephen Marshall, *A Peace Offering to God* (1641), 33, 40, 42, 45. For other references to 1641 as a year of Jubilee see John Vicars, *Jehova-jireh . . . Or*

Englands Remembrancer (1642), title page; *The Rat-Trap; or the Jesuites taken in their owne Net, &c. Discovered in this yeare of Jubilee or Deliverance from the Romish faction, 1641* (1641).

54. Edmund Calamy, *God's Free Mercy to England* (1642), 47–48.

55. *The Oxinden Letters, 1607–42,* ed. D. Gardiner (London, 1933), 162. A record of the speech can be found in *Proceedings of the Short Parliament of 1640,* ed. E. S. Cope and W. H. Coates, 140–43 (London: Royal Historical Society, 1977), with the reference to Egypt on 143.

56. Edward Symmons, *Scripture Vindicated* (Oxford, 1644), 84.

57. For examples, see J[ohn] P[rice], *A Spiritual Snapsacke* (1643), 4; Clement Walker, *History of Independency* (1649), 49; John Fenwick, *England's Deliverer* (1651); John Flowre, *Englands Late Miseries* (1651); Edward Barber, *The Storming and Total Routing of Tythes* (1651); Thomas Manley Jr. and Fisher Payne, *Veni, Vidi, Vici* (1652).

58. *The Letters and Speeches of Oliver Cromwell,* ed. W. C. Abbott, 4 vols. (Cambridge, Mass.: Harvard University Press, 1937–47), vol. 3, 434–35, 442.

59. Clement Walker, *The History of Independency, Part Two* (1649), 153.

60. Skinner, "Rethinking Political Liberty," 158–59; "Surveying the Foundations," in *Rethinking the Foundations of Modern Political Thought,* ed. Brett, Tully, and Hamilton-Bleakley, 259.

61. *Anti-Cavalierisme,* 38–39, 46.

62. See J. Coffey, *John Goodwin and the Puritan Revolution: Religion and Intellectual Change in Seventeenth-Century England* (Woodbridge: Boydell and Brewer, 2006).

63. Skinner, "John Milton and the Politics of Slavery," 307.

64. See *The Complete Prose Works of John Milton,* D. Wolfe et al. 8 vols. (New Haven, Conn.: Yale University Press, 1953–82), vol. 1, 545, 701, 706, 793; vol. 3, 496, 509–10, 520, 580; vol. 4, part 1, 386–87, 401; vol. 7, 387, 463.

65. In the last few years, scholars have started to explore the biblical sources of Milton's republicanism: W. Chernaik, "Biblical Republicanism," *Prose Studies* 23, no. 1 (2000): 147–60; G. Ferdon, "New-Modelling English Government: Biblical Hermeneutics, Jewish Polity and Constitutional Forms during the Interregnum (1649–1660)" (PhD diss., University of Leicester, 2004), chap. 3; W. S. H. Lim, *John Milton, Radical Politics and Biblical Republicanism* (Newark: University of Delaware Press, 2006); E. Nelson, "'Talmudical Commonwealthsmen' and the Rise of Republican Exclusivism," *The Historical Journal* 50, no. 4 (2007): 809–35.

66. See J. Morrill, "The Attack on the Church of England," in *The Nature of the English Revolution,* chap. 4.

67. *A Remonstrance in Defence of the Lords and Commons in Parliament* (1642), 3–5.

68. See Henry Burton, *The Protestation Protested* (1641), sigs. B3v, C3v.

69. See for example Henry Parker, *The Trojan-Horse of Presbyteriall Government* (1646), 15, 17–18.

70. William Walwyn, *Tolleration Justified* (1646), in *The Writings of William Walwyn*, ed. J. R. McMichael and B. Taft (Athens: University of Georgia Press, 1989), 156.

71. John Goodwin, *Two Hymns, or Spiritual Songs* (1651), 10–11.

72. John Lilburne, *The Legall Fundamental Liberties of the People of England* (1649), 64; *The Levellers (Falsely so called) Vindicated* (1649), in A. L. Morton, ed., *Freedom in Arms: A Selection of Leveller Writings* (London: Lawrence and Wishart, 1975), 316–17.

73. *Winstanley: The Law of Freedom and Other Writings*, ed. C. Hill (Harmondsworth: Penguin, 1973), 275.

74. John Spittlehouse, *Rome Ruin'd by Whitehall* (1649), dedicated "To his Excellency the Lord Generall Fairfax"; *A Warning-Piece Discharged, or Certain Intelligence communicated to his Excellencie the Lord General Cromwel* (1653), 6–25.

75. George Wither, *British Appeals* (1651), 24.

76. Henry Stubbe, *Malice Rebuked* (1659), 1–4.

77. Algernon Sidney, *Court Maxims*, ed. H. W. Blom, E. C. Mulier and R. Janse (Cambridge: Cambridge University Press, 1996), 197–98.

78. John Locke, *Political Essays*, ed. M. Goldie (Cambridge: Cambridge University Press, 1997), 40.

79. Walzer, *Exodus and Revolution*, 7.

80. C. Hill, "The Norman Yoke," in *Puritanism and Revolution* (London: Secker and Warburg, 1958), 58–125. The Norman Yoke myth had religious dimensions of its own, since Protestants like Matthew Parker imagined a pure Anglo-Saxon church later corrupted by Rome.

81. Henry Stubbe, *Essay in Defence of the Good Old Cause* (1659), 7.

82. For a useful attempt to do this for American revolutionary thought, see A. Tuckness, "Discourses of Resistance in the American Revolution," *Journal of the History of Ideas* 64, no. 4 (2003): 547–63.

83. See Noll, *America's God*.

4   "Sie Stinken Beide," or How to Use Medieval Christian-Jewish Disputational Material

ANNA SAPIR ABULAFIA

    Over two hundred years ago Heinrich Heine wrote a very long poem about disputatious Jews and Christians, which he entitled *Disputation*. He depicted a grand disputation held at Toledo before the king and queen of Castile between Rabbi Juda of Navarre for the Jews and Friar José for the Christians. What Heine thought of religious discussions like these is plain from the final verses:

> They have fought twelve hours already;
> Still remote the end desired;
> And the audience has grown weary,
> And the women hot and tired.
>
> Even the Court is now impatient;
> Ladies try to yawn unseen;
> And the king, Don Pedro, turning,
> Puts the question to the queen:
>
> "Tell me frankly what opinion
> You have come to; who is right?

Has the monk or has the Rabbi
Won the honors of the fight?"

Donna Blanca gazes puzzled;
Fingers twined, as if in thought,
Presses hard against her forehead,
Then she answers, as besought:

"Which is right," she says, "I know not,
But there's one thing I can tell:
I am sure both monk and rabbi
Have a most offensive smell."[1]

Heine's impatience with religious squabbling resonates well with our own western secular society. But it is hardly a fruitful attitude for anyone interested in tracing Christian ideas about Jews. This chapter will demonstrate how rich Christian-Jewish disputational material can be for historians of Christian-Jewish relations if they are read with respect for their setting and if they are interpreted within their full intellectual, religious, and social contexts. My examples will be taken from predominantly eleventh- and twelfth-century Latin material, which forms the basis of most of my own research.

A large subset of the *adversus Iudeos* literature is comprised of so-called Christian-Jewish disputations. First, we must determine what these are. As far as the eleventh and twelfth centuries are concerned, they are simply the literary form that many Christian scholars used for their academic discussions of Judaism. The literary genre of the academic dialogue was well known to them from classical sources and was adopted by them regularly for their theological writings. Disputational exercises were also a common teaching method in the schools. Scholastic scholars were trained to produce arguments and counterarguments on all kinds of issues, and dialogues were a particularly appropriate method of recording them. Literary disputations were often given the cut and thrust flavor of a judicial duel. This means that the aggressive language used to denigrate opponents is part of the genre. Finally, the author of any particular literary dialogue was in full control of the line of argument and the outcome of his production.[2]

All of this means that the *disputationes* or *dialogi* between Christians and Jews that we have from the eleventh and twelfth centuries are not real in the sense that they are not records of actual discussions that took place at a definable time and place between a specific Christian and Jew. They are, in other words, fictitious. Some have argued that this means they can tell us little about Christian-Jewish relations. But that is not the case. Even though these sources might not tell us much about medieval Jews themselves, they can be most instructive about what their Christian authors knew about Judaism and what they thought a real Jew would say. Apart from that, the fact that they are fictitious does not, of course, mean that no conversations between protagonists of either religion underlie the text. Gilbert Crispin, abbot of Westminster (d. 1117), for example, claims that his *Disputatio Iudei et Christiani* records the discussion he had with a Jew who visited him in his abbey. This is patently not the case. Gilbert has his Jew use the definition of God that Anselm of Canterbury (d. 1109) coined for his ontological proof of the existence of God in his *Proslogion*. It is obvious that Gilbert composed the whole text of the disputation for the purpose of proving the validity of the Christian faith and that he put the words that suited him into his literary antagonist's mouth. But this does not mean that Gilbert never spoke to the Jew he mentioned. Westminster Abbey was undergoing building work in Abbot Gilbert's day and it is very probable that he did business with a Jew to finance this. However Christian his disputation is, it is more than likely that his Jewish acquaintance had quizzed him about the Incarnation. As we shall see, Jewish sources leave us in no doubt about how unacceptable Jews found this doctrine to be.[3]

Together with other *adversus Iudeos* works that were not shaped as dialogues, Christian-Jewish disputations are particularly useful in making us aware of what Christian scholars imagined the major issues to be in the confrontation between Christians and Jews. The fact that so many Christian anti-Jewish writings were produced from the second half of the eleventh century shows us just how interested Christian scholars were in defining their stance towards Jews and Judaism. The topics that keep coming up in these works make us aware of the issues that engaged the minds of scholars within their own Christian communities. These include the oneness of the triune God; the feasibility and appropriateness of the Incarnation and the Virgin Birth; the correct interpretation of the Bible in conjunction with the continuing validity of the rules and regulations of the Law of Moses, in particular the dietary laws, circumcision, and the Sabbath; and the supersession of the Jewish people by Christians as God's chosen people. This makes us wonder for whom these works were intended and the intellectual context in which they need to be read.

Apology or polemic lies at the heart of the question about the intended audience for this kind of disputational material. Or to put it differently, were Christian authors writing this material with an eye to convert the Jews of their day, or were they writing in order to reassure their own coreligionists about the validity of Christian dogma? The fact that all of the Christian anti-Jewish material of this period was written in Latin must mean that it was not meant in the first place for a Jewish readership. To return to Gilbert Crispin, his closing words admonishing his Jew to reread the Hebrew Bible so that he could see that everything Gilbert had said was true are clearly rhetorical.[4] Gilbert would have spoken French to the Jew he did business with at Westminster. He would not have written a Latin text for this Jew's benefit. His disputation was for internal Christian consumption, exploring issues that we know occupied his teacher Anselm of Canterbury. One of Anselm's most important projects was to prove that the Incarnation was not just possible but also necessary. This resulted in his magisterial *Cur Deus Homo* (*Why God-man?*), which he completed by 1098. In this work, which incidentally was written as a dialogue between Anselm and one of his pupils by the name of Boso, Anselm has so-called unbelievers (*infideles*) ask tough questions about the rationale of God assuming flesh. Boso is made to say:

> The unbelievers who scoff at our simplicity raise against us the following objection: that we dishonor and affront God when we maintain that He descended into the womb of a woman, that He was born of a woman, that He grew, being nourished by milk and food for human beings, and—not to mention many other things which seem to be unsuitable for God—that He experienced weariness, hunger, thirst, scourging, and (in the midst of thieves) crucifixion and death.[5]

These words echo the criticism uttered by the Jew in Crispin's *Disputatio*:

If God is without measure, how could his dimension be circumscribed by the lowly and small dimensions of human members? If God cannot be circumscribed, by what kind of argument can it be proclaimed that he was totally circumscribed by a body and could be contained in one narrow womb of his mother? Further, if God is that than which nothing greater or more sufficient can be thought [cf. Anselm, *Proslogion* ii], by what necessity would he have been forced to participate in human misfortune and share and suffer so many ills?[6]

This would seem to indicate that Gilbert's anti-Jewish disputation is closely linked to Anselm's theological work. Anselm states explicitly in the *Cur Deus Homo* that his "unbelievers" ask the same kind of questions believers ask. By this he meant that "unbelievers" suspended their faith until they found the answers they sought concerning Christian doctrine. Believers like Boso kept on believing, however puzzled they were about the rational underpinnings of their beliefs.[7] We know from many sources that Christians did not just wonder about the feasibility of God assuming flesh and the possibility of Jesus being man and God. They also struggled to understand how it was possible for the majesty of God not to be corrupted by God's assumption of flesh. The overlap between the questioning of the Incarnation ascribed to Jews and the internal Christian questions that were being asked of this complicated piece of theology is instructive. For it shows how Christian-Jewish disputations were written as much as anything else in order to quell internal disquietude within the Christian community.[8] This impression is reinforced by the disputation by Odo of Cambrai (d. 1113) entitled *Disputation with the Jew, Leo, Concerning the Advent of Christ, Son of God*. Odo composed this work for Acard of Fémy because the monks of Fémy wanted to have in writing the exposé he had delivered on the Incarnation in their chapter just before Christmas. He claims that he put it into the format of a dialogue with a Jew called Leo because since then he had had a discussion with Leo on the same matter. In the introduction he claims that he managed to convince the Jew. At the end of the disputation Leo does not convert, but he does acknowledge that Odo has presented many reasoned arguments. It is very likely that Leo is a figment of Odo's imagination. The significant passage for us at this point is the question Odo has Leo ask at the start of the second part of the disputation:

> In one thing especially we laugh at you and think that you are crazy. You say that God was conceived within his mother's womb, surrounded by a vile fluid, and suffered enclosure within this foul prison for nine months when finally, in the tenth month, he emerged from her private parts (who is not embarrassed by such a scene!). Thus you attribute to God what is unbecoming, which we would not do without great embarrassment.[9]

The similarity to the questions asked by Anselm's *infideles* is obvious. Whether or not Leo is a real Jew, it should be noted that the harshly negative tone of the text does accord with the tenor of Jewish criticism of the Virgin Birth. In ca. 1170 Joseph Kimhi in southern France writes:

> How can I believe of this great God, who is hidden and secret, that He would enter completely unnecessarily into the belly of a woman, into her filthy and stinking entrails; or of the living God, that He would be born of a woman, a child without knowledge and understanding, a fool not knowing the difference between his right and left hand, who defecates and urinates and sucks at his mother's breasts from hunger and thirst.[10]

For Odo the harshness was probably meant as a rhetorical ploy to emphasize the clarity of Odo's rational explanation of the Virgin Birth that follows, in the course of which he accuses Jews of being irrational. Once again a Christian-Jewish disputation is shown to be geared to internal Christian usage. Jewish criticism of Christianity is addressed because it coincides with internal Christian doubts about the Virgin Birth.[11]

But this does not mean that Christian-Jewish polemics were never written with Jewish conversion in mind. Joachim of Fiore (d. 1202) was absolutely convinced that the End was nigh and that, therefore, Paul's prophecy of the final conversion of Gentiles and Jews was imminent. He expected all of this to have happened by, at the latest, 1260. He claimed that his *Adversus Iudeos* was written in order to convince at least some Jews to convert before the general conversion took place. The treatise is remarkably irenic, and Joachim goes out of his way to find common ground between Judaism and Christianity. Joachim set great store in the force of preaching, and it is possible that he hoped that his work would be used by preachers trying to convert Jews.[12] The otherwise unknown Odo, who wrote the theological compendium *Ysagoge in Theologiam* sometime in the 1140s in England, is quite sure that Christians would have no success against the Jews as long as they lacked Hebrew. That is why he decided to quote all his biblical texts not just in Latin but also in Hebrew and in addition to give a Latin transliteration of the Hebrew for the benefit of those who could not read Hebrew.[13] But use of Hebrew does not always prove that an author has Jewish conversion in mind. The poet Walter of Châtillon (d. 1180 or 1202/03) derived almost all of the Hebrew he used in his *Treatise Against the Jews* from Jerome. His purpose was to show that a simple, straightforward, literal reading of the Old Testament concerned the life, passion, and resurrection of Jesus Christ. His knowledge of Judaism was minimal. It was as if he wanted to quiet the objections he knew Jews would bring to his reading of the Bible.[14]

The many examples I have already given indicate many of the contexts that need to be taken into account in order to understand what Christian-Jewish disputational material is about. From our last example concerning Walter of Châtillon's use of Jerome it is clear how important is awareness of previous models. Indeed, the torturous relationship between Christianity and Judaism goes back to the beginning of the common era, when Christians established their own identity independent from the mother religion. The main topics of the debate of the twelfth century are in themselves not new. What is important is that they coincide with many of the major intellectual issues of the day. This means that old arguments received a new lease on life and that new ideas were brought to bear on traditional concerns. For example, Christians had been using biblical arguments against Jews for centuries. In the twelfth century, however, this exegetical debate coincided with greater Christian expertise in reading the Bible on account of renewed emphasis on the subjects of the trivium, that is, grammar, rhetoric, and dialectic. Scholars began to be extremely interested in the structure and meaning of language. The language they were most interested in was that of the Bible. Late eleventh- and twelfth-century northern Europe witnessed a tremendous expansion in learning, stimulated by the (re)discovery of many classical texts. Encouraged by Ciceronian and Aristotelian texts to use their reason, European scholars were determined to explore the doctrines of their faith through reason in order to understand better what they believed. The theological sources of this period give out an atmosphere of excitement tempered with concern that reason might not concur with faith. In the event, twelfth-century scholars were incredibly optimistic about what they could achieve with reason. They interpreted reason as a God-given faculty with which they could perceive truth. It was for them an extra route to God alongside the route of faith. They thought that it enabled them to achieve all kinds of insights about God, nature, and human society. It is within this context that Christian scholars poured over the teachings of the church concerning the Trinity and the Incarnation. As we have seen, the question *Cur Deus Homo* stimulated research into the feasibility of the Incarnation and the consideration of how divine majesty could concur with human frailty and death. One of the results of this line of inquiry was an increased respect for the dignity of man. After all, if majestic God deigned to become man, there must be something worthwhile in the human condition. Christ's death on behalf of mankind was used to explore the brotherhood of man. These ideas were woven together with classical ideas on human fellowship based on human capacity for reason. All of this put discussions concerning the question whether Christians had supplanted Jews as the chosen people into a new light. God's chosen people were the Christians who comprised the brotherhood of man saved by Christ. New Israel (Christians) became identified with the concept of Christian universality from which Old Israel (Jews) were excluded. Jewish rejection of all of the fundamental tenets of the Christian faith was not just a continuation of the challenge Judaism had always presented to Christianity. It brought into question everything twelfth-century scholars were trying to achieve. This is why so many Christian-Jewish polemics were written in this period and why the texts teach us so much about what was going on within the Christian community. The Christian-Jewish debate was intimately linked to internal Christian theological and intellectual developments.[15]

Gilbert Crispin's *Disputatio Iudei*, for example, spawned further works by him in which he explored issues concerning the persons of the Trinity, free will, the Fall, and the redemption of man.[16] Abelard's (d. 1142) analysis of Judaism falls within the framework of a discussion of natural law, the law written on human hearts and known to them through reason. Abelard concluded that Jewish observance did not accord with reason and the teaching of natural law.[17] Peter Alfonsi (fl. 1106–26) used reason in a different way. He wrote his dialogue to defend his own conversion from Judaism to Christianity and conceived it as a disputation between his former self, Moses, and his new identity, Peter. One of his goals is to prove that of the three religions Christianity is the most rational. He castigates Judaism as the most irrational on account of the anthropomorphic language used in the Talmud to describe God. Peter is the first polemicist of this period to employ passages of the Talmud. Peter the Venerable, abbot of Cluny (d. 1156), would do so too in his diatribe against the Jews in which he claimed that the Talmud was diabolical and blocked the faculty of reason in Jews. The Talmud would become much more important in the Christian-Jewish debate of the thirteenth century. Peter Alfonsi's discussion on the crucifixion ties in with new exegetical work on the meaning of the role assigned to the Jews in the Gospels. Gradually Jews were accused of killing Christ not out of ignorance but deliberately. Peter Alfonsi is the first polemicist to accuse Jews of deliberate deicide. He claimed they knew who Jesus was and that they killed him out of jealousy.[18] Peter of Blois (d. 1211/12) includes the accusation that Jews capture Christian boys and crucify them in secret in his *Contra Perfidiam Judaeorum*. This ties in with the circulation of the accusation of ritual murder from the 1150s onwards.[19] Joachim of Fiore's anti-Jewish treatise fits squarely into his vast corpus of apocalyptic scholarship.[20]

So what can we learn from Christian-Jewish disputational material about Christian-Jewish relations? We must certainly guard ourselves in concluding from the overwhelming negative language of the disputations that no good relations existed between them. As we have seen, harsh language is very much part of this literary genre. We know from other sources that Christians and Jews could be peaceful neighbors. Christian exegetes, for example, benefited much from their interaction with Jews concerning literal readings of the Hebrew Bible. The flowering of Jewish culture in this period must indicate that there was room for Jews to develop within their own communities.[21] Having said that, we also know from our sources that attitudes towards Jews were hardening, especially in northern Europe from the latter part of the eleventh century. This has to do with an intricate interplay of political, economic, intellectual, and religious factors. Analysis of Christian-Jewish disputational material can help us understand better what some of the issues were. We have already seen how Jewish rejection of Christian teachings was a particularly sensitive issue in the budding intellectual climate of the twelfth century. Exacerbating the problem was the fact that twelfth-century theology greatly emphasized religious or spiritual identification with Jesus and the Virgin Mary. In response, *ratio* or "reason" became a Christian weapon used against Jews. Odo of Cambrai equated Jews with animals, as did Peter the Venerable, because they would not accept the truth of Christian teaching. As we have seen, Peter Alfonsi made Jews out to be deliberate Christ killers. For Peter of Blois Jews were actively evil. Yet all of these examples should not make us forget the calmness of Gibert Crispin's *Disputation* at the very end of the eleventh century and the peaceful discussion by Joachim of Fiore at the end of the twelfth. Paul's prophecy of the final conversion of the Jews meant that Christians could never turn their backs entirely on Jews. This is why Augustine (d. 430) coined his witness theory that stated that God had ordained that Jews should continue to exist so that they could serve Christians. They carried for Christians the books of the Hebrew Bible, which contained all the prophecies concerning Jesus. Although Augustine's witness theory remained valid, by the twelfth century we do find scholars wondering whether they really wanted to avail themselves of Jewish service. With the growth of Christian expertise in Hebrew and with the advances made with the help of reason, many seemed to think that Christians did not really need that much assistance from Jews.

So far we have only spoken about the academic work of Christian scholars. The huge question that remains is, of course, what impact these elite works had on society at large. How did the ideas generated in Christian-Jewish disputational works reach the ecclesiastics who were not scholars and, indeed, the laity. Sermons would have been one route of transmission. Recent research has shown close contacts between the elite clergy and the aristocratic courts. Aristocratic men and women received letters of admonition and copies of sermons for their moral erudition. Hymns would be another route. I have recently investigated how Walter of Châtillon's Christmas hymns reflect even more sharply than his anti-Jewish treatise his conclusion that Jews are completely outmoded. In his hymns this message is conveyed without any of the theological considerations for the implications this might have for the validity of Augustine's witness theory. Hymns are meant to convey theological conundrums by way of evocative messages to the faithful. I am sure that further research on hymns will teach us more about how anti-Jewish ideas were disseminated.[22] The Latin and especially the vernacular miracle stories of the Virgin would have been another important route for spreading these ideas, at least to the upper echelons of lay society.[23]

From the above it will be clear that in my view the arguments contained in Christian-Jewish disputational material should be "seen their way" and not set aside as manifestations of religious squabbling. In other words, I am seriously engaging with late eleventh- and twelfth-century beliefs and analyzing them within their various historical contexts. This approach differs sharply from the one adopted by Gavin Langmuir in his important book *History, Religion, and Antisemitism,* which appeared in 1990. Langmuir argued that we cannot properly discuss the development of medieval anti-Semitism without first defining in objective terms what religion is and how it relates to terms like religiosity, nonrational thinking, rational empirical thinking, rational and nonrational doubt, and irrational thought. He defines religion as: "those elements of relgiosity that are explicitly prescribed by people exercising authority over other people." For Langmuir religiosity is "the dominant pattern or structuring of nonrational thinking—and the conduct correlated with it—which the individual trusts to establish, extend, and preserve consciousness of his or her identity." Nonrational thinking "fluidly indicates and establishes for us a universe of relations between symbolized aspects of experience that could not be expressed if the symbols were employed unambiguously. It is our understanding of what we cannot express as knowledge." On the other hand, rational empirical thinking "denote[s] the kind of thinking . . . that has enabled human beings to develop tools and demonstrate their efficacy by results in principle observable and repeatable by anyone else." Nonrational doubt is taken to mean "uncertainty about beliefs, values, or a cosmology that is inspired, not by any conflicting rational empirical knowledge but by the appeal of other beliefs." Rational doubt on the contrary is "the result of consciousness of a conflict between nonrational beliefs and rational empirical knowledge." Finally, Langmuir claims that irrational thought arises when individuals keep to belief "by the suppression or compartmentalization of their capacity to think rationally and empirically about segments of reality and the projection on those realities of associations created by their nonrational thinking." Using these concepts Langmuir argues that many twelfth-century Christian scholars had rational doubts about the doctrines of their faith. When they suppressed these doubts, irrational thinking set in, which went on to become social irrationality when society accepted their views. This in turn led to irrational accusations against Jews because the objections Jews posed to Christianity concurred with internal Christian doubt. Langmuir dubs irrational accusations against Jews anti-Semitic rather than anti-Judaic. He classifies accusations as irrational when they cease to have any basis in fact, as for example in the case of accusations of ritual murder and host desecration, as opposed to the accusation of Christ killer, which he calls rational, because it does go back to some kind of Jewish involvement in the crucifixion.[24]

There are a number of very attractive aspects to Langmuir's thesis. He distinguishes most helpfully between the religious beliefs of individual medieval scholars and the official teachings of the medieval church. And he releases the highly emotive topic of the Christian-Jewish debate from any subjective feelings stemming from an historian's own religious or lack of religious identity. But it seems to me that the price of Langmuir's approach is too high. For it robs twelfth-century theological activity of one of its main hallmarks, that of *ratio* or reason. In Langmuir's terminology most of what medieval scholars called rational was in fact nonrational or even irrational. Most of their endeavors to understand rationally the intricacies of the Virgin Birth, the Incarnation, and so on would have to be classified as the suppression of rational doubt by nonrational conclusions. But does this enable historians to understand any better what mattered to twelfth-century thinkers? To be sure, religious doubt did play an important role. It triggered a great deal of frenetic intellectual activity. As we have seen, the Christian-Jewish debate often served to lay to rest internal Christian questions about the Christian faith. But it seems to me to do an injustice to the medieval past to deny these scholars any success under their own terms of reference. It is clear from the closing words of the *Cur Deus Homo*, for example, that Anselm was convinced he had achieved what he set out to do, which was to prove the possibility and necessity of the Incarnation *sola ratione* (by reason alone).[25] Also it must be realized that twelfth-century Jews were just as convinced of the validity of Judaism as Christians were of the truth of Christianity. The sharpness of the Christian-Jewish encounter stems partly from the conviction on both sides that there was only one truth. It seems to me that one cannot come to a genuine understanding of the thinking of people if one eliminates from their thought its core principle, which is that there is a reality that exists beyond what is empirically discernable. Imposing a modern secular paradigm on medieval religious thinking might well help historians find their way, but it does not, in my view, make for better history.

To return to Langmuir's definition of anti-Semitism, I agree with him that accusations of ritual murder and host desecration contained irrational aspects. But I have argued that they are understood more fully if one understands how the development of rational thought in the twelfth century prompted some Christian scholars to doubt whether Jews were partners in the human fellowship of reason. The idea that Jews lacked reason contributed to a process of dehumanizing Jews. Accusations that Jews crucified Christian boys and tortured the consecrated host fit well into the image of inhuman Jews preying on Christian society.[26] A sharper understanding of the potential of late eleventh- and twelfth-century inquiry is useful not just for an historical understanding of the past, it is equally important for gaining insights into some of the most pressing problems facing us today.

NOTES

1. Translation taken from *The Works of Heinrich Heine*, vol. 12, *Romancero Book III, Last Poems*, trans. M. Armour (London: Heinemann, 1905), 66–67. I prefer this translation to the rendering by Aaron Kramer in *The Poetry and Prose of Heinrich Heine*, selected and ed. F. Ewen (New York: Citadel, 1948), 280.

2. On disputations, see for example H. Walther, *Das Streitgedicht in der Lateinischen Literatur des Mittelalters* (Munich: Beck, 1920); A. Cantin, "Sur Quelques Aspects des Disputes Publiques au XIe Siècle Latin," in *Etudes des Civilisation Médiévale (XIe–XIIe siècles): Mélanges offerts à Edmund-René Labande*, 89–104 (Poitiers: C.E.S.C.M., 1974); and P. I. von Moos, "Le Dialogue Latin au Moyen Age: L'exemple d'Evrard d'Ypres," *Annales* 44, no. 4 (1989): 995–99.

3. Gilbert Crispin, *Disputatio Iudei et Christiani*, 3–6 and 81, in *The Works of Gilbert Crispin, Abbot of Westminster*, ed. A. Sapir Abulafia and G. R. Evans (London: Oxford University Press for the British Academy, 1986); A. Sapir Abulafia, "The *Ars Disputandi* of Gilbert Crispin Abbot of Westminster (1085–1117)," in *Christians and Jews in Dispute: Disputational Literature and the Rise of Anti-Judaism in the West (c. 1000–1150)* (Aldershot: Ashgate, 1998), VI.

4. Crispin, *Disputatio*, 162.

5. Anselm, *Cur Deus Homo*, I, 3, in *S. Anselmi Cantuariensis Archiepiscopi Opera Omnia*, vol. 2, ed. F. S. Schmitt (Edinburgh: Thomas Nelson, 1946), 50; translation taken from Anselm of Canterbury, *Why God Became Man*, in *Anselm of Canterbury*, vol. 3, ed. and trans. J. Hopkins and H. Richardson (Toronto: Edwin Mellen, 1976), 52.

6. Crispin, *Disputatio*, 80–82.

7. Anselm, *Cur Deus Homo*, I, 1, 3; Anselm, *Why God Became Man*, ed. and trans. Hopkins and Richardson, 49, 52.

8. See A. Sapir Abulafia, "St Anselm and Those Outside the Church," in Abulafia, *Christians and Jews*, IV. R. W. Southern analyzed the collaboration between Anselm and Gilbert Crispin on this question in "St Anselm and Gilbert Crispin, Abbot of Westminster," *Mediaeval and Renaissance Studies* 3 (1954): 78–115. See also J. Cohen, *Living Letters of the Law: Ideas of the Jew in Medieval Christianity* (Berkeley: University of California Press, 1999), 177–79.

9. Odo of Cambrai, *Disputatio contra Judeum Leonem Nominee de Adventu Christi*, Patrologia latina 160, col. 1110; translation taken from, Odo of Tournai, *On Original Sin, and A Disputation with the Jew, Leo, Concerning the Advent of Christ, Son of God: Two Theological Treatises*, trans. I. M. Resnick (Philadelphia: University of Pennsylvania Press, 1994), 95.

10. See H. Trautner-Kromann, *Shield and Sword* (Tübingen: Mohr, 1993). On 70–72, Trautner-Kromann discusses the criticism leveled against the Virgin Birth by Joseph Kimhi in his *Sefer ha-Brit* (Joseph Kimhi, *The Book of the Covenant and Other Writings*, ed. F. Talmage [Jerusalem: Bialik Institute, 1974]). See also A. Sapir Abulafia, "Invectives against Christianity in the Hebrew Chronicles of the First Crusade," in Abulafia, *Christians and Jews in Dispute*, XVIII.

11. See A. Sapir Abulafia, "Christian Imagery of Jews in the Twelfth Century: A Look at Odo of Cambrai and Guibert of Nogent," in Abulafia, *Christians and Jews in Dispute*, X.

12. *Adversus Iudeos di Gioacchimo da Fiore*, ed. A. Frugoni (Rome: Nella Sede Dell'Istituto, 1957); see A. Sapir Abulafia, "The Conquest of Jerusalem: Joachim of Fiore and the Jews," in *The Experience of Crusading*, vol. 1, *Western Approaches*, ed. M. Bull and N. Housley, 127–46 (Cambridge: Cambridge University Press, 2003).

13. *Ysagoge in Theologiam*, in *Ecrits théologiques de l'Ecole d'Abélard, textes inédits*, ed. A. Landgraf, 61–289 (Louvain: Spicilegium Sacrum Lovaniense, 1934). The fact that the unique manuscript of the text only gives the transliteration for one biblical citation is probably the fault of the scribes involved in preparing the manuscript. See A. Sapir Abulafia, "Jewish Carnality in Twelfth-century Renaissance Thought," in Abulafia, *Christians and Jews*, XII.

14. Walter of Châtillon, *Tractatus contra Judaeos*, Patrologia latina 209, coll. 423–58; see A. Sapir Abulafia, "Walter of Châtillon: A Twelfth-Century Poet's Engagement with Jews," *Journal of Medieval History* 31, no. 3 (2005): 265–86.

15. See A. Sapir Abulafia, *Christians and Jews in the Twelfth-century Renaissance* (London: Routledge, 1995).

16. *The Works of Gilbert Crispin*, ed. Abulafia and Evans.

17. Peter Abelard, *Collationes*, ed. and trans. J. Marenbon and G. Orlandi. (Oxford: Clarendon, 2001). See A. Sapir Abulafia, "*Intentio Recta an Erronea?* Peter Abelard's Views on Judaism and the Jews," in Abulafia, *Christians and Jews*, XIII. But see also P. von Moos, "Les *Collationes* d'Abélard et la Question Juive au XIIe Siècleo," *Journal de Savants* 2 (July–Dec. 1999): 449–89.

18. Peter Alfonsi, *Dialogi*, Patrologia latina 157, coll. 535–672; Peter the Venerable, *Petri Venerabilis Adversus Iudeorum Inveteratam Duritiem*, ed. Y. Friedman (Turnhout: Brepols, 1985). Also see A. Sapir Abulafia, "Bodies in the Jewish Debate," in Abulafia, *Christians and Jews*, XVI; and J. Cohen, "The Jews as Killers of Christ in the Latin Tradition, From Augustine to the Friars," *Traditio* 39, no. 1 (1983): 1–27. For Peter Alfonsi see J. Tolan, *Petrus Alfonsi and His Medieval Reader* (Gainesville: University of Florida Press, 1993). A recent discussion on Peter the Venerable can be found in D. Iogna-Prat, *Ordonner et Exclure: Cluny et la Société Chrétienne Face à L'Hérésie, au Judäisme et à L'Islam 1000–1150* (Paris: Aubier, 1998), translated as *Order and Exclusion: Cluny and Christendom Face Heresy, Judaism and Islam, 1000–1150*, trans. G. R. Edwards (Ithaca, N.Y.: Cornell University Press, 2002).

19. Peter of Blois, *Contra Perfidiam Judaeorum*, Patrologia latina 207, col. 861; see A. Sapir Abulafia, "Twelfth-Century Christian Expectations of Jewish Conversion: A Case Study of Peter of Blois," *Aschkenaz* 8, no. 1 (1998): 45–70.

20. See note 12.

21. See for example S. Benner and A. Reverchon, "Die Champagne vom 11. bis Frühen 14. Jahrhundert," in *Jüdische Gemeinden und ihr christlicher Kontext in Kulturräumlich vergleichender Betrachtung von der Spätantike bis zum 18. Jahrhundert,* ed. C. Cluse, A. Haverkamp, and I. J. Yuval, 151–213 (Hannover: Hahnsche Buchhandlung, 2003), where they discuss the favorable position of the Jews in Champagne before 1254. Champagne is where Rashi (d. 1105) set up his famous school of exegetes of the Bible and Talmud.

22. See note 14. My PhD student Sarah Lamm has investigated the poetry of Peter Abelard, Peter the Venerable, and Peter of Blois.

23. J. Shea, "Adgar's *Gracial* and Christian Images of Jews in Twelfth-century Vernacular Literature," *Journal of Medieval History* 33, no. 2 (2007): 181–96.

24. See G. Langmuir, *History, Religion, and Antisemitism* (Berkeley: University of California Press, 1990), quotations from 136, 162, 154–55, 46, 240, 245, 157, 275–305. See also G. Langmuir, "Doubt in Christendom," in G. Langmuir, *Toward a Definition of Antisemitism,* 100–133 (Berkeley: University of California Press, 1990); G. Langmuir, "Faith of Christians and Hostility to Jews," in *Christianity and Judaism,* ed. D. Wood, 77–92 (Oxford: Blackwell, 1992); and G. Langmuir, "At the Frontiers of Faith," in *Religious Violence Between Christians and Jews: Medieval Roots, Modern Perspectives,* ed. A. Sapir Abulafia, 138–56 (Basingstoke: Palgrave Macmillan, 2002). See also my discussion of Langmuir's ideas in Abulafia, *Christians and Jews,* 4–7.

25. *Cur Deus Homo,* II, 22.

26. See Abulafia, *Christians and Jews,* 5, 134–35.

5 Anti-Semitism, Philo-Semitism, Apocalypticism, and Millenarianism in Early Modern Europe: A Case Study and Some Methodological Reflections

HOWARD HOTSON

In assessing methodologies for studying the history of religious ideas, the form of religious thought and behavior known as "apocalypticism" raises particularly interesting difficulties. In origin, the word "apocalypse" means "revelation." More particularly, it refers to the supernatural disclosure of mysteries outside the scope of ordinary experience, generally communicated in symbolism so mysterious as to be almost incomprehensible.[1] Moreover, since the most notable mysteries revealed in the New Testament Apocalypse pertain to the end of the world, "apocalypse" has also become virtually synonymous in common parlance with cosmic catastrophe, with destruction and disruption on the greatest imaginable scale. These combined connotations pose a standing challenge to historical understanding. While apocalypticism's association with violent cataclysm demands historical attention, its still more fundamental association with mysticism and irrationality seem to defy historical comprehension. If both the mysteries of the Apocalypse and the symbolism in which they are expressed surpass ordinary human comprehension, how can they and the behavior they provoke be comprehended by the ordinary tools of humanistic research?

Half a century ago, a compelling answer to this question was provided by perhaps the most influential book ever published on the history of apocalyptic expectation: Norman Cohn's *The Pursuit of the Millennium*. In focusing on what he loosely termed "millenarianism," Cohn drew attention to a fascinating variation of these deep-seated associations in which the irrationality of apocalypticism is compounded by the "phantasy" of an imminent terrestrial golden age, and the destructive dimension of apocalypticism is transformed into a fanatical zeal to prepare for this epoch by violently purging the world of evil. To make sense of this baffling material, Cohn fortified the tools of ordinary historical scholarship with methods and concepts derived from psychology and sociology; and this social-scientific approach allowed him not only to explain these "millenarian" movements in terms of concrete social, economic, and cultural conditions but also to derive from the study of obscure medieval religious sects a generalized pattern of behavior of explosive contemporary relevance. The "revolutionary millenarians and mystical anarchists" of the medieval period, in his account, were "rootless and desperate men" in a disintegrating society who attempted to purify their world and create a society "wholly unanimous in its beliefs and wholly free from inner conflicts" by destroying the "great ones," the clergy and the Jews. This emphasis on the Jews was by no means adventitious: the book had been stimulated by Cohn's dawning awareness of the Holocaust during the Second World War and his access to a library full of Nazi ideology and propaganda while awaiting demobilization in Germany during the winter of 1945. In a revised second edition of the book published in 1961 Cohn made explicit the argument that the dynamics at work in these obscure millenarian movements directly paralleled what he called "the great revolutionary fanaticisms of our time," communism and Nazism.[2] In a sequel published four years later, he sought to demonstrate more particularly how the medieval fear of an anti-Christian Jewish conspiracy was resurrected in the infamous *Protocols of the Elders of Zion*, "how it swept the world in the 1920s; and how, in the 1930s, it provided the ideology for an international movement and prepared the way for the near-extermination of European Jews by the Nazis."[3]

Translated into seven languages and reprinted over twenty times, *The Pursuit of the Millennium* became an extremely influential book, and not without good reason.⁴ As a means of exposing the deeper socio- and psychopathological roots of Nazi anti-Semitism, Cohn's approach was extraordinarily revealing. More generally, the striking parallels it suggested between obscure medieval religious sects and crucially important modern secular movements appeared to invest his social-scientific conception of millenarianism with enormous explanatory power. Millenarianism, previously dismissed by historians as an inexplicable aberration, could now be regarded as a social phenomenon so well understood that it could illuminate other developments associated with it. The obvious period in which to apply this new interpretive paradigm was the early modern one, situated as it was between the medieval and contemporary material analyzed by Cohn himself; and work on early modern millenarianism subsequently proliferated rapidly. While some of this attention was directed at the apocalyptic revolts in early Reformation Germany and the great revolutions in France and America, the most sustained attention focused on the groundswell of millenarianism that accompanied the dramatic disruptions of mid-seventeenth-century England. From the late 1960s to the early 1980s, a generation of historians produced a torrent of literature thoroughly integrating the history of English apocalypticism into a basically Marxist interpretation of the "English Revolution" and pioneering in the process the application of social scientific methods and terminology to English intellectual and religious history.⁵

After this dramatic surge of interest, however, the rapid pursuit of seventeenth-century millenarianism ground abruptly to a halt. In part this was due to extrinsic factors, to a turn in the underlying historiographical tide. If, as Conrad Russell and the revisionists of the 1980s maintained, the insular disturbances of the mid-seventeenth century cannot accurately be described as a "revolution," then they had no need for a revolutionary proto-ideology, and millenarianism thereby lost its basic historiographical function.⁶ Yet the sudden abandonment of this field was also prepared by developments within it, for the voluminous literature from the 1970s onwards had also invalidated many of the assumptions, largely derived from Cohn, that had provoked work on this topic in the first place. The figureheads of seventeenth-century millenarianism, it turned out, were not an impoverished, surplus population from the margins of society; they did not typically preach a doctrine of revolution to the masses; in no case did the masses respond with the genocidal fervor described in Cohn's work; and their tradition did not simply vanish with the return of political stability to the British Isles after 1660. The career of English millenarianism, in short, no longer made much sense either in the broader context of English history or in the theoretical framework provided by Cohn. Deprived both of its external historiographical foundation and its internal conceptual coherence, the flood of works on seventeenth-century English millenarianism dried up almost overnight. For the past twenty years, research in this field has been almost completely blocked by a conceptual and methodological impasse.

The main exception to this disheartening conclusion, however, is a striking one: a topic in which ongoing empirical research has yielded results diametrically opposite those suggested by Cohn's model. In the early modern period, it has emerged, millenarianism was persistently associated, not with anti-Semitism, but with its less familiar antithesis: philo-Semitism.[7] Five years before the appearance of Cohn's book, in fact, Hans Joachim Schoeps published a remarkable survey of some of the most extreme manifestations of millenarian philo-Semitism in seventeenth-century Germany, the Netherlands, and Scandinavia.[8] In subsequent decades, Johannes van den Berg, Richard Popkin, and their students and friends began exploring the closely interrelated groups of philo-Semitic millenarians in mid-seventeenth-century Holland and England. The Dutch connection, the special interest of Jewish scholars, its place outside the mainstream of English historiography, and Popkin's place on the editorial boards of two key Dutch monograph series in the field sustained the study of this aspect of English millenarianism beyond the watershed of the early 1980s and produced a voluminous specialized literature that, when combined with more episodic interest elsewhere, documents the existence of philo-Semitic millenarianism from the uplands of Transylvania to the Highlands of Scotland.[9] A survey of this remarkable conjunction of millenarianism with the very opposite of anti-Semitism offers a valuable cautionary tale on the dangers of premature importation of alien interpretative frameworks into early modern European intellectual history. Moreover, if the link between millenarianism and philo-Semitism can be identified with precision, it might also reveal a means of surmounting the methodological impasse that has hindered progress on the broader history of seventeenth-century millenarianism for two decades.

Here, however, we encounter a crucial weakness in the existing literature on this subject: although the constant conjunction of millenarianism with philo-Semitism has now been widely documented, the causal connection between them has not, to my knowledge, been precisely or convincingly identified. Here too the social-scientific model underlying much of this literature may be at least indirectly to blame. To a loose definition of millenarianism, derived more or less explicitly from Cohn, this literature has joined a still looser conception of philo-Semitism, thereby frustrating at the outset any attempt to identify a tight fit between these two doctrines. If, as critics have argued, philo-Semitism within this literature generally refers merely to an increased expectation of a final conversion of the Jewish nation to Christianity, redoubled efforts to effect that conversion, and an enhanced interest in things Jewish, then it is unworthy of the name.[10] Zealous efforts to convert the Jews have often been provoked by the most anti-Semitic of motives and can no more logically be equated with philo-Semitism than desire to convert heretics can be identified as love of heresy. Moreover, since the expectation of a final, national conversion of the Jews is incomparably more widespread in medieval and Reformation theology than millenarianism, if such a vague definition of philo-Semitism is employed then its tight association with millenarianism dissipates immediately.[11] In order for this link to be understood and sustained, a more precise definition of philo-Semitism as well as millenarianism is urgently needed. Any philo-Semitism worthy of the name must by definition involve an attitude of positive approbation or heightened goodwill towards the Jewish people and religion. In order for its link with millenarianism to be readily identifiable and historically significant, this heightened goodwill must also be viritually unprecedented within the previous Christian tradition but widespread amongst millenarians. A closer analysis of the relationship between philo-Semitism and millenarianism can therefore help to define the former phenomenon as well as its relationship with the latter one.

In exploring these issues, the following chapter is therefore intended to operate on two separate levels. On its first and most substantive level, it seeks to analyse the much studied yet still imperfectly understood early modern tradition of millenarian philo-Semitism. More specifically, it aims to identify with greater precision the basic theological logic linking millenarianism with philo-Semitism and in doing so to specify more precisely the intrinsic nature of millenarian philo-Semitism. Its basic argument on this level is that the specifically millenarian form of apocalyptic expectation radically altered Christian interpretations of Jewish messianic expectations. This alteration can best be clarified by contrasting it with the interpretations of Jewish messianism implicit in the other main apocalyptic scenarios current in the Reformation era: the standard medieval view, reasserted in the Counter-Reformation, which identified the Messiah awaited by the Jews with the biblical Antichrist; the standard Protestant view, which identified the Antichrist with the Roman Papacy; and (most fully) the Protestant millenarian view, which turned the implications of the medieval view inside out and provided a far more sympathetic perspective for embracing Jewish messianic yearnings than ever before. Having thereby identified a robust theological as opposed to sociological link between these two conjunct traditions, this chapter concludes by attempting briefly to derive from this case study a few basic suggestions regarding the most profitable methodology for studying religious ideas of this kind.

THE MEDIEVAL VIEW: ANTICHRIST AND ANTI-SEMITISM

That the dominant patristic and medieval conception of the Antichrist contained virulent anti-Semitic associations is a fact too well known to require lengthy demonstration here.[12] Many of these associations were derived, ironically, from ancient Jewish traditions regarding a final tyrant or false prophet from which the Antichrist myth gradually emerged. Others were fashioned by the logic of inversion, implicit in the concept of an "anti-Christ," which organized these sources into a coherent image. The Greek word *antichristos* denotes not merely one who is "opposed to Christ" but also a "false Christ," one who puts himself "in place of Christ." The final great opponent of Christ, it clearly followed, will also be a false Christ, who will disguise his evil intentions by mimicking or feigning all the acts prophesied of the true Christ in his first or second advent. From such a concept, the association of the Antichrist with the

Jews emerged almost inevitably. The true Christ, that is to say, the Messiah, the Redeemer of the Chosen People, must himself be a Jew, a member of the Chosen People. In order to perpetrate his deception and insinuate himself into Christ's place, the false Messiah or Antichrist must likewise be of Jewish origin. In ancient Judaism a loose chain of scriptural passages related the false Messiah more specifically to the tribe of Dan, and Christian theologians happily adopted this detail into their emerging conception of the Antichrist into a kind of Satanic parody of the origins and life of Jesus. Although born in Babylon, the Antichrist, like Jesus, would be raised in Galilee. At the age of thirty he would travel to Jerusalem, circumcise himself, and reveal himself to the Jews as their Messiah. There he would proclaim Jesus to have been an impostor and preach a new Law; but far from being the truth, his doctrine would be a kind of monstrous synthesis of all previous blasphemies and heresies. Sorcerers and witches would initiate him into the secrets of black magic, and through these he would begin to ape the miracles of Christ. His apostles, once initiated into these arts and doctrines, would perform further miracles and multiply his converts. He would fulfil the dearest of Jewish hopes by rebuilding the temple at Jerusalem, destroyed by the Romans; but (like Antiochus Epiphanes) would set up an image of himself in the most holy place and make himself the centre of the cult. Through such means, augmented by bribes and violence, he would convert almost all the people of the earth to his diabolical religion and would begin a persecution of the small remnant of faithful Christians more pitiless even than that of the ancient Roman emperors. After three and one-half years he would pretend to die and, after three days, to rise again. Finally, having triumphed over virtually the entire Christian world, he would attempt to mimic Jesus' ascension to heaven from the Mount of Olives, borne aloft by demons; but the Archangel Michael would be dispatched to destroy him, and the true Christ would then descend to judge a world almost completely lost in sin.

Since the life of Antichrist was in large part a parody of Jewish messianic expectations, it was only natural that the Jews themselves were expected to be amongst his earliest and most avid supporters. "I came in the name of my Father," Jesus had scolded the Jews (in John 5:43), "and you did not receive me; if another comes in his own name, him you will receive." This became a key proof-text demonstrating that the Jews, having rejected the true Christ, the Son of God, would joyously accept the Antichrist, the Son of Satan. The Jews were therefore the most important allies of Christ's greatest enemy; and in the final phase of world history they would play the same active role in tormenting Christians as they had played in the death of Christ himself. As if to drive the point home, the medieval Antichrist plays, from which much of this detail is ultimately drawn, were performed during Easter week. The anti-Jewish riots and massacres, which occurred most often during the Easter season, were among other things a kind of preemptive strike, intended to reduce the Antichrist's crack legions before it was too late. The most extreme form of the myth went further still: in the accounts of the "Red Jews," which circulated in vernacular texts especially in Germany, the ten lost tribes of Israel were equated with Gog and Magog, the destroying armies of the Antichrist that would encircle the camp of the saints in the final, climactic crisis of history.[13]

"Anti-Semitism and apocalypticism are so inextricably intertwined in medieval Europe," it has recently been emphasized, "that they must be studied together if a coherent and accurate picture of both phenomena is to emerge."[14] The end of the world would be immediately preceded by the tyrannical reign of Antichrist, and in that most terrible persecution the Jews would play a leading role. When eschatological expectations swelled in the latter middle ages, anti-Semitism naturally intensified as well. One need only recall that the most notorious of all anti-Semitic writings, *The Protocols of the Elders of Zion*, was originally published in Russia in a volume entitled *Antichrist as an Imminent Political Possibility* to grasp something of the anti-Semitic potential of this intimate association of the Jews with the figure of Antichrist.[15] Within the medieval frame of reference, Cohn's association of anti-Semitism with apocalypticism—though not precisely with millenarianism—is both broadly valid and highly significant.

THE PROTESTANT VIEW: ANTICHRIST AND ANTI-CATHOLICISM

Scarcely less well studied is the Protestant alternative to the traditional image of the Antichrist, and there is no need to dwell at length on the basis of this now familiar exegesis.[16] Second Thessalonians 2:3–4 prophesied that the second coming would not occur "except there come a falling away first, and that man of sin be revealed, the son of perdition; who opposeth and exalteth himself above all that is called God, or that is worshipped; so that he as God sitteth in the temple of God, shewing himself that he is God." The standard reference for English Calvinists, the Geneva Bible, did not even see the need to explicate the reasons for identifying this figure with the papacy: "All men know who he is that saith he can shut up heaven and open it at his pleasure, and took upon him to be Lord and Master above all kings and princes, before whom kings and princes fall down and worship, honouring that Antichrist as a God." No more difficult was the identity of the Whore of Babylon described in Revelation 17, seated on the beast with seven heads, drunken with the blood of saints, with a golden cup in her hand full of abominations with which she had corrupted the kings of the earth: this terrible figure, Protestants maintained, prophesied the papal church, seated upon the seven hills of Rome, polluting all the countries of Christendom with its blasphemous, abominable sacrifice of the Mass.[17]

More important even than the plausibility of this identification, however, was its enormous utility in fashioning an amorphous movement of protest into churches with a strong sense of identity. The revelation of the papacy as the Antichrist simultaneously explained the lapse of the established church, justified the most uncompromising rejection of its innovations, stiffened Protestant determination to resist counterreformation at all cost, and lent itself to the kind of vivid graphic representation needed to spread the new faith to an uneducated populace. Wherever the Protestant rejection of the Roman church spread, therefore, the notion of the papal Antichrist spread with it, not least because it was one of the most potent bearers of that message.[18] In a wide range of authoritative confessional documents—including Melanchthon's apology for the Augsburg Confession, Luther's Schmalkald Articles, and the confessions of the Bohemian Brethren and the English, Scottish, Irish, and French Protestant churches—we find the identification of the papacy as the Antichrist treated virtually as an article of faith.[19]

This conviction amongst Protestants that the papacy was the Antichrist had the potential to remove the crucial link between apocalyptic expectation and anti-Semitic violence characteristic of the late middle ages; but this potential was not immediately realized. The Jews' central role in the medieval Antichrist myth was of course only one cause of medieval anti-Semitism, and the reapplication of the texts concerning the Antichrist from Jews to Catholics did not therefore put an end to Protestant anti-Semitism. Nor did this reconceptualization of Antichrist immediately decouple anti-Semitism from its apocalyptic setting, although the reasoning necessary to connect the two was increasingly labyrinthine. In a series of notorious writings, the aged Luther expanded his notion of the Antichrist to include the Jew and the Turk along with the pope as a kind of diabolical, eschatological trinity.[20] Others reached a similar conclusion by reviving the old notion of the "Red Jews" as Gog and Magog, the armies of the Mohammedan Antichrist.[21] Even a century later in England, opponents of the readmission of the Jews would play upon their old associations with Antichrist.[22] Moreover, in one indirect way the new Protestant antichristology strengthened the old anti-Semitic eschatology: faced with the Protestant application of the figure of Antichrist to the papacy, Catholics responded by redoubling their emphasis on the traditional interpretation.

THE COUNTER-REFORMATION RESPONSE: REASSERTION OF THE MEDIEVAL VIEW

Unlike their medieval and Reformation predecessors, conceptions of the Antichrist in post-Reformation Catholicism have not yet attracted sustained attention.[23] If the scraps of existing literature on this subject are gathered together, however, it immediately becomes evident that the rhetoric of eschatological vituperation was not symmetrical. Catholics did not for the most part merely hurl the epithet "Antichrist" back at Protestants. On the contrary, while they ransacked the Apocalypse for other eschatological epithets[24] and routinely described their enemies as *precursors* of the Antichrist, they manifested an astonishing reluctance to declare Luther and his followers the final great Antichrist himself.[25] Given the heat of contemporary polemics, Catholic restraint in this regard is remarkable. The English Cardinal Reginald Pole, for instance, found that every word of the biblical description of the Antichrist applied to Henry VIII "so closely that a painter could never present a more exact image of anyone"; yet he still refused to regard the apostate king as anything more than a type or precursor of the final Antichrist.[26] The pioneering French polemicist Florimond de Raemond claimed that Luther's name contained "the number of the Beast" in all three sacred languages, but he explicitly refused to draw the conclusion that Luther was anything more than a precursor of Antichrist.[27] After rehearsing Luther's antichristian attributes for four folio columns, the Dominican Tomaso Malvenda nevertheless concluded that he was "not the *Antichristus verus* himself; but among all the heresiarchs since the foundation of God's Church, this man above all was the great forerunner of the Antichrist."[28] Similar self-discipline is manifest, for instance, in Francisco Suarez, in Cornelius à Lapide, and in the annotations of the English Catholic New Testament published in Rheims in 1582.[29]

A key factor distorting this unequal exchange was the profoundly asymmetrical relationship of Catholicism and Protestantism. While Protestants opposed a single great enemy that had mysteriously infested the heart of the institutional church, Catholics faced a constantly proliferating swarm of heretics and schismatics. To single out one of this swarm as the *Antichristus magnus* would only bestow undue distinction upon it. Moreover, the Catholic polemicist's truly vital task was not the aggressive one of answering Protestant invective in kind but the defensive one of rebutting the Protestant consensus that the papacy was the biblical Antichrist. In doing so, Catholic polemicists found no strategy more valuable than to turn Protestant preference for scriptural literalism against them. While the Protestant conception of the Antichrist was inconsistent with the obvious, literal meaning of key scriptural texts, they argued, a thousand years of theological tradition had painted a very different portrait of the Antichrist. Rather than fling the gravest of apocalyptic aspersions back against the heretics, the most senior Catholic polemicists therefore set about refurbishing the traditional image of the Antichrist with a more up-to-date and defensible scholarly apparatus.

In 1586 the greatest of Catholic polemicists, Cardinal Roberto Bellarmino, unveiled this strategy in a treatise on the Antichrist embedded in his epoch-making *summa* of polemical theology.[30] A defensible presentation of this argument required, to be sure, that the most unsubstantiated accretions to the Antichrist legend be pared away; but Bellarmino nevertheless deemed it "valde probabilis" that the Antichrist would be the son of a whore and a descendent of the tribe of Dan and "certissima" that the Antichrist would be of Jewish origin, circumcised, observe the Sabbath, rebuild the Temple in Jerusalem, reestablish the Jewish state, be received by the Jews as their Messiah, and would come, in short, "praecipue propter Iudaeos."[31] A few years later Francisco Suarez displayed a similar mixture of superficial caution and underlying conviction: Suarez regarded most of the prophecies concerning the Antichrist as "perobscura," the traditional account of Antichrist's tribe and mother as "incerta," his Jewish birth and religion as merely the most likely opinion ("inter omnia verisimillium"), and the Jews' reception of him as a mere "conjectura"; yet he adopted this conjecture as the basic premise of his account of the mores, doctrine, and reign of Antichrist and developed the anti-Semitic potential of the traditional view in far greater detail than Bellarmino.[32] Under such leadership, the scholarly refurbishment of medieval tradition grew rapidly, sweeping aside such inconsequential hesitations as it did so. In a work of almost two thousand folio columns, which culminated Counter-Reformation writing on the Antichrist, the Dominican Tomaso Malvenda buried these doubts under huge piles of biblical, patristic, medieval, and modern authorities unequivocally asserting the certainty of the Antichrist's origin from the tribe of Dan and acceptance by the Jews as their Messiah.[33] This conception of the Antichrist also thoroughly permeated two otherwise antithetical Catholic interpretations of the Apocalypse as a whole that sought, in two very different ways, to shield the papacy from association with the Antichrist by applying the prophecies of the Apocalypse to an era other than the medieval past, the present, and the immediate future. The "futurist" school interpreted almost the entire Apocalypse as a prophecy of the brief, future, three-and-one-half-year interval of Antichrist's reign, therefore effortlessly incorporating and indeed elaborating the traditional conception of the Jewish Antichrist.[34] The "praeterist" school referred most of the prophecies of the Apocalypse instead to a brief period in the distant *past*—the three centuries before Constantine—and applied the central section of the book to the earliest persecutions of the nascent Christian church by the Jews. The most massive statement of this praeterist tradition—the thousand-page folio volume by Luis de Alcázar—accordingly developed a portrait of the Jewish people as "la suma de las injusticias, el colmo de todas las maldades" and "el atributo metafísico del mal en la historia."[35] Vernacular writers in other Catholic countries naturally exercised no more restraint than their more learned Spanish contemporaries. The first Counter-Reformation treatise on the Antichrist in French, according to two independent studies, contained "un élément antisémitique extrêmement marqué et virulent."[36] In direct riposte to the antipapal woodcuts in the Wittenberg Bible and marginalia in the Geneva Bible, the English Catholic Bible printed in Douay in 1609 predicted that the Antichrist "will ioyne himself vvith the Iewes pretending to obserue the law of Moyses and so they vvil reciuiue him as their Messias."[37] In a German treatise of 1682, Dionysius von Lützemberg argued *in extenso* that every aspect of the Messiah awaited by the rabbis identified him instead as the Antichrist, thereby surpassing even the most elaborate of the medieval treatises in the profusion of anti-Semitic detail: the faith in which the Antichrist will instruct his messengers, for instance, will include the thirteen articles of Jewish belief taken from Moses Maimonides.[38]

More surprising than the revival of the Jewish Antichrist within post-Tridentine Catholicism is its adoption on precisely the point of the confessional spectrum where one might least expect to find it: in the moderate group of Protestant irenicists who sought to repair the terrible schism in the church. Under Charles I and his anti-Calvinist archbishop, William Laud, the widespread assertion that the papacy had been revealed as the Antichrist was temporarily silenced in England and replaced in at least one case with the positive assertion that when the Antichrist did come he would be a Jew.[39] The great Arminian intellectual and Protestant ecumenist Hugo Grotius adopted de Alcázar's praeterism and was followed by other leading irenicists such as Charles I's chaplain, Henry Hammond, Jean Le Clerc, and the young Gottfried Wilhelm Leibniz.[40] Developing this praeterism further, Grotius and his fellow Arminian Jacobus Batalerius were among a tiny minority of Dutch theologians who denied that Romans 11:26 prophesied a future conversion of the Jews to Christianity.[41] Leibniz's correspondent, Hermann von der Hardt, professor of oriental languages at the famously irenical University of Helmstedt, proposed an even more radically praeterist reading of the Apocalypse, which fully exposed its anti-Semitic potential. By arguing that the Apocalypse was composed before the destruction of the Second Temple in 70 A.D., von der Hardt proposed that virtually the entire book, rather than merely its central section, described the persecution of the earliest Christians by the Jews and the subsequent divine vengeance on the Jewish people.[42] Sixteen years later he added the argument that all the references to "Antichrists" in the New Testament referred to "le Chef et les autres Presidens des Juifs & de leur Republique & Eglise, avec tout le Senat de Jerusalem, & toute la nation de Juifs."[43] Once the association of the Antichrist with the papacy was removed, therefore, its association with the Jews rapidly reestablished itself in moderate Protestant as well as Catholic eschatology. In a revealing demonstration of the economy of hatred in the confessional age, some of Europe's most moderate theologians sought to help reconcile Protestants with Catholics by channelling their eschatological animosities outside the Christian community and against the Jews.

MILLENARIAN VIEW: ONE MESSIAH, TWO ADVENTS

The standard Protestant identification of the Antichrist with the papacy, then, decoupled the longstanding direct association of the Antichrist with the Jews; but it did not thereby neutralize other sources of anti-Semitism within the Protestant world, and it tended to reinforce the anti-Semitic associations of the Antichrist within the Catholic world, associations which then reentered the Protestant one as well. Eventually, however, the Protestant apocalyptic tradition did develop a major variant with a far more positive relationship to the Jews: millenarianism.

The term "millenarianism," as is well known, derives from the Latin "mille annis" meaning "a thousand years." The *locus classicus* for this term is the thousand-year period, described in Apocalypse 20, during which Satan is hindered from persecuting the church and the resurrected saints reign on earth. The established interpretation of this passage, advanced by Augustine and adopted by virtually all major theologians for a thousand years after him, held that this passage was to be understood spiritually. The elect, he argued, would never reign over an earthly kingdom: their sovereignty applied only to the spiritual plane, where Christ's death had made them invulnerable to the assaults of Satan. The number one thousand was likewise not to be understood as a literal thousand-year period: rather it was a perfect number, designating the entire period of the Christian church, between the first and second advents of Christ. Millenarians, on the other hand, maintained that this prophecy would be fulfilled in the future, when Satan would be restrained for a long period from persecuting the church and the saints would in some sense be resurrected and reign on earth.

Given the defining importance of this passage, historians often appear to assume that millenarianism is based more or less exclusively on a revised interpretation of the twentieth chapter of the Apocalypse. But this is a serious misconception; and nothing could reveal the gravity of this error more fully than one of the earliest and most important works in the mainstream Protestant millenarian tradition: the *Diatribe de Mille Annis Apocalypticis,* published in 1627 by a leading professor of the Calvinist academy in Herborn, Johann Heinrich Alsted (1588–1638). Alsted's path-breaking work begins with a brief commentary on Apocalypse 20, but the core of the book consists of a detailed consideration of sixty-five other scriptural prophecies of a period of unparalleled felicity for the church on earth.[44] Only ten of these are from the two main apocalyptic books of the Bible, Daniel and Revelation. Fifty-four are taken from the Old Testament against only eleven from the New; and the Old Testament passages range from Genesis 17 to the last verse of Malachi, with special emphasis on Isaiah, Jeremiah, and the minor prophets.

An adequate examination of Alsted's millenarian reinterpretation of each of these sixty-five passages is obviously beyond the limits of this chapter, but the basic hermeneutical shift is clear enough. Like the twentieth chapter of the Apocalypse, these Old Testament passages had traditionally been interpreted spiritually by Christians and regarded as having been fulfilled by Jesus of Nazareth. The Jews, on the other hand, had traditionally interpreted them literally and therefore regarded them as remaining unfulfilled. Alsted's interpretation, and the basis of his millenarianism, splits the difference, arguing that the prophecies are part spiritual and part literal and therefore have only been partially fulfilled. Jesus, he insists, in his first advent fulfilled all those Old Testament prophecies that concern our eternal salvation; but there remain other prophecies pertaining to the happiness of the church on earth that have yet to be fulfilled. The result is a revolution in prophetic exegesis, a sea change in the interpretation not merely of Daniel or Revelation, but of the whole of scriptural prophecy. Passages that Protestants had traditionally applied to the past and Catholics to the present were applied to the future; passages that had traditionally been applied to the spiritual plane or the eternal state of the church in heaven were applied to secular, temporal events on earth; and passages that were traditionally applied to the early state of the Christian church were now applied to the future conversion and felicity of the Jews.

Moreover, in a second work published in 1627—the revised second edition of his *Theologia polemica*—Alsted made explicit the compromise with Judaism left tacit within the *Diatribe* itself. Within a rewritten opening section on controversies between Christians and Jews, Alsted inserted two entirely new chapters that constitute a kind of synopsis of the central section of the *Diatribe* with its implications for the Jews in mind.[45] The first of these chapters considers the question "Whether there is to be expected any particular period of felicity for the Christian church on this earth." Alsted's response to this question begins with the extraordinary concession to an imaginary Jewish interlocutor that not all the messianic prophecies of the Old Testament have been fulfilled in Jesus of Nazareth. Although Jesus fulfilled all those prophecies that concern our eternal salvation, there remain others pertaining to the happiness of the church on this earth which have *not* yet been fulfilled.[46] In this and the following chapter, thirty-four of the fifty-four Old Testament prophecies discussed in the *Diatribe*, and five from the New are repeated and their general meaning summarized in a fashion highly reminiscent of the *Diatribe*: the church on earth still awaits a future period of liberation from persecution, a thousand years of peace, augmentation through the conversion of Jews and Gentiles, majesty, glory, and great joy.

The implications of this interpretation for Jewish-Christian relations are brought out in the second of these two chapters, which considers the question "Whether the Jews are to be converted to faith in Christ." Here

Alsted proposes two remarkable rules that should be held continually in mind by all those concerned with the conversion of the Jews. The first is that "the first advent of the Messiah is to be distinguished from the second." The Jews fail to do this when they turn their eyes and minds from the first advent and apply all messianic prophecies to the second. Yet Christians have also erred in attempting to apply all messianic prophecies to the first advent, averting their eyes from the afflictions of their age and acknowledging only its blessings.[47] Unlike the orthodox Augustinian, the millenarian Christian, in effect, offers to meet Jewish messianic expectations half way. The second of these two rules, although formulated in a rather less generous fashion, proposes a similar compromise regarding the *nature* of this messianic period. This period of future happiness for the church on earth will be blessed, Alsted concedes, with temporal goods far greater than any which have previously been enjoyed. He immediately cautions that the kingdom of Christ proper will not consist of these things, "lest we seem to do as the Jews do, who expect nothing from the Messiah but carnal things." This qualification is necessary in order to defend himself against the charge not merely of "Judaizing," but also of following ancient heretics such as Cerinthus, whose description of the thousand years consisted chiefly in the most voluptuous abundance of food, drink, and other pleasures.[48] But it also represents a major departure from the standard Augustinian interpretation, which interpreted the millennium entirely in inward, spiritual terms.[49] The revolution in prophetic exegesis underlying Alsted's millenarianism therefore brings in its wake a revolution in the relationship of Christians and Jews.

Alsted's *Diatribe de Mille Annis Apocalypticis* is the first work by an established Reformed authority dedicated exclusively to defending the expectation of a future millennium. His *Theologia polemica* is in all likelihood the first compendium of mainstream Protestant theology to defend millenarianism and related ideas. But as Alsted was well aware, the ideas just outlined can be traced with confidence to earlier writers: alongside a list of twenty-four biblical passages on the conversion of the Jews, his *Diatribe* itself lists ten recent authorities on this topic. Inspection of them all reveals that Alsted's key source for these doctrines was the final entry on the list: the first independent treatise on the conversion of the Jews published in seventeenth-century Germany, written by the professor of jurisprudence in Tübingen, Christoph Besold (1577–1638).⁵⁰ The treatment of the conversion of the Jews within the *Diatribe,* in fact, is drawn very largely from Besold's dissertation: nine of the ten recent authorities on this doctrine are copied from Besold's first pages, and fifteen of Alsted's twenty-four scriptural passages on the conversion of the Jews stem from the body of his pamphlet.⁵¹ More remarkably still, Besold's little treatise is also the immediate source of the more radically philo-Semitic doctrine simultaneously introduced into Alsted's *Theologia polemica.* The last of the ten authorities listed by Besold is the work on the two advents of the Messiah published in 1581 by the Italian Joachimist and heterodox "Huguenot" Jacopo Brocardo (d. 1594).⁵² As its full title indicates, Brocardo's work pursued a dual strategy identical to that spelled out in Alsted's *Theologia polemica.*⁵³ On the one hand Brocardo sought to convince his nonmillenarian fellow Christians that many messianic prophecies traditionally applied to the first advent remain in fact unfulfilled and await their realization in the second. On the other hand, he sought to persuade the Jews that many of the most important messianic prophecies had in fact already been accomplished by Jesus of Nazareth, who would fulfil the others when he returned a second time. Besold included a brief summary of Brocardo's main thesis at the end of his list of authorities on the conversion of the Jews, and the key passage of Alsted's *Theologia polemica* is essentially a *verbatim* transcription—without acknowledgement either of Brocardo or of Besold—of this summary.⁵⁴

Alsted's two Latin treatises of 1627, then, gave more authoritative expression to ideas previously circulating in more suspect and ephemeral publications. Sixteen years later, the wave of English interest in Alsted's millenarianism accompanying the outbreak of civil war enhanced that circulation further still. In the preface to his English translation of the *Diatribe* published in 1643, the obscure schoolteacher William Burton highlighted precisely the ideas that Alsted had derived via Besold from Brocardo: the identification of the returning Christ as the Jewish Messiah and the utility of this identification in facilitating the conversion of the Jews. "Seeing that there are so manifest proofes of a glorious Kingdome of the *Saints* here on earth out of the old Testament," Burton wrote, there will be no better or easier way, to deale with the *Iewes* in matter of their conversion, then not to wrest the plaine prophecies of a second and glorious appearance of Christ, to his first comming; but rather to perswade them, that they must expect no other *Messias . . .* besides that *Jesus of Nazareth,* whom their Ancestors crucified. And this way is every where almost through the whole *Revelation* diligently insisted upon. For whilst we force these most cleare prophecies concerning things promised in the second, to his first comming, the *Iewes* scorne and deride us, and are more and more confirmed in their infidelity. But for the cours which I have here set doune, I am much mistaken if it be not the same which was observed among them by *Peter* himselfe, *Act.* 3. 19, 20, 21 *Repent ye therefore, and be converted, that your sins may be blotted out, when the* times of refreshing *shall come from the presence of the* Lord, *And he shall send* Jesus Christ, *which before was preached unto you whom the Heaven must receive, until the* times of restitution of all things, *which* God *hath spoken by the mouth of all his holy* Prophets *since the World began.*[55]

Given the similarity of this statement with the writings just discussed, one might suppose that Burton derived it from Alsted, Besold or Brocardo; but his source—which can be identified with virtual certainty—is in fact the other main fountainhead of the Calvinist millenarian tradition: Joseph Mede (1586–1638). In 1627, the same year as the first edition of the *Diatribe* and the revised *Theologia polemica,* Mede published in Cambridge his *Clavis apocalyptica,* which includes a firm and forceful exposition of millenarianism within a highly original and influential interpretation of the Apocalypse as a whole. The passage quoted from Burton's preface above is in fact an abbreviated but only slightly modified translation of the two concluding paragraphs of Mede's famous book.[56] Small wonder, then, that when Alsted himself encountered this passage in the anonymous second edition of Mede's *Clavis apocalyptica* published in 1632, he should have embraced it with enthusiasm.[57]

Alsted and Mede are rightly acknowledged as the joint founders of the Calvinist millenarian tradition, and their remarkable consensus on this point therefore has two important implications. In the first place, the equation of the Christian millennium with the Jewish messianic kingdom and the hopes raised by this for an easy conversion of the Jews were clearly established at the outset of the mainstream Protestant millenarian tradition. In the second place, while Brocardo and Besold probably exercised little direct influence on subsequent millenarians, the seminal works of Alsted and Mede rapidly spread their ideas throughout the diverse branches of the Calvinist millenarian tradition—British and continental, learned and popular, moderate and radical. A full demonstration of the speed and extent of this diffusion would require a comprehensive survey of this huge tradition; but even a more superficial sounding reveals the importance of these ideas in the origins of millenarian philo-Semitism.

A useful point of departure is the important philo-Semitic tract, *The Glory and Salvation of Jehudah and Israel*, published in 1650 by the prominent Independent pastor and politician Henry Jessey (1601–1663).[58] As the full title of the work stressed, Jessey's purpose was to reunify the Christian and Jewish religions by demonstrating their conformity in many fundamental principles, especially those regarding the Messiah. Jessey addressed his treatise simultaneously to Jews and nonmillenarian Christians, and his reasoning is highly reminiscent of Alsted. While many Old Testament prophecies regarding the Messiah and his glorious reign have undoubtedly been fulfilled by Jesus in his first advent (he insists to the Jews) there are others (he urges his nonmillenarian fellow Christians) that equally undoubtedly have *not* yet been fulfilled— prophecies such as the destruction of all idolatry, the increase of the knowledge of the Lord as the waters cover the sea, the calling of the Jews from all quarters of the world and their restoration to great privileges, the outpouring of the Holy Spirit upon the Jews, the destruction of all their oppressors, and the establishment of the Messiah's Fifth Monarchy. Christians, he concludes, cannot hope to convert the Jewish nation until they concede that many of their dearest messianic hopes remain unfulfilled and have no right to persecute them when their own position is indefensible. Millenarianism, on the other hand, acknowledges the truth of both parties and will greatly facilitate the conversion of the one to the other. The source of these now familiar ideas is further suggested by the recent authorities that Jessey cites in support of it: almost all of the more exotic ones are derived from the list of writers on the conversion of the Jews that Alsted borrowed from Besold. In addition to Alsted himself, these include Petrus Cunaeus, Johannes Ferus, "Seraphim Firmianus" (Seraphino da Fermo), Martinus Cellarius (*alias* Borrhaus), Johannes Dobricius (cited by Alsted but not Besold), and "Christianus Resoldus" [*sic*]. As Ernestine van der Wall has commented regarding this list, "It was quite unusual to put the Leiden professor of theology André Rivet, the Roman Catholic exegete Johannes Ferus, and Firmianus (whose identity is unknown to me) on the list of Christian millenarian authors. Cellarius and Resoldus also did not belong to the popular group of millenarians. It is noteworthy that Jessey does not mention Joseph Mede or his friend Nathaniel Homes."[59] In sum, this is a highly distinctive list, clearly not derived from Mede; the garbling of Christoph Besold's name into "Christianus Resoldus" suggests that Jessey's direct source for these names cannot be Besold, and the inclusion of Dobricius confirms that it must therefore have been taken from Alsted.

Jessey was a central figure in the circle of Anglo-Dutch millenarian philo-Semites, which represent the best-studied climax of the tradition in the 1650s and 1660s; and whether through him, Alsted, Mede, or their sources similar conceptions quickly became commonplace in this circle. A prime example is the work described by Hans Joachim Schoeps as "das für die Geschichte des Philo-Semitismus im 17. Jahrhundert *bedeutsamste* Dokument":[60] the *Bonum Nunciam Israeli de Messiah*, published in Amsterdam in 1655 by Paul Felgenhauer (1593–ca. 1677). The very title page of the work emphasizes the key idea that Christians and Jews await the coming of the same savior: the work is described as written "à Quodam Christiano, qui Adventum Messiae cum Iudaeis exspectat."[61] The "Good News" that Felgenhauer wished to communicate to the Jews was that the Christian scriptures indicated that the advent of this shared savior was imminent; and his desire to communicate this was clearly enhanced by the expectation that his message would help convert the Jews to Christianity.[62] Two years later, Jessey's friend Petrus Serrarius (1600–1669) voiced similar ideas: "What Jews and Christians are now anticipating so keenly is the appearance of the true Messiah in the glory of God." He also drew the direct philo-Semitic consequence from this: "We must show them love and respect because of the inheritance which was promised to them, and was, through grace, bestowed on us by the Lord Jesus, who is their Messiah and ours."[63] As his most sustained student has concluded recently, for Serrarius "Chiliasm is thus a synthesis of the partial truth which the Jews and the Christians have each appropriated. The idea that Christianity and Judaism are in a sense complementary can be regarded as one of the basic features of Serrarius's millenarianism."[64] Very similar ideas are found in the chief millenarian work of Serrarius's friend, the expatriate Huguenot preacher and spiritualist Jean de Labadie (1610–1674). The doctrine of the coming millennial reign of Jesus Christ and that of the conversion of the Jews, de Labadie wrote in 1667, "are joined in such a way that the knowledge of the one implies the other, and both are equally necessary and useful. . . . This doctrine will exceedingly facilitate their conversion to Jesus Christ and their reunion with the Christian Church, because by this means we concede to them things which are incontestable."[65]

Such ideas clearly circulated widely in mid-century Anglo-Dutch millenarian circles; but they did not die out after the critical middle decades of the seventeenth century. After the revocation of the Edict of Nantes in 1685, millenarianism welled up in figures central to the French Protestant church. The chief work of this mainstream Huguenot millenarian tradition was a huge, two-volume commentary on the Apocalypse written by the leader of the *refuge,* Pierre Jurieu (1637–1713), and heavily indebted to Mede. A prominent letter on the first page of that work, addressed "TO THE NATION OF THE JEWS," outlined the link between millenarianism and the conversion of the Jews in still greater detail:

> I Desire of that People [the Jews], that they would please to read this *book* attentively, and without prejudice; especially from the middle of the second part to the end;[66] they will find nothing there that can irritate 'em. I confess the hopes of the *Messiah,* which shall be chiefly for them, is built upon express and unquestionable *Prophecies;* that even their *Ierusalem* should be *rebuilt,* and that they shall be again gathered together in their own Land. And if any thing be capable to recover them from their obstinacy, for the establishment of the Law of *Moses,* and against the Law of *Christ;* this is certainly the most likely method, which we make use of, because it grants them almost all the advantages which they expect.[67]

As Jurieu's statement suggests, Jewish expectations were most closely approximated by those millenarians who interpreted the Old Testament prophecies of the messianic kingdom most literally. The Jews expected the literal coming of the Messiah at the beginning of the messianic kingdom, the literal reunion of the twelve tribes, their literal restoration to their own state in the Holy Land, the literal rebuilding of the temple, and a literal kingdom to bless the whole earth. As the orthodox denunciation of millenarians generally as "Judaisers" implies, these expectations were most closely mirrored by millenarians such as Jurieu who entertained the literal fulfilment of these and other prophecies in the literal reign of the saints over a peaceful, just, and godly kingdom. But even far more spiritualizing millenarians saw their doctrine as a key to the reconciliation with and conversion of the Jews. An important example is the father of German Pietism, Philipp Jakob Spener (1635–1705), one of the most subtle of chiliasts and most passionate exponents of a future general conversion of the Jews. Spener derived relatively early from the pseudonymously published commentary on the Apocalypse of Christian Knorr von Rosenroth (1639–1689) the idea that the Jews "probably have many truths in their books regarding the opinion of the glorious reign of Christ in this world" and "that from them the Jews should be shown that they await the Messiah not in vain but rather the same one whose first coming they failed to regard."[68] He later expressed similar ideas himself. Christians, he urged, should seek opportunities to show the Jews "from God's word . . . that God will once again show mercy to them and fulfil his promises to them so that then they with us will acknowledge and worship the one Messiah."[69] In addition, he advised that if the Jew's messianic hopes were frequently and movingly expounded to them, this "might form a preparation in their heart, to their greater good in the future."[70]

The idea that adoption of millenarianism would facilitate the conversion of the Jews was therefore widespread. Opponents of millenarianism were also aware of the link: Moise Amyraut, for instance, devoted an entire chapter of his classic assault on millenarianism to an "Examen de l'auantage que ces Messieurs pretendent tirer de leur opinion, pour faciliter la conuersion des Iuifs."[71] The crucial point, however, is the underlying one: millenarianism could facilitate the conversion of the Jews because it conceded the validity of many of the Jews' dearest messianic expectations. The importance of this concession can be seen from the fact that it often replaces the fervent expectation of a future national conversion with a still more striking form of eschatological expectation more worthy of name "philo-Semitism": some millenarians concede the validity of Jewish messianic expectations so fully that they foresee *no need* for a future conversion of the Jews.

An early example is the little book *Du Rappel des Juifs* [*On the Calling of the Jews*] published in 1643 by the Huguenot secretary to the prince of Condé, Isaac La Peyrère (1596–1676). While Alsted, his great Moravian student Jan Amos Comenius, Comenius's friend Samuel Hartlib, and their mutual friend Henry Jessey based their millenarian expectations very largely on Old Testament messianic prophecies,[72] La Peyrère's expectations were based almost *exclusively* on the Hebrew scriptures, especially the prophet Joel.[73] In a certain sense La Peyrère still gave precedence to Christianity: just as expiation precedes sanctification, the humble spiritual mission of expiating the sins of the world, performed in the first advent, needed to precede the establishment of a glorious terrestrial kingdom at the second. But this historical precedence did not imply a soteriological superiority, and La Peyrère seems to have held that Jewish faith and practice were sufficient to gain salvation. Such ideas naturally appealed to the leading ecumenical rabbi in Amsterdam, Menasseh ben Israel (1604–1657), who succinctly summarized the Frenchman's teaching in 1656 as follows: "the Jewes, saith he, shall be saved, for yet we expect a second coming of the same Messias, and the Jewes believe that that coming is the first and not the second, and *by that faith they shall be saved,* for the difference consists onely in the circumstance of the time."[74]

Later millenarians drew similar conclusions still more explicitly. A striking example is found in the "Schreiben an die Juden" written in 1699 by the radical pietist Ernst Christoph Hochmann von Hochenau (1669/70–1721) and republished by Count Nicolaus Ludwig von Zinzendorf.[75] Hochmann does not first expound a Christian millenarianism, then emphasize its similarities to Jewish messianic expectations, and finally urge a campaign to convert the Jews to reformed, chiliastic Christianity. He does not even mention that the Messiah whom the Jews await has already come. Still less does he stress that the Jews can only enter the messianic kingdom after conversion to Christianity. Rather, he suspends his Christian perspective almost completely, formulates his vision in an almost entirely Jewish idiom, and concedes the sufficiency of the Jewish religion as a means of recognising the returning Messiah and entering his kingdom. As Heinz Renkewitz observed, upon a first reading of this remarkable document "one might suppose oneself to be reading the sermon of a Jew regarding the coming Messiah." Further study by Hans Schneider has revealed more subtle traces of New Testament theology underlying this text; but Renkewitz and Schneider agree, "that according to Hochmann the Jewish path to salvation does not lead through a preparatory conversion to Christianity and therefore no mission to convert the Jews is necessary. The separate paths of Christianity and Judaism only meet in the Last Days in the revelation of the *one* Messiah of Jews *and* Christians."[76] Far from equating philo-Semitism with zeal for the conversion of the Jews, the most advanced form of millenarian philo-Semitism saw no need for a campaign of Jewish conversion whatsoever.

The notable English scientist and Unitarian dissenter Joseph Priestley (1733–1804) carried these ideas two stages further still. On the one hand, he introduced a further distinction regarding the awaited Messiah. By the late eighteenth century when Priestley wrote, philo-Semitic millenarians had long urged both Christians and Jews to divide Old Testament messianic prophecies into two categories—those pertaining to the "suffering Messiah" and those relating to the triumphant Messiah—and to apply them respectively to the two separate advents of the same Christ, one in the distant past, the other in the near future. Priestley, in effect, reworked this division into a distinction between two quite separate individuals. The Old Testament prophets, he claimed, had foretold two entirely distinct figures: a "suffering Messiah," who would later return in glory, and a prince of the House of David, who would restore the Jewish state and worship before the second advent of the Messiah. These two personages, Priestley argued, adapting the arguments of his millenarian predecessors, had been confounded by both Christians and Jews "from the age of the apostles to the present day." Christians, rightly recognising in Jesus the attributes of the suffering Messiah, had wrongly identified him as the prince of the House of David as well. Jews, rightly failing to find in Jesus the attributes of the prince of the House of David, had wrongly rejected his status as the Messiah.[77]

In recognizing an independent prince of the House of David, Priestley granted even greater independence to the Jewish nation in the final eschatological events than his predecessors had. His second novel concession, regarding the nature of Jewish "conversion," extended similar independence to the Jewish religion. The Jews, he argued, would convert to Christianity insofar as they would recognize Jesus of Nazareth as the suffering Messiah foretold in their scriptures and accept him as their Christ upon his return. But even thereafter they would remain distinguished as Jews: within the messianic kingdom they would form a separate church, which would continue "to the end of time" to keep the Sabbath, holy feasts, sacrifices, circumcision, and other commandments of the Mosaic law.[78] Thus while the Jews will convert *to* Christianity, Priestley saw no need for them to convert *from* Judaism.

Priestley's vision may represent a kind of limiting case in which Christian philo-Semitism reaches its fullest possible accommodation with Judaism without sliding into a radically Judaized Christianity. Rejecting the traditional view that the prophecies of the messianic kingdom are fulfilled spiritually in the present, Priestley's millenarianism (like that of his many predecessors) conceded to the Jews the validity of their messianic expectations. Rejecting the orthodox teaching of the three persons of the Trinity and the dual nature of Christ, Priestley's Unitarianism also removed the greatest obstacle preventing the Jews from recognizing Jesus as their Messiah when he returns. This also allowed him to assert the permanent, independent validity not only of the Jewish people but of the Jewish religion as well, without compromising the permanent, independent validity of Christianity. In a genuinely pluralistic vision, both would prosper in the millennial age, without further Christianization of Judaism or further Judaization of Christianity. Far from issuing in fanatical intolerance of the kind documented by Cohn, this form of millenarianism went far beyond mere toleration to affirm the essential, religious unanimity of Judaism and Christianity and their consequent everlasting coexistence, not only in this imperfect life but also in the perfect world to come.

Millenarian philo-Semitism could, to be sure, be taken to even greater extremes, but only by further reducing the difference between Christianity and Judaism through a radical Judaization of Christian thought and practice. A concluding example, emerging from the earlier stages of the Unitarian tradition exemplified by Priestley, also demonstrates that at the radical boundaries of Christendom such ideas could work themselves out far more swiftly than the narrative treatment just sketched suggests. The example concerns the radical form of philo-Semitic millenarianism that arose directly from the "non-adorantist" antitrinitarianism particularly widespread in Transylvania in the latter sixteenth century. Jesus of Nazareth, these early Unitarians maintained, was neither divine (as Athanasian Christians believed) nor a superangelic being (as Arians maintained): he was a human being, a man of the house and lineage of David chosen by God to fulfill the Old Testament messianic prophecies. Jesus was therefore truly the Messiah awaited by the Jews; but since the Jews of his day had failed to recognize him as such, he in turn had failed to fulfill the prophecies of a messianic kingdom on earth. Lest these divine promises remain unfulfilled, God had taken him into heaven as his adopted son, where he now waits patiently at his right hand for a second opportunity to complete his divinely appointed mission. Throughout the current era, therefore, Jesus is entirely passive: prayers to him are not only idolatrous (since he is not divine) but fruitless, since he does not yet enjoy the dominion which was promised to him (hence the designation of this form of antitrinitarianism as non-adorantist). But the day will come when these promises will be fulfilled: Christ will come a second time to establish on earth for a thousand years the kingdom that was denied him at his first advent.[79]

The basic premise underlying this radical vision is that shared by all the philo-Semitic millenarians just discussed: Jesus of Nazareth, the Christian Messiah, is also the Messiah awaited by the Jews, who will fulfil in his second coming those things left unfinished by his first. The difference is that here it is not merely the prophecies regarding the happiness of the church here on earth that are regarded as unfulfilled but those regarding the means of salvation as well. Some non-adorationist antitrinitarians carried this reasoning still further. The outstanding example is Matthias Vehe-Glirius (ca. 1545–1590), one of the early circle of antitrinitarians in Heidelberg who gravitated to Transylvania for a time before dying in prison near Emden.[80] More explicitly even than La Peyrère, Vehe-Glirius struck all the books of the New Testament from the canon of Holy Scripture (with the single exception of the Apocalypse) and based his expectations not merely *largely* but *almost entirely* on the Old Testament and Jewish commentaries on them. Moreover, since the messianic kingdom had failed to materialize, he inferred that Jesus had inaugurated no new dispensation whatever; and from this it followed that even those who recognized Jesus's status as God's chosen Messiah (in other words, Christians) were obliged to fulfill all the prescriptions of the law of Moses, with the possible exception of circumcision. Particularly in thinkers liberated from the basic constraints of Christian orthodoxy by such fundamental heresies as antitrinitarianism, the philo-Semitic counterpart of millenarianism was capable of provoking the most extreme Judaization of Christian thought and practice.

While such views horrified more conservative antitrinitarians and millenarians alike, they nevertheless won a scattered following in east-central Europe, and their history records a particularly striking inversion of Norman Cohn's association of millenarianism with anti-Semitism. The Transylvanian nobleman Andreas Eössi translated Vehe-Glirius's strange theological principles into Hungarian prose and verse, applied them to practical life, and helped build a Sabbatarian sect in Transylvania of which chiliasm was a fundamental tenet.[81] When Eössi's adopted son, Simon Péchi, further diluted the future role assigned to Jesus in this theology, the result was a millenarian sect, stripped of most of the attributes of Christianity and progressively resembling Judaism, which survived in the upland regions of Transylvania until "the last representatives of the sect were dragged off to concentration camps by the Nazis in the summer of 1944."[82] If the link between modern "millenarianism" and anti-Semitism postulated by Cohn helped inspire those who planned and executed the Holocaust, the link between early modern millenarianism and philo-Semitism also helped inspire some of those who suffered from it.

RETHINKING MILLENARIANISM, PHILO-SEMITISM, AND METHODOLOGIES FOR THE HISTORY OF RELIGIOUS IDEAS

To those who view "millenarianism" as a generalized form of human behavior manifested with relatively superficial differences in fundamentally different cultures throughout the world, this collision of radically philo-Semitic and radically anti-Semitic species of "millenarianism" within the limited cultural field of central Europe may appear highly problematic. To those, however, who define "millenarianism" in more traditional and precise theological fashion as the expectation of an extended future period of felicity for the church on earth prophesied in Apocalypse 20, this apparent problem dissipates immediately. The reason is, quite simply, that most of the "mystical anarchists" and "revolutionary messianists" discussed in both the medieval and the modern sections of Cohn's book are not millenarians at all in the strict theological sense of that term. With this terminological ambiguity resolved, two quite different sets of explanations can then be applied to two quite distinct (if by no means unrelated) phenomena. On the one hand, powerful psychosocial forces of the kind invoked by Cohn can help account for the generation of extreme anti-Semitism amongst disorientated populations seduced by apocalyptic visions of various kinds, including what one might term "quasi-millenarian" ideologies. On the other hand, a series of clear and compelling theological inferences can be shown to link extraordinary expressions of philo-Semitism throughout the Protestant world no less forcefully to an underlying tradition of strict millenarianism.

This millenarian philo-Semitism, moreover, is not exhausted merely in a heightened expectation of the conversion of the Jews to Christianity; nor does it involve merely a more general enhancement of the expected Jewish role in the events of the last age: the gathering of the twelve tribes, their restoration to the Holy Land, the rebuilding of the Temple, and their recognition of the returning Christ. Within Protestant millenarianism the role of the Jews in the Last Days was not merely enhanced but transformed: it is scarcely too much to say that millenarianism could overturn the traditional Christian interpretation of Jewish messianism completely. Jews, it was traditionally argued, had rejected the true Messiah and were therefore awaiting a false one: the greatest enemy of Christ's church, the Antichrist. Protestants, however, had now firmly identified the Antichrist as the papacy, and millenarian Protestants were now awaiting the fulfilment of many of the same Old Testament prophecies as the Jews. Rather than awaiting the Antichrist, Jews could now be seen as awaiting Jesus Christ himself, who would fulfil in his second coming those prophecies of terrestrial felicity left unfulfilled by his first. That the Jews themselves did not realize that the Messiah whom they awaited was in fact the same one whom they had failed to recognize many centuries earlier was not an insuperable difficulty: Brocardo, Besold, Alsted, Mede, and numerous later millenarians clearly hoped that many might be convinced of this fact before the second advent, and the fulfilment of *all* Old Testament prophecies in the return of the Messiah would surely convince the rest. The crucial point was this: Protestant millenarians had discovered uniquely important expectations that they shared more fully with the Jews than with their nonmillenarian fellow Christians. Jews, in praying for the advent of the Messiah, could for the first time be seen as allies rather than adversaries in the great eschatological struggle. The apocalyptic framework that had previously exacerbated many of the most extreme expressions of anti-Semitism could now help nurture unprecedented expressions of philo-Semitism throughout the Protestant world. Indeed when combined with other heterodox doctrines such as antitrinitarianism or sabbatarianism, millenarianism could help stimulate a philo-Semitism so radical as to precipitate, not the conversion of Jews to Christianity, but the conversion of Christians to virtual Judaism.

A precise definition of "millenarianism" thus helps to distinguish between related species of apocalyptic expectation to produce a more adequate conception of "philo-Semitism" and to establish its intrinsic link with Protestant millenarianism. What more general methodological guidelines can briefly be drawn from this case study in conclusion?

The most basic one is that the erudite tradition of Protestant millenarianism in the early modern period is not in fact "irrational" or unintelligible in its own terms. Ancient apocalyptic texts, to be sure, purportedly originating from supernatural visions, were filled with dark and mysterious symbols and therefore lent themselves to innumerable contradictory interpretations. In the early modern period, moreover, disciplined philological exegesis of these difficult texts was often supplemented with numerological speculations, astrological theorizing, claims to personal revelation or supernatural insight, and highly emotive rhetoric, all of which were frequently shaped and distorted by confessional polemics and political agendas. The superficial level of the early modern millenarian tradition therefore teems with such a chaotic profusion of detail as initially to seem virtually unintelligible. Yet if the clear and powerful inferences binding Protestant millenarianism and philo-Semitism are any indication, at a deeper level this tradition has its own internal logic that is easily robust enough, once identified, to provide a clear understanding of the general shape of early modern millenarianism in its own terms.

In the context of this case study, this methodological conclusion carries several others in its train. If the basic shape of the early modern millenarian tradition is intelligible in its own terms, then historians do not need immediate recourse to imported theoretical frameworks in order to understand it, but can rely primarily on the traditional tools and methods of intellectual history. Indeed, as the case of millenarian philo-Semitism further suggests, these traditional tools and methods are sufficiently powerful to shatter even the most apparently powerful theorizations when they conflict with widespread empirical evidence. If, moreover, as the historiography of English millenarianism suggests, the hasty imposition of imported theoretical constructions led two generations of historians down a methodological blind alley, then historians should be very wary of placing too much reliance on alien interpretative frameworks. In sum, a half-century of historiographical experience has convincingly demonstrated that the enthusiastic importation of theoretical models from cognate disciplines is not the most productive or reliable starting point for an accurate and enduring analysis of early modern millenarianism.

It would be equally hasty, to be sure, to conclude from this limited case study that social-scientific perspectives have no place whatever in a holistic account of millenarianism in western culture. Even though the impetuous and uncritical importation of entire theoretical frameworks has proved an unsound point of departure for work in this field, social-scientific insights might still prove useful when employed patiently, carefully, critically, sensitively, selectively, and heuristically. The fatal error of much previous historiography on millenarianism, in other words, has been to regard these frameworks as independently validated explanatory paradigms of such scientific authority that they obviated historians' most basic obligation to ground their work in a serious and sustained encounter with the basic empirical evidence—that is, in this case, in the plentiful surviving records of what early modern millenarians actually thought and did. With this obligation fulfilled, historians may sometimes find social scientific models useful, not as substitutes for the sources, but as means of deepening their understanding of them. "Seeing things their way" may therefore not be the ultimate endpoint of all investigations into the history of religious ideas, but it is clearly the indispensable place to begin.

NOTES

1. For a splendid overview along these lines, see Christopher Rowland, *The Open Heaven: A Study of Apocalyptic in Judaism and Early Christianity* (London: SPCK, 1982).

2. Norman Cohn, *The Pursuit of the Millennium* (London: Secker & Warburg, 1957); 2nd rev. ed. subtitled *Revolutionary Messianism in Medieval and Reformation Europe and Its Bearing on Modern Totalitarian Movements* (New York: Harper & Row, 1961); 3rd. rev. ed. subtitled *Revolutionary Millenarians and Mystical Anarchists of the Middle Ages* (London: Paladin, 1970; New York: Oxford University Press, 1970; London: Pimlico, 1993). It has also been translated into German, French, Spanish, Portuguese, Italian, Japanese, Greek, and Norwegian.

3. Cohn, *Warrant for Genocide: The Myth of the Jewish World-Conspiracy and the Protocols of the Elders of Zion* (New York: Harper & Row, 1967; London: Eyre & Spottiswoode, 1967; London: Seriff, 1996; Harmondsworth: Penguin, 1970; Chico, Calif.: Scholars Press, 1981), quoting here from the dust jacket. Further translations into German, French, Spanish, Portuguese, Italian, Russian, Serbian, Hebrew, and Japanese. The origin of Cohn's researches is made explicit in the autobiographical forward to this book.

4. It is listed, for instance, amongst the hundred most influential books published since the war in Timothy Garton Ash, ed., *Freedom for Publishing—Publishing for Freedom: The Central and East European Publishing Project* (Budapest: Central European University Press, 1995); and the *Times Literary Supplement,* November 6, 1995. A still more general formulation of Cohn's thesis has been applied to contemporary politics in John Gray, *Black Mass: Apocalyptic Religion and the Death of Utopia* (London: Allen Lane; New York: Farrar, Straus and Giroux, 2007).

5. William Lamont, *Godly Rule: Politics and Religion, 1603–60* (London: Macmillan, 1969); P. Toon, ed., *Puritans, the Millennium and the Future of Israel: Puritan Eschatology 1600 to 1660* (Cambridge: James Clarke & Co., 1970); J. A. De Jong, *As Waters Cover the Sea: Millennial Expectations in the Rise of Anglo-American Missions, 1640–1810* (Kampen: Kok, 1970); C. Hill, *Antichrist in Seventeenth-Century England* (London: Oxford University Press, 1971); C. Hill, *The World Turned Upside Down* (London: Temple Smith, 1972); B. S. Capp, *The Fifth Monarchy Men* (London: Faber, 1972); Tai Liu, *Discord in Zion* (The Hague: Nijhoff, 1973); B. W. Ball, *A Great Expectation: Eschatological Thought in English Protestantism to 1660* (Leiden: Brill, 1975); Charles Webster, *The Great Instauration: Science, Medicine and Reform, 1626–1660* (London: Duckworth, 1975); Margaret C. Jacob, *The Newtonians and the English Revolution, 1689–1720* (Ithaca, N.Y.: Cornell University Press, 1976); R. Bauckham, *Tudor Apocalypse: Sixteenth Century Apocalypticism, Millenarianism and the English Reformation* (Appleford: Sutton Courtenay Press, 1978); Paul Christianson, *Reformers and Babylon* (Toronto: University of Toronto Press, 1978); K. R. Firth, *The Apocalyptic Tradition in Reformation Britain* (Oxford: Oxford University Press, 1979); William M. Lamont, *Richard Baxter and the Millennium* (Totowa, N.J.: Rowman and Littlefield, 1979); C. A. Patrides and Joseph Wittreich, eds., *The Apocalypse in English Renaissance Thought and Literature* (Manchester: Manchester University Press, 1984).

6. Obvious points of reference are the collection of Russell's key papers on *Unrevolutionary England, 1603–1642* (London: Hambledon Press, 1990) and his overview of *The Causes of the English Civil War* (Oxford: Clarendon Press, 1990). Subsequent revisionist and counterrevisionist literature is now enormous.

7. As will be apparent in the following discussion, the link between millenarianism and what I am calling "philo-Semitism" can be traced back at least to the seventeenth century and has been discussed in these terms for over half a century. This phenomenon must therefore not be confused with the very recent application of the terms "philo-Semitism" or "Judeophilia" to an enhancement

of gentile interest in, respect for, and appreciation of the Jewish people and their role in western history, which some journalists have noted during the past decade.

8. Hans Joachim Schoeps, *Philo-Semitismus im Barock* (Tübingen: J. C. B. Mohr, 1952); on the later period see also his *Barocke Juden, Christen und Judenchristen* (Bern and Munich: Franke, 1965); summarized in Karl Heinrich Rengstork and Siegfried von Kortfleisch, eds., *Kirche und Synagoge: Handbuch zur Geschichte von Christen und Juden*, 2 vols. (Stuttgart: Klett, 1968), esp. vol. 2, 23–86.

9. The pioneering Dutch work was Johannes van den Berg, *Joden en christenen in Nederland gedurende de zeventiende eeuw* (Kampen: Kok, 1969), summarized in his "Eschatological Expectations Concerning the Conversion of the Jews in the Netherlands during the Seventeenth Century," in *Puritans*, ed. Toon, 137–53. A programmatic introduction is Richard H. Popkin, "Jewish Messianism and Christian Millenarianism," in *Culture and Politics from Puritanism to the Enlightenment*, ed. Perez Zagorin, 67–90 (Berkeley: University of California Press, 1980). Other key English works are Mel Scult, *Millennial Expectations and Jewish Liberties: A Study of the Efforts to Convert the Jews in Britain, up to the Mid Nineteenth Century* (Leiden: Brill, 1978), and especially David S. Katz, *Philo-Semitism and the Readmission of the Jews to England 1603–1655* (Oxford: Clarendon Press, 1982). The most important publications include Menasseh ben Israel, *The Hope of Israel*, ed. Henry Méchoulan and Gérard Nahon (Oxford: Oxford University Press, 1987); Johannes van den Berg and E. G. E. van der Wall, eds., *Jewish-Christian Relations in the Seventeenth Century* (Dordrecht: Kluwer Academic, 1988); R. H. Popkin, ed., *Millenarianism and Messianism in English Thought and Literature, 1650–1800* (Leiden: Brill, 1988); Yosef Kaplan, Henry Méchoulan, and R. H. Popkin, eds., *Menasseh ben Israel and His World* (Leiden: Brill, 1989); David S. Katz and Jonathan I. Israel, eds., *Sceptics, Millenarians and Jews* (Leiden: Brill, 1990); R. H. Popkin and G. M. Weiner, eds., *Jewish Christians and Christian Jews: From the Renaissance to the Enlightenment* (Dordrecht: Kluwer Academic, 1994); M. Goldish, *Judaism in the Theology of Sir Isaac Newton* (Dordrecht: Kluwer Academic, 1998); A. P. Coudert, S. Hutton, R. H. Popkin, and G. M. Weiner, eds., *Judaeo-Christian Intellectual Culture in the Seventeenth Century* (Dordrecht: Kluwer Academic, 1999); Martin Mulsow and R. H. Popkin, eds., *Secret Conversions to Judaism in Early Modern Europe* (Leiden: Brill, 2004). Most of these latter works appeared in the series "International Archives of the History of Ideas" (Dordrecht) or "Brill's Studies in Intellectual History" (Leiden).

10. See for instance Todd. M. Endelmann's review of Katz, *Philosemitism*, in *American Jewish History* 72 (1982/83): 410–12. For more positive contributions

to a definition, see also the suggestive but undeveloped typology in Schoeps, *Philo-Semitismus*, 1; the discussion in Martin Friedrich, *Zwischen Abwehr und Bekehrung; Die Stellung der deutschen evangelischen Theologie zum Judentum im 17. Jahrhundert* (Tübingen: Mohr, 1986), 10–13; and Wolfram Kinzig, "Philosemitismus, Teil I: Zur Geschichte des Begriffs," *Zeitschrift für Kirchengeschichte* 105, no. 3 (1994): 202–28, which deals mostly with the later period.

11. In the very book of *De civitate Dei* (xx.29) in which he offers his epoch-making critique of millenarianism, Augustine looked forward to the return of Elias to convert the Jews in the last days. Throughout the middle ages this theme remained among "the most popular and widespread" apocalyptic expectations: R. K. Emmerson, *Antichrist in the Middle Ages* (Manchester: Manchester University Press, 1981), 41, 99–101, 144, 170, 217, 220. The German Reformation left this largely unchanged: cf. the thirty-eight leading Lutheran theologians excerpted in Philipp Jakob Spener, *Pia Desideria* (Frankfurt am Main, 1680), 356–85; facs. repr. in Spener, *Schriften*, ed. Erich Beyreuther (New York: Olms, 1979–), vol. 1, 502–31; and the thorough discussion in Friedrich, *Zwischen Abwehr und Bekehrung*, here citing 28. The same expectation was shared by "virtually all Dutch theologians of the seventeenth century"; in England it "was doubtless very widely accepted" by the end of the sixteenth century; while in Scotland it flourished amongst established court figures about the same time: see respectively J. van den Berg, "Eschatological Expectations," 139–40; Bauckham, *Tudor Apocalypse*, 225–27; and Arthur H. Williamson, "The Jewish Dimension of the Scottish Apocalypse: Climate, Covenant and World Renewal," in *Menasseh ben Israel and His World*, ed. Kaplan, Méchoulan, and Popkin, 7–30. For similar evidence from the Catholic world see the material collected in Tomaso Malvenda, *De Antichristo Tomus Primus [/Secundus]* (1604; rev. edn. Lyon, 1647), lib. XI. "De conversione Iudaeorum ad fidem Christi sub finem saeculi," vol. 2, 171–204.

12. Classic treatment of this themes include Wilhelm Bousset, *Der Antichrist in der Überlieferung des Judentums, des Neuen Testaments under der alten Kirche* (Göttingen, 1895); H. Preuß, *Die Vorstellungen vom Antichrist im späteren Mittelalter, bei Luther und in der konfessionellen Polemik* (Leipzig, 1906), 10–44; and Joshua Trachtenberg, *The Devil and the Jews: The Medieval Conception of the Jew and Its Relation to Modern Antisemitism* (New Haven, Conn.: Yale University Press, 1943; Cleveland, Oh.: Meridian Books, 1961; 2nd ed., Philadelphia: Jewish Publication Society of America, 1983), chap. 2. For more recent discussions, see Horst Dieter Rauh, *Das Bild des Antichrist im Mittelalter* (Münster: Aschendorff, 1973); Emmerson, *Antichrist;* Bernard McGinn, *Antichrist: Two Thousand Years of the Human Fascination with Evil* (San Francisco, Calif.: HarperSanFrancisco, 1994), chaps. 1–7; Otto Böcher and Gustav Adolf

Benrath, "Antichrist .II. Neues Testament," in *Theologische Realenzyklopädie*, vol. 3 (Berlin: de Gruyter, 1978), 21–28.

13. Andrew Colin Gow, *The Red Jews: Antisemitism in an Apocalyptic Age, 1200–1600* (Leiden: Brill, 1994).

14. Ibid., 3.

15. See also Claus-E. Bärsch, "Der Jude als Antichrist in der NS-Ideologie: Die kollektive Identität der Deutschen und der Antisemitismus unter religionspolitischer Perspektive," *Zeitschrift für Religions- und Geistgeschichte* 47, no. 2 (1995): 160–88.

16. See for instance Preuss, *Vorstellungen vom Antichrist*, 83–210, 220–47; Gottfried Seebaß, "Antichrist .IV. Reformations- und Neuzeit," in *Theologische Realenzyklopädie*, vol. 3, 28–43; Hill, *Antichrist*, chap. 1; David Brady, *The Contribution of British Writers between 1560 and 1830 to the Interpretation of Revelation 13.16–18 (The Number of the Beast)* (Tübingen: Mohr, 1983); Emmerson, *Antichrist*, 206–21; McGinn, *Antichrist*, chap. 8.

17. Cf. for instance Ph. Schmidt, *Die Illustrationen der Lutherbibel, 1522–1700* (Basle: F. Reinhardt, 1962), 110–11, 125, 214; and John Calvin, *Institutio Christianae religionis* (1559), IV.xviii.18.

18. R. W. Scribner, *For the Sake of Simple Folk: Popular Propaganda for the German Reformation* (Cambridge: Cambridge University Press, 1981), 149–89.

19. *Die Bekenntnisschriften der evangelisch-lutherischen Kirche*, 4th. ed. (Göttingen: Vandenhoeck & Ruprecht, 1959), 234, 239–40, 246, 300, 364, 424, 430; cf. 484–9; *Die Bekenntnisschriften der reformierten Kirche*, ed. E. F. Karl Müller (Leipzig: Deichert, 1903), 263, 264, 536, 599; cf. 32, 290, 666; [Jean] Aymon, *Tous les synodes nationaux des églises reformées de France*, 2 vols. (The Hague: Charles Delo, 1710), vol. 1, 258–59.

20. See for instance Heiko A. Oberman, *The Roots of Anti-Semitism in the Age of Renaissance and Reformation* (Philadelphia: Fortress Press, 1983), 116–22, and *Luther: Man between God and the Devil*, trans. Eileen Walliser-Schwarzbart (New Haven, Conn.: Yale University Press, 1982), 292–7.

21. Gow, *The Red Jews*, chap. 6.

22. Hill, *Antichrist*, 180; Katz, *Philo-Semitism*, 163, 174, 221.

23. Brief surveys include Wilhelm Bousset, *Die Offenbahrung Johannis* (1859; 6th rev. edn. Göttingen, Vandenhoeck & Ruprecht, 1906; facs. repr. Göttingen: Vandenhoeck & Ruprecht, 1966), 91–95; Preuß, *Vorstellungen vom Antichrist*, 210–17, 247–61; Leroy Erwin Froom, *The Prophetic Faith of Our Fathers: The Historical Development of Prophetic Interpretation*, 4 vols. (Washington, D.C.: Review and Herald, 1946–54), vol. 2, 484–509; Hill, *Antichrist*, 178–81; Claude-Gilbert Dubois, *La Conception de l'histoire en France au XVIe siècle*

(1560–1610) (Paris: Nizet, 1977), 501–74, esp. 556–62; Philipp Schäfer, *Eschatologie: Trient und Gegenreformation* (Freiburg: Herder, 1984), 62–63; Jean-Robert Armogathe, "Dall'escatologia alla storia: l'esegesi cattolica dell'Apocalisse nel Seicento," in *Storia e figure dell'Apocalisse fra '500 e '600*, ed. Roberti Rusconi, 302–13 (Rome: Viella, 1996); Armogathe, "Interpretations of the Revelation of St. John, 1500–1800," in the *Encyclopedia of Apocalyptic*, vol. 2, ed. Bernard McGinn (New York: Continuum, 1998), 186–97; McGinn, *Antichrist*, 226–33; Karl A. Kottman, ed., *Catholic Millenarianism: From Savonarola to the Abbé Grégoire* (Dordrecht: Kluwer Academic, 2001).

24. Cf. for instance Marjorie Reeves, *The Influence of Prophecy in the Later Middle Ages: A Study in Joachimism* (Oxford: Clarendon Press, 1969; repr. Notre Dame, Ind.: University of Notre Dame Press, 1993), 276, 357, 363–64, 370, 447, 469–70; Marjorie Reeves, ed., *Prophetic Rome in the High Renaissance Period* (Oxford: Clarendon Press, 1992), 194, 274, 299; E. G. Gleason, "Sixteenth-Century Italian Interpretations of Luther," *Archiv für Reformationsgeschichte* 60, no. 2 (1969): 160–73; Barbara Sher Tinsley, *History and Polemics in the French Reformation: Florimond de Raemond; Defender of the Church* (London: Associated University Presses, 1992), 90; François Laplanche, *L'Écriture, le sacré et l'histoire: Erudits et politiques protestants devant la Bible en France au XVI-Ième siècle* (Amsterdam-Maarssen: Holland University Press, 1986), 176–77; John M. Headley, *Tommaso Campanella and the Transformation of the World* (Princeton, N.J.: Princeton University Press, 1997), 296.

25. Preuß, *Vorstellungen vom Antichrist*, 215, 259–61, and J. J. I. von Döllinger, *Christentum und Kirche in der Zeit der Grundlegung* (Regensburg: Manz, 1868), 438n.1, state unreservedly that no Catholic exegete "Luther und sein Werk als den von Paulus gemeinten Antichrist bezeichnet hätte."

26. Peter S. Donaldson, "Machiavelli, Antichrist and the Reformation: Prophetic Typology in Reginald Pole's *De Unitate* and *Apologia ad Carolum Quintum*," in *Leaders of the Reformation*, ed. Richard L. DeMolen, 211–46 (London: Associated Universities Presses, 1984), esp. 219–22.

27. Tinsley, *History and Polemics*, 91, citing F. de Raemond, *L'Antechrist et l'anti-papesse*, 2nd. ed. (Paris, 1599), 133–34.

28. Malvenda, *De Antichristo*, lib. I, cap. xxvi, 60–63, here 62–63.

29. Francisco Suarez, *Defensio fidei Catholicae adversus Anglicanae sectae errores* (1613), lib. 5, "De Antichristo"; repr. in *Opera omnia*, ed. Charles Bertin, 28 vols. (Paris, 1856–78), 616.a–b.; Cornelius à Lapide, *Commentarii in Apocalypsin S. Johannis* (1627), on Apocalypse (Revelation) 17:3; repr. in *Commentarii in sacram scripturam*, 19 vols. (Milan, 1857–70), xix, 1098; Brady, *Contribution*, 22–3.

30. Roberto Bellarmino, *Disputationes de controversiis Christianae fidei adversus hujus temporis haereticos*, 3 vols. (Ingolstadt, 1586–93), vol. 2, 329–467, i.e., tomus I, contr. III, lib. iii, "Disputatio de Antichristo."

31. Bellarmino, "Disputatio de Antichristo," chap. 12. See also the synopses in Preuß, *Vorstellungen vom Antichrist*, 248–52; Laplanche, *L'Écriture*, 165–66.

32. Francisco Suarez, *Commentariorum ac disputationum in tertiam partem Divi Thomae, tomi quinque* (1594–96), quaest. 59, art. 6, disp. 54, "De Antichristo"; in *Opera omnia*, ed. Bertin, vol. 19, 1025–44, esp. 1025.a, 1031.b–1032.a, 1034–41; see also disp. 56, 1062.b. Cf. Preuß, *Vorstellungen vom Antichrist*, 252–53; McGinn, *Antichrist*, 227.

33. Malvenda, *De Antichristo*, esp. vol. 1, 138–62, 592–603; vol. 2, 66–70.

34. Francesco de Ribeira, *In sacram beati Ioannis Apocalypsin commentarij* (1591; Antwerp, 1593), on Apocalypse (Revelation) 7:4, 13:16, 20:7, on 220–25, 351, 526. Blasius Viegas, *In Apocalpsim Joannis Apostoli comentarii exegetici* (1599, Cologne, 1603), on Apocalypse (Revelation) 13, 688–711. Cornelius à Lapide, *Commentarii in sacram scripturam*, on John 5:43, 2 Thessalonians 2:4–11, and Apocalypse (Revelation) 11:8, in vol. 16, 418; vol. 18, 171–84; vol. 19, 1007.

35. Luis de Alcázar, *Vestigatio arcani sensus in Apocalypsin* (Antwerp, 1614), quoting the most comprehensive study of this work to date, Francisco Contreras, C.M.F., "*Vestigatio arcani sensus in Apocalypsi* (1614): Presentatión, estudio y comentarios," *Archivo Teológico Granadino* 52 (1989): 51–168, esp. 84, 107, 167. See also Bousset, *Offenbahrung*, 93–94; Laplanche, *L'Écriture*, 174–76.

36. Florimond de Raemond's *L'Antechrist* (Lyon, 1597), as described by Dubois, *La Conception de l'histoire*, 562 (cited here); and Tinsley, *History and Polemics*, 85–87.

37. *The Holie Bible faithfully translated into English* [from the Latin by the English College of Douai], 2 vols. (Douai: Laurence Kellam, 1609–10; facs. repr., Ilkley: Scolar, 1975), preface.

38. Dionysius von Lützemberg, *Leben Antichristi . . . Es seynd auch alhie jene Zeichen, so nach der Rabbiner Meynung vor der Ankunfft deß Judischen Messiä, sambt allem dem, so die blinde Juden von ihrem zukünfftigen Messia dem Antichrist hoffen, trewlich verzeichnet* (Frankfurt am Main, 1682), here chap. 27; cf. Preuß, *Vorstellungen vom Antichrist*, 254–56; McGinn, *Antichrist*, 231–32.

39. R. Shelford, *Five Pious and Learned Discourses* (Cambridge, 1635), 314. Cf. Hill, *Antichrist*, 38, 180; Anthony Milton, *Catholic and Reformed: The Roman and Protestant Churches in English Protestant Thought, 1600–1640* (Cambridge: Cambridge University Press, 1995), chap. 2.

40. Johannes van den Berg, "Grotius' Views on Antichrist and Apocalyptic Thought in England," in *Hugo Grotius, Theologian*, ed. H. J. M. Nellen and

E. Rabbie, 169–83 (Leiden: Brill, 1994); John William Packer, *The Transformation of Anglicanism, 1643–1660, with Special Reference to Henry Hammond* (Manchester: Manchester University Press, 1969); Maria Rosa Antognazza and Howard Hotson, *Alsted and Leibniz on God, the Magistrate and the Millennium* (Wiesbaden: Harrassowitz, 1999), esp. 130–48.

41. Grotius, *Annotationes in Novum Testamentum toums secundus* (Paris, 1646), 299. Batalerius, *Dissertatio de Israelitarum conversione* ('s-Gravenhage, 1669), esp. 102–39. See van den Berg, "Eschatological Expectations," 140–41.

42. [H. von der Hardt,] *Brevis et perspicua enarratio locorum scripturae Ezech. cap. XXXIIX. et cap. XXXIX. Apocal. cap. XX. ad fontium sacrorum tenorum* (n.p., n.d.); 2nd rev. ed., *Conjectura de millenario* (Helmstedt, 1691).

43. [H. von der Hardt] *L'Antichrist* ([Helmstedt, 1707?]), [3] (copy in Wolfenbüttel HAB, sign. Jm 309). For further detail, see Antognazza and Hotson, *Alsted and Leibniz*, 165–66.

44. Alsted, *Diatribe de mille annis apocalypticis, non illis Chiliastarum et Phantastarum, sed BB. Danielis et Johannis* (Frankfurt am Main, 1627), 33–53, 80–219. On Alsted generally, see Howard Hotson, *Johann Heinrich Alsted 1588–1638: Between Renaissance, Reformation and Universal Reform* (Oxford: Clarendon Press, 2000).

45. Alsted, *Theologia polemica*, 2nd ed. (Hanau, 1627), 111–19.

46. Ibid., 111: "Iesus Nazarenus implevit omnia V. T. vaticinia, quae concernunt aeternam nostram salutem *Dan. 9. v. 24*. Quantum vero attinet ad felicitatem ecclesiae his in terris, implebit vaticina V. et N. T. suo tempore."

47. Ibid., 119: "Atque haec habuimus quae breviter commentaremur de conversione Iudaeorum: ubi velim duas istas regulas perpetuo obversari oculis. 1. *Adventus Messiae primus distinguendus est à secundo.* Hoc non faciunt Iudaei, quando mentem et oculos à primo Christi adventu avertunt atque ad secundum duntaxat respiciunt, refugientes quae fuerunt primi afflictiones, et amplectentes solum bona, quae proponentur in seculo."

48. This necessity is emphasized by the full title of the *Diatribe* (see note 44 above) and within it on 246–51.

49. Alsted, *Theologia polemica*, 119: "2. *Tempus felicitatis ecclesiae in his terris futurae, etsi complectitur bona temporalia longe maxima, non tamen in iis oportet constituere regni Christi proram et puppim.* Ne scilicet videamur facere cum Iudaeis, qui nil nisi carnalia expectant à Messia."

50. Christoph Besold, *Dissertationum philologicarum PENTAS* (Tübingen, 1622), diss. IV (dated 1620), "De Hebraeorum ad Christum salvatorem nostrum conversione conjectanea." On Besold, see most recently Martin Brecht, "Christoph Besold: Versuche und Ansätze einer Deutung," *Pietismus und*

Neuzeit 26 (2000): 11–28; on the work, Friedrich, *Zwischen Abwehr und Bekehrung*, 55–56.

51. For a full comparison, see Howard Hotson, *Paradise Postponed: Johann Heinrich Alsted and the Birth of Calvinist Millenarianism* (Dordrecht: Kluwer Academic, 2000), 144–53, with an edition of Besold's dissertation on 187–202.

52. On Brocardo, see Delio Cantimori, "Visione e speranze di un ugonotto italiano," *Rivista storica italiana* (1950): 199–217; Jürgen Moltmann, "Jacob Brocard as Vorläufer der Reich-Gottes-Theologie und der symbolisch-prophetischen Schriftauslegung des Johann Coccejus," *Zeitschrift für Kirchengeschichte* 71 (4. Folge 9) (1960): 110–29, here esp. 113–14, 123–24; Reeves, *Influence of Prophecy*, 494–99.

53. Brocardo, *Libri duo: alter ad Christianos de prophetia, quae nunc compleatur in his, quae sunt secundi adventus Domini: alter ad Hebraeos de primo, et secundo eiusdem adventu* (Leiden, 1581).

54. Aside from a few grammatical changes, Alsted's text is essentially a transcription of the following excerpt from Besold, "Conjectanea," 2 (Hotson, *Paradise Postponed*, 188): "Confert pariter hûc tractatus Jacobi Brocardi, de primo et secundo Messiae adventu, ad Hebraeos: ubi probare conatur, Judaeos mentem et oculos à primo Christi adventu avertisse, atque ad secundum tantùm respexisse; refugientes quae fuerunt primi adflictiones, et amplectentes solùm bonum, quod proponebatur in secundo. Quâ eâdem de re, agit etiam idem, in praefat. interpretat. Bibliorum, *quae praefixa est mysticae et propheticae Geneseos enodationi, fol. 4.* ac pariter conversiones Judaeorum, *in cap. 45. et seq.* mentio fit ibidem."

55. Alsted, *The Beloved City, or the Saints Reign on Earth a Thousand Years* (London, 1643), preface by Burton (missing from some copies), vi–vii.

56. Joseph Mede, *Clavis apocalyptica* (1632), 293–4: "His ità habentibus, viris doctis, et de hujusmodi in Theologia mysteriis judicare valentibus, expendendum relinquo; annon haec optima et facillima cum Judaeis agendi ratio esset; non ut clarissimae illae de rebus in secundo et glorioso Christi adventu prophetiae ad primum torqueantur; verum ut illis persuadeatur, nullum alium Messiam ipsis expectandum esse . . . quàm Jesum illum Nazarenum, quem Majores ipsorum crucifixerunt. [I]d quod Apocalypsis passim, tàmque studiosè inculcat. . . . Dum enim nos clarissimas illas, de rebus in secundo Christi adventu, prophetias ad primum torquemus, Judaei nos derisui habent, et in infidelitate sua magis obfirmantur. / Hanc Judaeos convertendi rationem, nisi nimiùm fallor, secutus est Apostolus Petrus, Act. 3. V. 19. *Resipiscite*, inquit [etc.]." On Mede there is at last an excellent monograph by Jeffrey K. Jue, *Heaven upon Earth: Joseph Mede (1586–1638) and the Legacy of Millenarianism* (Dordrecht: Springer, 2006).

57. Alsted's *Prodromus religionis triumphantis* (Alba Julia [Gyulaferhérvár / Weissenburg], 1635 [actually 1641]), 1038-40, summarizes, abridges, and reproduces Mede's *Clavis* (1632), 22-30, 276, 277-80, 286-88, 289, 292-94. There is a rare copy in the university library in Göttingen (sign. 4° Theol.polem. 454/5).

58. Although originally written in English, Jessey's work survives in a single known copy of the Dutch translation in the Herzog August Bibliothek, Wolfenbüttel (sign. 916.2Th.[3]): *De heerlickheydt en heyl van Jehuda en Israel, zijnde een tractaet streckende tot vereeniginge der Jooden en Christenen . . . mits aenwijsende hoe sy beyde in veele fundamentele grond-stucken der religie, insoderheydt noopende den MESSIAM eein zijn* . . . (Amsterdam, 1653). On this text, see E. G. E. van der Wall, "A Philo-Semitic Millenarian on the Reconciliation of Jews and Christians: Henry Jessey and his 'The Glory and Salvation of Jehudah and Israel' (1650)," in *Sceptics, Millenarians and Jews,* ed. Katz and Israel, 161-84.

59. E. G. E. van der Wall, "A Philo-Semitic Millenarian," 180-73.

60. Schoeps, *Philo-Semitismus,* 21 (his emphasis).

61. János Bruckner, *Abraham von Frankenberg: A Bibliographical Catalogue with a Short List of His Library* (Wiesbaden: Harrassowitz, 1988), 65.

62. Cf. Popkin, "Jewish Messianism and Christian Millenarianism," 75.

63. Serrarius, *Assertion du règne de mille ans* (Amsterdam, 1657), 16; as quoted in Méchoulan and Nahon's introduction to Menasseh ben Israel, *The Hope of Israel,* 50.

64. Ernestine van der Wall, "Mystical Millenarianism in the Early Modern Dutch Republic," in *Continental Millenarianism: Protestants, Catholics, Heretics,* ed. Richard H. Popkin and John Christian Laursen, 37-47 (Dordrecht and Boston: Kluwer Academic, 2001), 41 (refering also to the *Assertion*).

65. Jean de Labadie, *Le Héraut du Grand Roy Jesus* (Amsterdam, 1667), 55, 76, 346-47; as quoted in van der Berg, "Eschatological Expectations," 149-50.

66. That is, part 2, chapters 16-25, which treat of the millennium.

67. Pierre Jurieu, *L'Accomplissement des Propheties, en la delivrance prochaine de l'Eglise,* 2nd ed. (Rotterdam, 1686), fol. A1^v; translated as *The Accomplishment of the Scripture Prophecies* (London, 1687), fols. *2^{r-v}.

68. Spener, *Theologische Bedenken,* 4 parts (Halle, 1700-1702), part 4, 256 (October 12, 1678); repr. in *Schriften,* Bd. XIV.1, IV. Theil (1999), 256. The source is A. B. Peganius [i.e. Christian Knorr von Rosenroth], *Eigentlich erklarung uber die gesichte der offenbarung Ioannis* (Amsterdam[?], 1670).

69. Spener, *Letzte Theologische Bedencken,* 3 parts (Halle, 1711), part 1, 293 (September 22, 1702); repr. in *Schriften,* Bd. XV, Teilband 1 (1987), 293.

70. Spener, *Letzte Theologische Bedencken* (1711), part 3, 720; *Schriften,* XV/2, 720.

71. Moise Amyraut, *Du regne de mille ans* (Saumur, 1654), chap. 14, 293–304.

72. Cf. for instance Comenius, *Via lucis* (Amsterdam, 1668), VI.8, 14, in *Dílo Jana Amose Komenského* (Prague: Akademia, 1974) vol. 14, 305, 307; Comenius, *De rerum humanarum emendatione consultatio catholica,* 2 vols. (Prague: Akademia, 1966), part 6, chap. 2, esp. vol. 2, 381–98; Charles Webster, ed., *Samuel Hartlib and the Advancement of Learning* (Cambridge: Cambridge University Press, 1970), 89; van der Wall, "A Philo-Semitic Millenarian," 170.

73. Richard H. Popkin, *Isaac La Peyrère (1596–1676): His Life, Work and Influence* (Leiden: Brill, 1987), 68.

74. Menasseh ben Israel's last work, the *Vindiciae Judaeorum, or a Letter in Answer to Certain Questions* (London, 1656), 18; quoted in Richard Popkin, "Jewish-Christian Relations in the Sixteenth and Seventeenth Centuries: The Conception of the Messiah," *Jewish History* 6, nos. 1–2 (1992):163–77, at 166; and idem, *La Peyrère,* 102. Emphasis mine.

75. Hochmann von Hochenau, "Schreiben an die Juden" (1699), reprinted in N. L. von Zinzendorf, *Ergänzungsbände zu den Hauptschriften,* ed. Erich Beyreuther and Gerhard Meyer, vol. 11 *Freywillige Nachlese (Kleine Schriften), I.-VI. Sammlung* (Hildesheim: Georg Olms, 1972), III. Sammlung, Nr. 4, 62–69.

76. Heinz Renkwitz, *Hochmann von Hochenau (1670–1721): Quellenstudien zur Geschichte des Pietismus* (Breslau, 1935; Witten, 1969), 52; Hans Schneider, "Ein 'Schreiben an die Juden' (Freiwillige Nachlese III.4): Hochmann, Zinzendorf und Israel," *Unitas Fratrum* 17, no. 1 (1985): 68–77.

77. Pamphilius (= Priestley), "Observations on the Prophecies relating to the Messiah, and the future Glory of the House of David," in [Priestley, ed.], *The Theological Repository* 5 (Birmingham, 1786): 210–42, 301–16; repr. in *The Theological and Miscellaneous Works of Joseph Priestley,* ed. J. T. Rutt (1817–32; repr. New York: Kraus Reprint, 1972), vol. 12, 411–442.

78. Hermas (= Priestley), "Of the Perpetuity of the Jewish Ritual," *The Theological Repository* 5 (1786): 403–44; 6 (1788): 1–21, esp. 19–20; *Works,* vol. 12, 442–82. On this whole theme, see Johannes van den Berg, "Priestley, the Jews and the Millennium," in *Sceptics, Millenarians, and Jews,* ed. Katz and Israel, 257–74, esp. 263–64.

79. On this tradition, see most recently Mihaly Balazs, *Early Transylvanian Antitrinitarianism (1566–1571): From Servet to Palaeologus* (Baden-Baden: Koerner, 1996); Mihaly Balazs, ed., *Ungarländische Antitrinitarier* (Baden-

Baden: Koerner, 2004); Howard Hotson, "Arianism and Millenarianism: The Link between two Heresies from Servetus to Socinus," in *Continental Millenarianism*, ed. Popkin and Laursen, 9–35.

80. See the splendid book by Robert Dán, *Matthias Vehe-Glirius: Life and Work of a Radical Antitrinitarian with His Collected Writings* (Budapest: Akadémiai Kiadó; and Leiden: Brill, 1982).

81. S. Kohn, *Die Sabbatarier in Siebenbürgen: Ihre Geschichte, Literatur und Dogmatic* (Budapest and Leipzig, 1894); and more recently L. M. Pákozdy, *Der Siebenbürgische Sabbatismus* (Stuttgart: Kohlhammer, 1973).

82. Dán, *Vehe-Glirius*, 172. See also Daniel Liechty, *Sabbatarianism in the Sixteenth Century* (Berrien Springs, Mich.: Andrews University Press, 1993), part 2, which strangely overlooks Robert Dán, *Az erdélyi szombatosok és Péchi Simon* [*The Transylvanian Sabbatarians and Simon Péchi*] (Budapest: Akadémiai Kiadó, 1987), with English summary 317–20.

6

Reflections on Persistent Whiggism and Its Antidotes in the Study of Sixteenth- and Seventeenth-century Intellectual History

RICHARD A. MULLER

The last several decades have seen a series of significant shifts in the study of sixteenth- and seventeenth-century intellectual history. These shifts in emphasis and method are based, moreover, on the recognition of problematic elements in the older scholarship on the Reformation and post-Reformation eras and consist largely in an attempt to remedy those problems along several identifiable lines of research and reappraisal. My emphasis will be on the study of theology and philosophy during the era, recognizing the interrelationships of these disciplines and also assuming the necessity of looking beyond specific modern disciplinary fields in order to examine either theological or philosophical ideas in a sixteenth- or seventeenth-century context. I would like to begin by identifying some of the problems in the older scholarship, then, second, move on to a summary of what I see to be significant altered patterns and new approaches in research, and, third, offer a few specific patterns of scholarly results and reappraisals.

SEVERAL PROBLEMS IN THE OLDER SCHOLARSHIP— NINETEENTH- AND TWENTIETH-CENTURY STUDIES, WHETHER IN THEOLOGY OR PHILOSOPHY

A fundamental problem of the older scholarship, even of some of the most seemingly objective studies, is what I was taught to call the "Whig interpretation of history," after the (one would hope, still famous) book of that title by Sir Herbert Butterfield.[1] The Whig party of the eighteenth century is the ancestor of modern British liberalism—with reference to historical method and to an underlying, often unanalyzed, assumption in historiography, the term indicates not only a sense of progress in history but a consistent reading of the past with primary reference to the present. There has been, in other words, a fundamental tendency in theological and philosophical historiography to identify what is important in a past era on the basis of the seeming importance, influence, or relevance of a person, idea, or event to the present-day self-understanding of the writer or the society, *rather than asking the documents of the past era what persons, ideas, or events were then understood as important or influential*—or, indeed, rather than asking the documents themselves what concepts, language, and contexts are requisite to the understanding of the documents!

An evident result of such a methodology, as Butterfield rather nicely pointed out with reference to the Reformation, has been an "over-dramatization" of certain historical moments and various historical personages—Luther symbolizes a full-scale rebellion against the Middle Ages; Calvin personifies a "transformationist" world-ethic; the posting of the *Ninety-five Theses* was a moment when all of history was changed; Protestantism provides the well-springs of modernity; and so forth.[2] Butterfield wisely countered,

> The large process which turned the medieval world into the modern world, the process which transformed the religious society into the secular state of modern times, was wider and deeper and stronger than the Reformation itself. The Reformation may have been something more than merely a symptom or a result of such a process, and

we should be assuming too much if we said that it was only an incident in the transition. But the historian would be very dogmatic who insisted in regarding it as a cause.³

One very simple way of documenting the problem is to examine the names and biographies of important seventeenth-century thinkers in a twentieth-century dictionary or encyclopedia, then to work through a list of seventeenth-century persons in a nineteenth-century encyclopedia like the Herzog-Plitt *Realencyklopädie für Protestantischen Theologie und Kirche,* and finally to work through the mid-eighteenth-century *Algemeines Gehlehrten Lexicon* of Jocher: the list has changed. In particular, many of the individuals deemed highly significant by Jocher, from the vantage point of under a hundred years, are absent from the more recent encyclopedias.

A further nuancing of this problem from the perspective of intellectual history is found in Quentin Skinner's remarkable and remarkably daunting essay of some three and a half decades ago, "Meaning and Understanding in the History of Ideas."[4] The essay ought to be regarded as a benchmark effort in the revision of methods and approaches in intellectual history—required reading for all in the discipline. Perhaps the most significant point of the essay, given both the internal or inherent problems in much intellectual history and the rising critique of the social historians, was its balance of two problems—not only critiquing the intellectual historians who act as if a document itself provides "the sole necessary key to its own meaning" but also the assumption that "religious, political, and economic factors" are the determiners of the meaning of any given text.[5] On the first of these issues, Skinner identified several "mythologies" accepted by practitioners of the trade, notably the belief in "perennial ideas" of "universal" relevance and application coupled with the assumption that "each classic writer" will naturally "enunciate some doctrine on each of the topics regarded as constitutive of his subject."[6] Of course, the full list of topics exists in the present construal of the historian, not necessarily in the mind of the historical subject of inquiry. A superb example of the problem in my own field is the extensive Anglo-American literature on the question of Calvin's approach to "limited" or "universal atonement"—given that Calvin himself did not address the subject and would not have recognized the word "atonement" as a suitable descriptor of the problem, namely, the value and extent of Christ's satisfaction. On the second point, the issue of religious, political, or economic (and, we can add, social) context, Skinner points out that a delineation of such contexts still will leave open the question of "how what was said was meant and . . . what relations there may have been between various statements within the same general context." Skinner points out that even when a social context can "explain" a text in the history of ideas, it will not be utterly sufficient to understand the text and its ideas.[7] The search for social contexts, albeit often highly illuminating of texts, also poses the danger of relegating ideas to a class of epiphenomena, indeed, epiphenomena that have no meaning except that which a particular context identifies for them: theological statements become expressions not of theology or religion but of economic or social forces of which the individual who made the statement may have been utterly unaware. After praising Skinner, I must confess here my own early naïveté—it took me a good decade to recognize that, in my own field, many practitioners of intellectual history are just dogmaticians in disguise; perhaps half a decade more to realize that the phrase "Barthian historiography" is an oxymoron; and several more years beyond that to come to grips with the datum that systematic theologians, taken as a group, do not read historical documents and, when they go so far as to cite historical documents, often evidence a deep aversion to the meaning intended by the original authors. On to some specifics in my own field.

First, by way of illustration, I note two examples of the "Whig interpretation" problem, broadly construed, with reference to the question of the continuity and discontinuity of the Reformation and post-Reformation eras with preceding history (medieval and Renaissance) and with one another: the neoorthodox reading of the Reformation, and the history of seventeenth-century philosophy that places Descartes at its center. In the case of the former problem, there is a large body of literature on the thought of the Reformers, particularly that of Calvin, that speaks of him as a "christocentric" theologian of piety, as having a dynamic understanding of scripture as a witness to the living Word, as a "humanist" or "biblical humanist" engaged in a nearly archetypal warfare against Aristotelianism and scholasticism, even as being a theologian of "crisis" whose thought was focused on the "event" of Jesus of

Nazareth.[8] Such language is wildly anachronistic, and what it represents is an isolation and reinterpretation of elements in Calvin's thought in such a way that he can be viewed as the influential predecessor of twentieth-century neoorthodoxy.[9] One of the clues to the problem is the consistent importation of twentieth-century theological jargon to the task of analysis, notably terms that bear with them the theological or philosophical freight of other eras, indeed, of their modern users, and impose that freight on the past. The methodological solution, here, is quite straightforward, albeit sometimes quite painful to the modern writer: avoid the use of such terms entirely and draw one's technical terminology out of the documents under analysis, with very close attention to the meaning of the terms in their historical context. There is, moreover, another, perhaps more subtle side to this linguistic problem, namely, the modern, that is, post-Enlightenment, loss of the older meaning of standard terms, such as seemingly stable terms like "real," "substance," "scholastic," "practical," "speculative"—the list could be made quite long. We need not only to recover the vocabulary of the older theology and philosophy, we need to observe the understandings of the terms that belong to the era. Among other things, intellectual historians must use sixteenth- and seventeenth-century dictionaries![10]

Reading thinkers like Calvin and Descartes by placing them into their context and examining their place and importance in their own contexts yields a rather different result—a view of their thought, not at all surprisingly, very little like twentieth-century thought. Calvin emerges not as the eminent founder of a great "ism" (that is, "Calvinism") but as one among several movers of a particular confessional line of thought, his version being nuanced, often, by his own sociopolitical context in Geneva; by the very particular angle of his connections with other movers of Protestantism, with whom he was engaged in an extensive and detailed correspondence; and by the way in which he received and appropriated the earlier theological and, most importantly, exegetical tradition. His thought, developed in dialogue and debate, is both less original than the literature has typically admitted and less amenable to use and adaptation in the twentieth or twenty-first century: rather than standing above a host of others, Calvin now fits in, shoulder to shoulder, with the likes of Bullinger, Vermigli, Hyperius, Viret, Laski, Musculus,

Melanchthon, Hardenburg, and various others. His thought, like theirs, has very specific locations and, beyond that, very specific uses, virtues, and demerits that were understood by his contemporaries. It is worth pointing out that the massive correspondence of these Reformers, presently gathered in no one place, offers as many clues (perhaps more) to the meaning of their major theological treatises as the treatises themselves. It is also worth pointing out that study of these other, less-famous thinkers offers the benefit of bringing to view sixteenth-century texts that have not been farded over with dogmatic misinterpretations and that, therefore, can offer a pathway into a more contextualized understanding of Calvin as well.

The issue of Descartes is analogous: he is typically examined in detail because he is viewed as one of the founders of modern philosophy (exemplifying the problems noted by Skinner) and has only seldom been discussed in terms of his education, the context of his debates, or the many late-Renaissance scholastic elements of his thought. In fact, many histories of philosophy examine Descartes as if his thought had no scholastic elements and, indeed, as if he were the one important philosophical thinker in the first half of the seventeenth century (without reference to the work of such revisionists as Verbeek and Ariew).[11] If, however, the question of importance were asked from a seventeenth-century perspective, it is clear that the majority understanding of Descartes would register the several ways in which his philosophical usage departed from what was understood to be normative and useful and rendered his thought problematic and, indeed, unfruitful—and it is entirely likely that Suárez, Timpler, Alsted, Heereboord, Burgersdijk, and even Keckermann would have been counted as more significant thinkers by contemporaries.[12] The fact that of these five only the first is relatively well known today makes the point: there is no easy line to be drawn from the work of these philosophers to the philosophies of the twentieth century. The history has been selective and, in Butterfield's language, quite Whiggish.

Second, such an approach to historiography often merges with what might be called the "great thinker" problem: many of the standard studies of the sixteenth and seventeenth centuries, by following out the selective, progressivist approach based on modern assumptions of relevance, have looked only to a series of great thinkers—Luther, Calvin, Rabelais, Montaigne, Descartes, Galileo, Bacon, and so forth. The problem with such an approach is that it ignores the "minor" or "lesser" thinkers of an era and examines only the thought of a major writer to the exclusion of the persons and events that surrounded him. This problem goes beyond the basic issue just noted as an element of the "Whig Interpretation," given that it is problematic even when the "great thinkers" selected for examination were significant in their own time. The problem here is the removal of one of the contexts of interpretation of the thought of a particular individual. To make the point simply, the writings of a Luther, Calvin, Montaigne, or Descartes do not provide the context for the interpretation of the writings of Luther, Calvin, Montaigne, or Descartes. And although this might appear to be a simple point, a rapid glance at studies of the theology or philosophy of these writers will demonstrate that the problem has been quite prevalent, even in studies received as major scholarly efforts. The problem with much of the older scholarship is that it did not worry about context at all, ignoring not only social, cultural, and political context, but *intellectual context* as well. The burden of a twenty-first century intellectual history of the sixteenth and seventeenth centuries is not only to overcome the critique, in particular, of social historians, but to identify the intellectual context of the thought being examined.

A third issue—oddly associated with the great thinker problem—is the apparent assumption of much older intellectual history that, as thoughts emanate from the decontextualized minds of great thinkers, they take on a life of their own and inhabit a realm that subsists independently like a Platonic realm of ideas, dipping down at significant moments to "influence" actors in the human drama. The human actors sometimes grasp the ideas correctly, sometimes misinterpret the ideas, and sometimes even, for example, create problems of ideological misrepresentation like the problems of predestination or assurance in later Calvinism. Don't disregard the comment as a caricature before you work through, as I have, notions of central dogmas, predestinarian systems juxtaposed with christocentrism, federalism in tension with predestinarianism, humanism taking on scholasticism—great reified "isms" in an ultimate conflict that far exceeds the importance of mere human beings in varied historical contexts! On such issues, intellectual history has (or at least could have) benefitted from the critique of social historians who (on those good days when they do not deny the existence of thought) have demanded attention to the human, social, cultural, political, and institutional contexts of all human expression.

Fourth, the older historiography often fell victim to an excessively strict periodization, most notably, in theology, a periodization created from the perspective of religious or "denominational" interests. Thus, there is the fairly common sense in the older scholarship that, circa 1517, Europe experienced the end of "scholasticism" and the beginning of the Reformation. Of course, the literature did not always make the point so blatantly and in so obviously problematic a form. What was commonly the case, however, was that older lines of scholarship discussed the Reformation as if it had no positive medieval antecedents other than the usually cited rebels—Wyclif, Hus, the Waldenses, and so forth. This was true of Roman Catholic scholarship that understood the Reformation as a massive break with church and tradition, and of Protestant scholarship that understood the Reformation as a rejection of medieval abuses, which was, in the view of this scholarship, nearly everything medieval.[13] If all this sounds terribly gauche, I simply remind you that it was, as recently as twenty or twenty-five years ago, the majority approach of intellectual historians of the Reformation, and it still has its practitioners. To make the point in a more specific way: there are still books written (although, I hope, they are increasingly in the minority) that discuss the thought of Reformers like Calvin and Bullinger without substantive consideration of medieval background.[14] On the issue of scholasticism and its relation to the Reformation there continues to be a line of scholarship that so associates scholasticism with the Middle Ages and, at times, with particular lines of medieval theology and philosophy that the idea of a post-Reformation Protestant scholasticism is treated as if it were quite intolerable and as if it were not a development following the Reformation, growing out of the thought-world of the sixteenth century, but as a throw-back to the Middle Ages and a rejection of the Reformation itself.

Fifth—less the direct result of problems in historical method than of the disciplinary structure of the modern academy—the older line of scholarship on the intellectual history of the sixteenth and seventeenth centuries evidences a distinct lack of interdisciplinary cooperation and what can only be called a narrow, even nationalistic geographical vision. In other words, it is typical that scholars have written or do their research within separate "histories" of theology, philosophy, rhetoric, biblical interpretation, political theory, and so forth, despite the fact that these disciplines not only overlapped and cross-fertilized one another but also that the thinkers of the era quite consistently worked in several disciplinary areas and, in the case of rhetoric, were nearly all trained in its use. Similarly, there has been a tendency to isolate thinkers nationally, as if British writers of the sixteenth and seventeenth centuries can be explained with reference only to Britain; as if Calvin were so Gallican that his frame of reference, properly considered, was the western fringe of Europe; or as if the Reformed version of Protestant orthodoxy fit rather neatly into the same geographical box as Calvin and could be explained as if it were merely the dogmatic aftergrowth of Calvin's own thought. Is all of that a caricature of older lines of scholarship on the history of sixteenth- and seventeenth-century thought? Would that it were.

ALTERED PATTERNS, NEW APPROACHES

In the strongest contrast to what I have referred to as the "Whig" and the denominational approaches to sixteenth- and seventeenth-century intellectual history, many scholars in the field have begun to follow the suggestions of Heiko Oberman and others of his generation for a more contextual, less anachronistic, and less denominationally biased approach to the continuities and discontinuities in the historical record. The first of Oberman's suggestions concerns revision of the concept of "forerunners" of the Reformation: rather than seek out the rebels and the heretics of the later Middle Ages, seek out the lines of intellectual conversation that run, quite unbroken, from the later Middle Ages into the sixteenth century and, we add, given our present purposes, into the seventeenth century as well.[15] In Oberman's approach, varieties of late medieval Augustinianism provide a background for the conceptions of grace found in the thought of Luther and other Reformers, and the lack of originality of sixteenth-century writers like Calvin becomes rather apparent. Of course, there remains the broad medieval background for the thought of the sixteenth-century Roman opposition to the Reformation as well, but neither the developing Protestant approaches nor the Roman Catholic models leading to the Council of Trent can be read apart from long-term trajectories of thought flowing out of the Middle Ages.

A useful example here is the issue of authority: both the approach of the Reformers, with their sense of the priority of the biblical norm over the traditionary interpretations, and the approach of the Council of Trent, with its sense of the coequality of scripture and tradition, have medieval antecedents and both belong to the western catholic tradition. Oberman identified the first as "Tradition I," which argued a single authority, namely, the canonical scripture, as understood in the churchly tradition of interpretation, and the second as "Tradition II," which, initially from the perspective of canon law, argued two parallel and coequal authorities of scripture and tradition.[16] Of course, the sixteenth century brought shifts in the paradigm: the Protestant heirs of Tradition I were more ready than their medieval predecessors to set various streams of the tradition over against scripture and point toward the capacity for error in the thought of the fathers and medievals, whereas the Tridentine heirs of Tradition II had already begun the process of identifying the contemporary magisterium as definitive interpreter of both scripture and tradition.

The issue of context is related to the sense of continuity with the past offered by Oberman and others. In my own analysis of the development in contemporary scholarship, there has been a two-pronged revision, driven by intellectual historians examining "lesser" figures in order to identify more contextually representative patterns of thought, and driven also by the social historians' critique of intellectual history: ideas do not float six feet off the ground across the stage of history, as much of the older discussion of the theology of the Reformation seemed to imply. Thus, by way of example, an idea expressed by Calvin in his famous *Institutio christianae religionis* of 1559 can no longer be viewed as legitimately presented and analyzed if the only references in the exposition and analysis are to Calvin; the backgrounds of his thought, albeit often notoriously difficult to establish, and its immediate contexts need to be presented as the proper basis for understanding.[17] One example: in the *Institutes,* Calvin has minimal recourse to traditional language concerning the merit and extent of Christ's death, whereas in his commentary on 1 John 2:2, he remarks that in the schools the text has been interpreted by way of the distinction between the sufficiency of Christ's death for all sin and its efficiency for the elect only. He then adds that, although he accepts the formula, it cannot be used as a proper interpretation of this text.[18] What is interesting here (far more interesting, by the way, than the anachronistic dogmatic discussion of whether Calvin held to "universal" or "limited atonement") is the fact that he cites a standard scholastic distinction without any negative comment about scholastics or scholasticism; perhaps even more interesting to the understanding of Calvin is the fact that his one citation of the distinction occurs not in the *Institutio* or in a dogmatic treatise, but in a commentary. This datum has a context—specifically, it indicates to us that, at least in this case, Calvin's positive reception of scholastic distinction probably came not from his reading of the dogmatic tradition of commentaries on Lombard but from his reading of the commentary tradition, which had tended to generate many of the distinctions in the first place.[19] The datum also serves to illustrate Calvin's relationship to the various models of commentary in his time: the use of the distinction by others points toward a purely topical approach to the commentary, to the presentation of *loci* or *topoi* in the commentary itself, whereas and Calvin's movement away from its use points as much to his unwillingness to oblige the topical approach to the text. His own argument is clarified and understood contextually through examination of other commentators, and thereby his originality (or lack thereof) is brought to light.[20]

SOME SPECIFICS

The medieval background of the Reformation must be examined in a nuanced manner. A recent study of the beginnings of Calvin's theology by a rather biased Roman Catholic writer took the position that Calvin's strictly Augustinian doctrine of predestination represented an element of Augustine's theology that had been rejected by all of the medieval teachers and that had only the single medieval antecedent of the heretic of the Carolingian era, Gottschalk of Orbais.[21] Here, of course, is an example of the all too neat line drawn between Middle Ages and Reformation on the basis not of data but of denominational bias—given that Calvin had numerous medieval antecedents in his predestinarianism, all quite orthodox in their time, such as Gregory of Rimini, Thomas Bradwardine, and, when his terms are rightly compared with Calvin's, even Thomas Aquinas.[22] What is more, the "Calvinists" were not the only Augustinian predestinarians of the era. On the Roman Catholic side, there are a series of theologians of the Dominican order (notably Baius and Bañez), plus Jansen and Pascal. Of course, these latter were censured. On the other hand, we need to be wary of hypothesizing and then reifying excessively neat connections—like the supposed *schola Augustiniana moderna* as an explanation of the Augustinian tendencies of the Reformers.[23]

Common ground can be found among late medieval Augustinians; Reformers, like Calvin, Wolfgang Musculus, and Peter Martyr Vermigli,[24] and their Protestant successors; various sixteenth- and seventeenth-century Dominicans and Augustinian thinkers; and the Jansenists; not to mention the common element found in various late medieval semi-Pelagians, the Canons of the Council of Trent, various early Reformation synergists, Arminius, and Jesuits like Molina and Bellarmine. Now that this common ground has been recognized, the intellectual map of the late Renaissance and Reformation has been substantially altered. We have found, in other words, that the modern "denominational" approach that neatly divides "Protestant" from "Roman Catholic" does not well represent the materials of history.

Therefore, part of the scholarly discussion must involve the removal of "denominationalism" in theological history. The understanding of "catholic" and "schismatic" thought in the sixteenth century must be revised away from the modern denominational approach that, on the side of historians of the Roman Church, has all too willingly denied patristic and medieval roots to the Reformation and that, on the side of older generations of Protestant historians, has tended to view the Middle Ages as harboring but few forerunners of the Reformation. The Reformers did not view themselves as schismatic; rather, they understood themselves as representative thinkers of the Catholic church. Nor can they be seen as radicals who allowed only the Bible as their foundation to the exclusion of tradition: their approach, as easily documented from their citations, was to use scripture as their ultimate norm and tradition as a subordinate, albeit fallible, support. This approach to the relation of scripture and tradition is, of course, contrary to the views of the Council of Trent, but it is surprisingly like the position of Thomas Aquinas and a great number of other major medieval thinkers. The Protestant use of patristic and medieval sources, moreover, became more explicit in the later generations of the Reformation; the nature of that reception should be a significant element of a revised historiography.[25]

This removal of denominationalism must also be ready to reckon with the point that the Reformers' understanding of their own task included a sense of catholicity and that the breach with Rome did not mean the rejection of a claim to catholicity or, indeed, to represent the Catholic Church. Among the Reformed, certainly, there was a self-identification as "Reformed Catholic" well into the seventeenth century. Thus, even the standard modern descriptors used in this essay, namely, "Protestant" and "Roman Catholic," need to be called into question as less than useful in the analysis of Reformation-era thought.

It is also quite impossible to draw neat lines between Protestant and Roman Catholic philosophy and method. Late medieval and Renaissance trajectories of thought were shared. A nearly identical point must be made with regard to scholasticism or scholastic method: as method, rhetoric, and logic passed through the Renaissance and were altered and adapted, the alterations and adaptations affected Protestant and Roman thinkers equally, with rather similar results. If there is a difference between the scholasticism and the Aristotelianism of the Protestants and the Roman thinkers, and an attendant methodological problem in addressing the Protestants, it has to do (at least in part) with the absence of religious orders or similar indicators of subtraditions of thought among the Protestants, yielding the still unanswered question of why individual Protestant writers were attracted to particular medieval thinkers. Why, for example, did Lambert Daneau cite (and use) Durandus of Sancto Porciano? Presumably not because Durandus was a renegade Dominican, but perhaps because of the ability to cite Durandus as paradigmatic for particular understandings of theology, the divine attributes, and the providential *concursus* that were beginning to be hotly debated in the mid- to late sixteenth century.[26]

There is also a need to "demote" great thinkers. A revised historiography of the intellectual history of the sixteenth and seventeenth centuries will need to overcome the tendency of older intellectual history to identify particular individuals as the great or, even more problematic, the emblematic thinkers of particular eras and to evaluate especially the purportedly great thinkers in their historical context and in terms of their own immediate impact and reputation.[27] The problem of "Calvinism" is a case in point: not only was the term initially a slur on the Reformed churches of the era invented by adversaries, it is, in addition, a term that does not well describe the fairly large group of thinkers to whom it is often applied. In Calvin's own generation, thinkers of fairly equivalent stature such as Bullinger and Vermigli can hardly be called "Calvinists," any more than Calvin, on grounds of similarities between his doctrine and theirs ought to be identified as a Bullingerian or Vermiglian. In fact, very few of the writers of the sixteenth and seventeenth centuries now commonly identified as "Calvinist" would have described themselves strictly as followers of Calvin. What is more, these other writers stand as thinkers in their own right within a tradition—and on certain issues and in various instances of biblical and theological interpretation are more important to the development of the tradition than Calvin: thus, Bullinger arguably had more impact on the development of covenant thought, while Vermigli and Musculus had more impact on the understanding of the category of divine permissive willing. And both Vermigli and Musculus were more instrumental in conveying elements of traditionary method, namely, scholasticism.[28]

Similarly, a study of the philosophy of the first half of the seventeenth century manifests a series of thinkers renowned in their own time and forgotten by later ages. The actual progress of thought in the era can only be understood when the broader patterns of thought, the shared traditions, and the diversity of individual positions in their own specific contexts have been examined. Descartes had less impact on his immediate contemporaries than Suárez; and Descartes' work on method, so famous in the nineteenth and twentieth centuries, was not as widely accepted and used as the works of Burgersdijk.[29] What is more, there is an entire line of recent scholarship that has placed Descartes into the context of the scholasticism of the era and shown that he is far less revolutionary than has often been claimed.

The disciplinary and geographical boundaries observed by modern scholarship frequently do not coincide with the boundaries observed in the sixteenth and seventeenth centuries. The modern divisions of specialty between philosophy and theology, between both of these disciplines and rhetoric, and between the history of biblical interpretation and Renaissance philology, need to be set aside, at least relatively speaking, given that the writers of the sixteenth and seventeenth centuries were typically adept at several, if not all, of these disciplines. Similarly, recognizing the different national and political realities of the sixteenth and seventeenth centuries is also a necessity: there was a broad central European intellectual community, linked by Renaissance Latinity. Scholars and students moved freely across the continent, and national boundaries did not serve as thought boundaries. Thus, the "Reformation in Germany" appears, when strictly argued, as a curious product of the modern nation-state, given that there was little or no political unity in the German lands, that there was theological diversity among the Reformers of the various principalities, and that there was interchange of ideas not only among the German Reformers but between the Reformers of nominally "German" principalities and Reformers in the Swiss cantons, the Low Countries, and England. The "Reformation in Poland," however, far less discussed in the last two centuries, perhaps because for more than a century there had been no Poland, takes on a rather more significant connotation, given (in contrast to "Germany") the more unified character of the geographically vast Polish-Lithuanian state. So too, the Reformation in Poland had an international character and can only be understood in terms of the international exchange of letters and the broader political framework of Europe.

A significant contemporary example of scholarship that breaks down both the disciplinary and the intellectual boundaries is Howard Hotson's monograph on Alsted, in which the theological and the philosophical belong together as aspects of a still larger encyclopedic project—and in which the broader central European culture and connection of Alsted's work is drawn out.[30] Certainly, whatever we might identify as the relevant sphere for the study of Protestant thought in the sixteenth and seventeenth centuries, the theological and philosophical histories belong to the broad geographical and intellectual swath of the northern Renaissance. Another salient example is the progress of English Protestantism and the rise of Puritanism: there was a consistent intellectual commerce between British Protestants and Protestant thinkers on the continent, with efforts on both sides of the Channel to publish and to translate writings of significant authors—evidencing both the broader European intellectual culture and the consistent interrelationship of the various disciplinary interests. It can even be argued that, whereas the British development followed the continent in matters of printing, philosophy, and scholastic method, the late sixteenth- and early seventeenth-century British (both English and Scottish) development of a full-scale federal or covenant theology came first and provided the basis for much of the continental development of federal models in the seventeenth century. Nor is tracing such a development merely a matter of riding high among the university trained intelligentsia of the early modern era when one considers that a largely untrained, popular writer like Bunyan could and did expound in good form for a lay audience such rarified notions as the *pactum salutis*.[31]

In sum, contemporary scholarship will not succeed in coping with the intellectual history of the early modern era unless modern writers develop competency in the various cognate disciplines, unless they overcome the imposition of modern national and geographical boundaries not observed by the intellectual culture of the era, and unless the guild structure of our historiography is superceded by increased levels of communication among experts in a broader spectrum of disciplines; in other words, not until the highly decontextualized methodologies—or ought one to say, mythologies—of the older literature have been set aside. All of these observations, finally, go to the question of context and return us to the issue posed early on in this essay in the words of Skinner—to arrive at an understanding "how what was said was meant and . . . what relations there may have been between various statements" and, we add, other impinging issues, whether religious, political, cultural, social, institutional, traditionary or of the moment, "within the same general context."[32] Or to make the point in a somewhat different way, our historiographical burden remains the determination of the proper context for understanding what was said rather than the imposition of a particular de- or re-contextualizing assumption based on our own stance in the present, whether that assumption be taken from social or economic theory or from some particular modern dogmatic or philosophical school of thought. There is really not a great distance between the error of claiming that all of one type of religious statement are expressions of economic forces and the error of claiming that all of one type of theological formulation are the result of the tension between predestinarianism and federalism in an archetypal clash of central dogmas. Some ideas are generated by immediate social and economic forces, but other ideas follow out long traditionary trajectories for which we cannot account on social and economic grounds or on grounds of any other reified "isms." In short, our burden is to avoid the enormous pitfalls of a decontextualized or badly contextualized intellectual history (which, in fact, is not history at all, but some sort of dogma) and find not the social, economic, political, or (why not?) agricultural meaning of what purported to be a theological or philosophical idea, nor indeed, the ultimate meaning of a theological statement as determined by the language and norms of modern dogmaticians. We must seek instead the suitable *intellectual context,* for the statements of living, breathing, eating, drinking, buying, selling, religiously expressive, *thinking* people in a past era.

NOTES

1. Herbert Butterfield, *The Whig Interpretation of History* (London: George Bell, 1931).
2. Ibid., 50–53.
3. Ibid., 54.
4. Quentin Skinner, "Meaning and Understanding in the History of Ideas," in *History and Theory* 8, no. 1 (1969): 3–53.
5. Ibid., 3.
6. Ibid., 7.
7. Ibid., 46–47.

8. See, for example, Alister McGrath, *Reformation Thought: An Introduction*, 2nd ed. (Oxford: Basil Blackwell, 1993), 129–30; Karl Barth, *The Theology of John Calvin*, trans. Geoffrey W. Bromiley (Grand Rapids, Mich.: Eerdmans, 1995), 165.

9. See further, Richard A. Muller, *The Unaccommodated Calvin: Essays in the Formation of a Theological Tradition* (New York: Oxford University Press, 2000), 6–8; Richard A. Muller, *After Calvin: Studies in the Development of a Theological Tradition* (New York: Oxford University Press, 2003), 92–102.

10. For example Johannes Altenstaig, *Lexicon theologicum quo tanquam clave theologiae fores aperiuntur, et omnium fere terminorum, et obscuriorum vocum, quae s. theologicae studios facile remorantur* (Cologne: Petrus Henningius, 1619), originally published in 1517 and frequently reissued in the sixteenth and seventeenth centuries; and John Withals, *A Dictionary in English and Latine* (London: Thomas Purfoot, 1634).

11. Theo Verbeek, *Descartes and the Dutch: Early Reactions to Cartesianism (1637–1650)* (Carbondale: Southern Illinois University Press, 1992); Theo Verbeek, "Descartes and the Problem of Atheism: The Utrecht Crisis," *Nederlands Archief voor Kerkgeschiedenis* 71, no. 2 (1991): 211–23; and Roger Ariew, *Descartes and the Last Scholastics* (Ithaca, N.Y.: Cornell University Press, 1999).

12. See the recent work of Aza Goudriaan, *Philosophische Gotteserkenntnis bei Suarez und Descartes, im Zusammenhang mit der niederländischen reformierten Theologie und Philosophie des 17. Jahrhunderts* (Leiden: E. J. Brill, 1999); Aza Goudriaan, *Jacobus Revius: A Theological Examination of Cartesian Philosophy; Early Criticisms (1647)* (Leiden: E. J. Brill, 2002); and Aza Goudriaan, *Reformed Orthodoxy and Philosophy, 1625–1750: Gisbertus Voetius, Petrus van Mastricht, and Anthonius Driessen* (Leiden: E. J. Brill, 2006). Also note Joseph S. Freedman, *European Academic Philosophy in the Late Sixteenth and Early Seventeenth Centuries: The Life, Significance, and Philosophy of Clemens Timpler (1563/4–1624)*, 2 vols. (New York: Olms, 1988); Joseph S. Freedman, "The Career and Writings of Bartholomew Keckermann," in *Proceedings of the American Philosophical Society* 141, no. 3 (1997): 305–64; Howard Hotson, *Johann Heinrich Alsted, 1588–1638: Between Renaissance, Reformation, and Universal Reform* (Oxford: Clarendon Press, 2000); and Howard Hotson, *Commonplace Learning: Ramism and its German Ramifications, 1543–1630* (Oxford: Oxford University Press, 2007).

13. For example, George Tavard, *Holy Writ or Holy Church: The Crisis of the Protestant Reformation* (New York: Harper & Row, 1959), 105 et passim.

14. For example, J. Wayne Baker, *Heinrich Bullinger and the Covenant: The Other Reformed Tradition* (Athens: Ohio University Press, 1980); T. H. L. Parker,

Calvin: An Introduction to His Thought (Louisville, Ky.: Westminster/John Knox, 1995); Kevin Kennedy, *Union with Christ and the Extent of the Atonement in Calvin* (New York: Peter Lang, 2002); B. A. Gerrish, *Grace and Gratitude: The Eucharistic Theology of John Calvin* (Philadelphia: Fortress, 1993); and Randall Zachman, *John Calvin as Teacher, Pastor, and Theologian: The Shape of His Writings and Thought* (Grand Rapids, Mich.: Baker, 2006).

15. See Heiko A. Oberman, *Forerunners of the Reformation* (New York: Holt, Rinehart, and Winston, 1966), 1–65; and *The Dawn of the Reformation: Essays in Late Medieval and Early Reformation Thought* (Edinburgh: T. & T. Clark, 1986).

16. Heiko A. Oberman, *The Harvest of Medieval Theology: Gabriel Biel and Late Medieval Nominalism*, rev. ed. (Grand Rapids, Mich.: Eerdmans, 1967), 365–412; also note Oberman's "*Quo vadis Petre?* Tradition from Irenaeus to *Humani Generis*," in his *Dawn of the Reformation*, 269–96, where he explicitly links the Reformation approach to scripture to Tradition I and the Council of Trent to Tradition II (286).

17. See David C. Steinmetz, *Calvin in Context* (New York: Oxford University Press, 1995); cf. the arguments in Muller, *Unaccommodated Calvin*, 4–8, 42–44, 94–95, 97–98, 108–11, 163–64, et passim.

18. John Calvin, *Commentarius in Iohannis Apostoli epistolam, CO* 55, col. 310; in translation, John Calvin, *Commentaries on the Catholic Epistles* (repr., Grand Rapids, Mich: Baker Book House, 1979), 173. The formula may perhaps also be reflected in Calvin, *De aeterna Dei praedestnatione, CO* 8, col. 336–37; in translation, *Concerning the Eternal Predestination of God*, trans. with an intro. by J. K. S. Reid (London: James Clarke, 1961), 148–49. Cf. the discussion in Muller, *Unaccommodated Calvin*, 55.

19. Calvin's approaches to scholasticism, both negative and positive, are reviewed in David C. Steinmetz, "The Scholastic Calvin," in *Protestant Scholasticism: Essays in Reassessment*, ed. C. Trueman and R. Clark, 16–30 (Carlisle: Paternoster Press, 1999); see also Muller, *Unaccommodated Calvin*, 39–61; and Armand Aime LaVallee, "Calvin's Criticism of Scholastic Theology" (PhD diss. Harvard University, 1967).

20. See the studies in Steinmetz, *Calvin in Context*.

21. George H. Tavard, *The Starting Point of Calvin's Theology* (Grand Rapids, Mich.: Eerdmans, 2000), 183–84; for a review of the problems in Tavard's work, see Richard A. Muller, "The Starting Point of Calvin's Theology: An Essay-Review," in *Calvin Theological Journal* 36, no. 2 (2001): 314–41.

22. Cf. the careful comparison of Augustine and Aquinas with Calvin in J. B. Mozley, *A Treatise on the Augustinian Doctrine of Predestination*, 2nd ed.

(New York: E. P. Dutton, 1878), 266–76, 393–401; and in Arvin Vos, *Aquinas, Calvin, and Contemporary Protestant Thought: A Critique of Protestant Views of the Thought of Thomas Aquinas* (Grand Rapids, Mich.: Eerdmans, 1985).

23. See the exhaustive history of the scholarship in Eric Leland Saak, *High Way to Heaven: The Augustinian Platform between Reform and Reformation, 1292–1524* (Leiden: E. J. Brill, 2002), 683–98.

24. See Frank James III, *Peter Martyr Vermigli and Predestination: The Augustinian Inheritance of an Italian Reformer* (Oxford: Clarendon Press, 1998); and "A Late Medieval Parallel in Reformation Thought: *Gemina praedestinatio* in Gregory of Rimini and Peter Martyr Vermigli," in *Via Augustini,* ed. Heiko A. Oberman and Frank James III, 157–88 (Leiden: E. J. Brill, 1991).

25. See the relevant essays in Irena Backus, ed., *The Reception of the Church Fathers in the West: From the Carolingians to the Maurists,* 2 vols. (Leiden: E. J. Brill, 1997).

26. Cf. Richard A. Muller, *Post-Reformation Reformed Dogmatics: The Rise and Development of Reformed Orthodoxy, ca. 1520 to ca. 1725,* 4 vols. (Grand Rapids, Mich.: Baker Book House, 2003), vol. 1, 195, 283, 319, 326, 350, 356, 376, 387; vol. 3, 114, 115, 166, 465.

27. See Freedman, *European Academic Philosophy.*

28. See, for example, Frank A. James III, "Peter Martyr Vermigli: At the Crossroads of Late Medieval Scholasticism, Christian Humanism and Resurgent Augustinianism," in *Protestant Scholasticism: Essays in Reassessment,* ed. Trueman and Clark, 62–78.

29. See, for example, Aza Goudriaan, *Philosophische Gotteserkenntnis dei Suárez und Descartes;* E. P. Bos and H. A. Krop, eds., *Franco Burgersdijk (1590–1635): Neo-Aristotelianism in Leiden* (Amsterdam: Rodopi, 1993).

30. Hotson, *Johann Heinrich Alsted.*

31. John Bunyan, *The Doctrine of Law and Grace Unfolded,* in *The Whole Works of John Bunyan,* ed. George Offor, 3 vols. (London: Blackie & Sons, 1862), vol. 1, 522–26.

32. Skinner, "Meaning," 46–47.

7 Scholasticism Revisited:
Methodological Reflections on the Study of Seventeenth-century Reformed Thought

WILLEM J. VAN ASSELT

THE PRIMACY OF QUESTIONS OVER ANSWERS

Historical theologians have commonly held that a rather negative connection exists between the two major intellectual movements in the Protestant world of the sixteenth and seventeenth centuries: the Reformation and Protestant scholasticism. These scholars have condemned the writings of the Protestant scholastics as an unfortunate survival of medieval traditions that could be safely disregarded, and argued that the true spirit of Protestantism was expressed in the literature of the Reformers. Protestant scholastics were condemned without a hearing and labelled as empty "quibblers," followers of a dead past who failed to understand the living problems of their new times. Characterized as the return of medieval dialectic and Aristotelian logic to the Protestant classroom, it was, therefore, considered a distortion or perversion of Reformation theology. Many recent works on the history of Protestant theology still repeat the common notion that scholasticism was a relapse into earlier "concept-splitting school philosophy," giving some of the charges made against scholasticism by the Reformers a much more extreme meaning than they originally had. The scornful way in which Luther and Calvin treated some forms of late medieval scholasticism is thus taken as an overall hermeneutical principle for this approach to discerning theological truth. As a result, too many historians have read the whole period of post-Reformation theology exclusively in light of a modern aversion to scholasticism, and not on its own terms or in light of its own concerns and context.[1] Thus, more than one hundred and fifty years of the history of Protestant theology were consigned to the museum of historical curiosities that are no longer worth studying, of use only to conservative Protestants who want to legitimize their own dogmatic prejudices.

In this chapter I want to suggest that the antischolasticism of Reformation theology is a later invention and that the assumptions this view makes about Protestant and, especially, Reformed scholasticism have been called into question by recent research. Instead of trying to reduce everything to one issue—Reformation or scholasticism—we should try to develop a sound historical method not influenced by all kinds of prejudices against scholasticism. Problems in historical theology require, first and foremost, historical solutions. Although complete objectivity may be impossible to achieve, it should be the permanent aim and standard of the historian of theology. As Paul Oskar Kristeller observed: "It is easy to praise everything in the past which happens to resemble certain favourite ideas of our own time, or to ridicule and minimize everything that disagrees with them. This method is neither fair nor helpful for an adequate understanding of the past."[2]

In a certain way, this new approach to Protestant scholasticism reflects the strategy promoted by Quentin Skinner in his historical study of moral and political theory. Following R. G. Collingwood, Skinner argues that in order to grasp the meaning of historical texts we have to ask "what their authors were doing in writing them."[3] Applied to the study of the texts of the Protestant scholastics, Skinner's method of stressing "the primacy of questions over answers" can be very useful to debunk all kinds of doctrinal mythology surrounding the Protestant scholastic authors. His method implies that our attention should not be devoted primarily to individual authors but to the more general and theological discourse of their times: what issues they were addressing, and to what extent they were accepting or questioning the prevailing assumptions or traditions of theological debate.

In this essay, my main contention is that we should pay close attention to the argumentative context of the post-Reformation scholastics in order to rediscover their intentions. To put the point in another way: we need to understand *why* a certain position was taken up if we wish to understand the position itself. As Carl Trueman put it, "Reformed theology is expressed in historical texts, whether confessions, commentaries, catechisms, or systems; and these are historical actions which need to be understood in context, not isolated from that context and treated as self-understanding, autonomous artefacts."[4]

Therefore, the claim made in this essay is that we should let the Reformed scholastics define for themselves what scholasticism stands for. For this purpose I will discuss some major methodological—and hence practical—implications for the study of Protestant scholasticism implied by this new approach.

CENTRAL RESEARCH THEMES

Research on Protestant scholasticism in the last few decades has reached the consensus that, in the past, the term "Protestant scholasticism" was insufficiently defined, and that the definitions that were given were often charged with value judgements. In contrast to the older research, which remained confined to a purely dogmatic approach, a strong plea has now made for a more contextualized approach by arguing that the contrast so often drawn between scholasticism, Reformation, and humanism is outdated. When these phenomena are studied in their context, they turn out to be closely related to each other.

This development was stimulated especially by new approaches in the study of Reformation history, which pointed to the medieval background of the Reformation. The work of the late H. A. Oberman drew attention to the continuities between the theology of the late Middle Ages and that of the reformers. David Steinmetz and Richard Muller pointed to continuities and discontinuities between the Reformation and Protestant scholasticism.[5] In his research project at Utrecht University, Antonie Vos combined systematic, analytical, and historical methods for the study of Reformed scholasticism and pointed to the significant impact of the metaphysics of Duns Scotus on Reformed theology.[6] In the writings of all these authors, the simplistic oppositions so characteristic of the older research (whether Roman Catholic or Protestant) were subjected to devastating criticism.

It is, however, no simple matter to give a final definition of the term scholasticism freed from any pejorative connotation. L. M. de Rijk made a good attempt at a clear definition of scholasticism in his book on medieval philosophy, in which he consistently interpreted scholasticism as no more than a method. According to de Rijk, scholasticism should be taken as a collective noun denoting an "approach, which is characterized by the use, in both study and teaching, of a constantly recurring system of concepts, distinctions, proposition analyses, argumentative techniques and disputational methods."[7] Although de Rijk writes on medieval scholasticism, his definition of scholasticism as a method applies just as well to Reformed (and Lutheran) scholasticism.

Richard Muller has offered a complementary account of the discussions concerning the place and significance of Reformed scholasticism in the history of theology. In his judgment, the central problem is the question of the continuity or discontinuity between, on the one hand, the Reformation and orthodoxy, and on the other hand, between orthodoxy and the whole tradition of western theology as such.[8] According to Muller, the core of the scholastic method, in every period, consists in the so-called *quaestio* technique characterized by presenting a thesis or a thematic question, followed by the treatment of objections against the adopted positions (*objectiones*), and, finally, the formulation of an answer (*responsiones*). When this structure, or some form of it, is found in a work, in Muller's judgement one ought to refer to it as scholastic. The definitions presented by de Rijk and Muller are argued or presupposed by an increasing number of scholars.[9]

Furthermore, both de Rijk and Muller have pointed to the fact that medieval and Reformed scholasticism exhibited far greater variety than the earlier research suggested. Against this background, Muller and de Rijk argue that the most adequate and useful definition of scholasticism seems to be the one that takes the term primarily as indicative of a method that supplied the broad argumentative framework within which the doctrines could be developed and which was not bound, in terms of both method and content, to any philosophy, such as Aristotelianism. According to these authors, this definition also guards against the idea that one particular doctrine or concept is necessarily moved to the foreground merely by the use of the scholastic method, such as the doctrine of predestination.

In sum: the most important of the theses put forward by the new research is that the term "scholasticism" refers primarily to a method, rather than any definite doctrinal content. This insight has resulted in a new approach to the study of Protestant scholasticism. In this chapter I will examine several issues and point to some of their implications. In my own work I have attempted to give concrete shape to this new approach, and to make it fruitful for the study of Protestant scholasticism in general and of Reformed scholasticism in particular.[10]

WHAT IS PROTESTANT SCHOLASTICISM?

Historically, the term "Protestant scholasticism" referred to the period of institutionalization and codification following the Reformation, which resulted in a theological interpretation of the Reformation within particular, confessionally determined bounds. This theology was taught in the new Protestant academies and universities with the help of the so-called scholastic method. As already noted, the term refers primarily to a method for education and research that had already been developed in the medieval period. Therefore, adherents of the new type of research claim that a study of the theology of the medieval, Reformation, and post-Reformation periods in isolation from one another belies the complexity of the historical and theological relations and connections between them. These scholars thus reject clear breaks and lines of demarcation, and emphasize the continuous development within the history of theology. As in the Middle Ages and during the period following the Reformation, it was the method that gave scholasticism a recognizable shape and lent it unity and continuity. In methodological terms this approach means taking leave of the accepted division into clearly demarcated periods of Middle Ages—Reformation—Protestant orthodoxy. For example, the observation that it is no longer possible to study Luther or Calvin without knowledge of the medieval background has by now been established as part of the *communis opinio* in Reformation studies.

Although the Reformation was rooted in the question of authority, a question that was answered with the language of *sola scriptura* (the priority of scripture as the ultimate norm of doctrine over and above all other grounds of authority), the phrase *sola scriptura* should not be taken as a condemnation of tradition as such. As Oberman has observed, the Reformation principle had as its point of departure the late medieval debate on the relation of scripture to tradition and assumed that tradition was a subordinate norm (*norma normata*) under the authority of scripture (*norma normans*).[11] In this way the Protestant mind respected the use of tradition and allowed for a churchly set of confessions and catechisms as a standard of belief. According to Muller, it is "entirely anachronistic to view the *sola scriptura* of Luther and his contemporaries as a declaration that all of theology ought to be constructed anew, without any reference to the church's tradition of interpretation."[12] For the reformers and their Protestant orthodox followers, the point of debate with their Roman Catholic opponents was not the authority of scripture as such; rather the question was how the scriptural rule functioned in the context of other claims of authority, whether of tradition or churchly *magisterium*.

At the same time, this observation raises the question of the reception and use of medieval traditions in post-Reformation theology. Studying this reception history, one is struck by a complex pattern of continuity and discontinuity. In order to explain the motives and intentions of the post-Reformation scholastic authors for adopting scholastic method for doing theology we can point to several external or contextual factors. The most significant of these was the quest for self-definition. After the Reformation, in the period extending roughly from 1565 to 1700, Protestantism faced the crisis of being forced to defend its nascent theology against attacks from highly sophisticated Roman Catholic theologians. This theology, which until the middle of the sixteenth century could be conceived in either scholastic or rhetorical terms, was driven by the Reformation and the Council of Trent (1545–1563) into a second period of scholasticism, a current of Catholic theology and philosophy that was dominated by the Spanish and Italian schools. First the Dominicans and later the Jesuits took the lead in this neoscholastic movement.[13] The Jesuit Cardinal Robert Bellarmine (1542–1621) in particular subjected the views of the Reformation to continuous and incisive criticism.[14] Bellarmine's offensive was scholastic in nature, so in order to combat him and other Roman Catholic polemical theologians, the Protestant theologians were pressed to use the same scholastic apparatus. And it was in the course of this debate that an increasingly detailed elaboration of the Reformed theological position came into being. By using scholastic tools, Protestant theologians built a theological system that excelled in the precision with which its ideas were formulated.

The ecclesial and pedagogical context were also important for the rise and development of Reformed scholasticism. Protestantism was facing the problem of institutionalization as it passed from its beginnings as a protest movement within the Catholic Church to a self-sufficient ecclesiastical establishment with its own academic, confessional, and dogmatic needs. After the first and second generation of theologians who had played such an important role in the establishment of the Reformed church had passed away, the new generation faced the task of giving expression to the significance of the Reformation in a new ecclesial and academic context. On the one hand, the quest was to find a way of showing forth, in the light of the Christian tradition, the catholicity of Reformed faith. On the other, the confrontation with the theological tradition of the Roman Catholic Church and the beliefs of Arminian and Socinian opponents obliged the Reformed thinkers of the seventeenth century to define their own identity in order to delineate its bounds. In this situation the need for self-definition became urgent. The scholastic method, therefore, provided the most reliable means by which they might define themselves over and against others.[15]

Thus it becomes clear why Reformed theologians in developing their theology could draw upon medieval sources. In order to point out and justify their own position within the Catholic tradition, they adopted a set of definitions and divisions of theology derived from the medieval tradition. This apparent regression to pre-Reformation scholasticism, however, was not a simple return to a medieval approach to theology: it was a move forward towards a critical reappropriation of aspects of the Western tradition in order to develop a restatement of the Catholic roots of Reformed thought. Moreover, far from breaking down at the close of the Middle Ages, scholasticism underwent a series of modifications that enabled it to adapt to the renewed Aristotelianism of the Renaissance.[16]

Methodologically speaking, this implies at the very least that the scholastic influence on Reformed theology is to be interpreted as a result of the Renaissance revival of scholasticism. The extensive reappropriation of the technical language of medieval and Renaissance scholasticism by Reformed theologians was also helpful in endowing their theological formulations with the precision needed to distinguish themselves from the tenets of Arminianism and Socinianism that confronted Reformed orthodoxy with deviant theologies. The point at issue with these opponents was not simply whether scripture was the authoritative foundation for theology, but how scripture was to be interpreted, a point that raised questions about logic and metaphysics, and about how individual passages of scripture are mutually related. In addition, the increasing methodological, metaphysical, and linguistic sophistication of post-Tridentine Catholic theology (represented by theologians such as Bellarmine) required the production of a precise response. At the same time, Reformed scholastics actually appropriated much of established Roman Catholic thought in a positive fashion, as can be seen in their doctrines of the divine attributes and the Trinity.[17]

In conclusion, representatives of the new approach to Reformed scholasticism place the emphasis on a double continuity, whereby attention is drawn, not only to a confessional continuity with the reformers, but also to a methodological continuity with medieval theologians. However, this theory also recognizes discontinuity: Reformed scholasticism was obviously no duplicate of the medieval systems, and no repetition of the Reformation. It is important to reject any such identification that denies historical development and places the statement of Reformed scholasticism on a timelessly normative level. Reformed scholasticism is seen as a form of (Protestant) Catholic theology bearing a distinctive stamp designed to meet the needs of the hour.[18]

HUMANISM VERSUS SCHOLASTICISM?

One of the fruits of the more recent scholarly reassessment of the development of Reformed scholasticism is a relativization of the opposition between scholasticism and humanism. In nineteenth-century historiography, humanism and scholasticism were portrayed as diametrically opposed intellectual movements. The classic formulation of this view can be found in Jacob Burckhardt's *Die Kultur der Renaissance in Italien* (1860). The rise of humanism, and the process by which it earned its place in the university, is portrayed in this perspective as a brutal conflict.

However, more recent research has shown that the opposition of humanism versus scholasticism was never as sharp as was often thought. Christian-oriented humanism was in continuity with medieval scholastic scholarship rather than in opposition to it. Paul Oskar Kristeller argued that the opposition between humanism and scholasticism came to be exaggerated beyond all proportion in light of the later appreciation of humanism. Furthermore, he pointed out that the origin of the humanist movement is not to be sought in the sphere of philosophy and science, but rather in the areas of grammar and rhetoric. The humanists should be understood as continuing the medieval traditions in these areas, adding new impulses from their study of the classics. This influence was important, "but it did not affect the content or substance of the medieval traditions in those sciences."[19] Moreover, other proponents of the revisionist thesis have pointed out that from accounts of the history of universities in Germany and France around 1500, it would appear that there was hardly any question of a fundamental struggle between scholasticism and humanism. Here one should rather speak of the (more or less) peaceful coexistence of humanism and scholasticism.[20] The two traditions had their locus and center in two different sectors of learning: humanism in the fields of grammar, rhetoric, and poetry and to some extent in moral philosophy, scholasticism in the fields of logic and natural philosophy.

The most recent work on the relations between humanism and scholasticism, however, offers further revision to the revisionist thesis by putting into perspective both the traditional view that emphasizes the antagonism between scholasticism and humanism and the revisionist view that claims that the controversies were mere periods in a long period of peaceful coexistence. According to Erika Rummel the latter view has some validity for the early Renaissance, but during the Reformation period things changed. Nevertheless, the result of the debate was that while humanism successfully reshaped educational institutions and aesthetic values, it failed to coalesce into a coherent epistemology and unified body of teachings. Scholasticism, by contrast, experienced a certain renewal under the pressure of humanist criticism. In addition, it could be argued that Renaissance humanists such as Lorenzo Valla, Rudolph Agricola, and Melanchthon developed dialectic into a tool of textual analysis and scriptural exegesis,[21] and, on the other hand, the scholastics of the Renaissance and their Reformed successors did not remain untouched by the new influence of humanism.[22] They began to make abundant use of the Greek text and the new Latin translations of Aristotle, his ancient commentators, and other Greek thinkers.[23]

The most important implication of this humanist-scholastic debate for the study of Protestant scholasticism is that we need to expand our bibliography in this area significantly, in order to get rid of the idea that the Renaissance as a field of research has no relation to post-Reformation Protestantism. So far, the influence of recent Renaissance scholarship on the study of the relation between the Reformation and Reformed scholasticism has been negligible.[24]

CALVIN AGAINST THE CALVINISTS?

A third issue concerns the discovery of diverse trajectories within Reformed theology itself. Here, I will point to the reappraisal of the role of John Calvin in the development of Reformed theology. In previous research the Geneva reformer was used as a benchmark for assessing the work of later theologians. Basil Hall has characterized this approach to Protestant scholasticism as "Calvin against the Calvinists."[25] A "non-scholastic Calvin" was contrasted with the later "scholastic Calvinists" and comparisons made between the treatment of a particular doctrine by a later scholastic author and Calvin's treatment of the same topic. Such a procedure is guaranteed to yield the desired result, given the difference in genre and context between the works of Calvin and the scholastic writings of seventeenth-century dogmaticians. Moreover, such research concentrates on the influence of a single individual theologian, who is then regarded as decisive for all later developments. By applying the methodology of scholars such as Oberman and Steinmetz to the question of Calvin's relationship to his successors, the new approach relativizes the status of Calvin within the Reformed tradition. Focusing on issues of exegetical and doctrinal continuity set within the much broader and variegated contexts of the development of Western theology as a whole, the new approach takes account of the complexity and wide variety of (post-Reformation) Reformed theology and its tradition-historical *Sitz im Leben*. The influential role of Calvin is not denied, but he was one among a number of influential theologians such as Peter Martyr Vermigli, John a Lasco, Martin Bucer, and Heinrich Bullinger. In some respects their thought exerted as much influence on the later Reformed tradition as the theology of Calvin did.

In addition, some have argued that there was not one, but several trajectories—a whole series of Reformed theologies of the sixteenth and seventeenth centuries. There are various lines of development within Reformed orthodoxy, such as the Swiss line of Francis Turretin and Johann Heidegger, the French approach represented by the academy of Saumur, the Northern German Reformed line of Bremen or the Herborn Academy, the Franeker theologians in the tradition of William Ames, and the Coccheian or federalist approach that was not identical with the Voetian project in Utrecht. In British Reformed theology John Owen and Richard Baxter can be identified as different types of Reformed teaching.[26]

Therefore, it seems more appropriate for the historian of theology to refer to the theologians from this post-Reformation period and the tradition in which they stood and of which Calvin was a part with the term "Reformed" rather than with the name "Calvinist" or "Calvinism." This indicates that we are dealing with a complex movement: the designation of this movement as "Calvinism" is suggestive, rather than illuminating, as it seems to ascribe this movement to one individual.[27]

Finally, apart from the lack of attention to the diversity within post-Reformation theology itself, the study of the interaction between Reformed scholasticism and post-Tridentine Catholic scholasticism (represented by thinkers such as Bellarmine, Cano, Molina, and Suárez) has also scarcely been addressed. For historians of Reformed theology, this literature is difficult to access and arduous to read but very helpful in explaining the context in which philosophical and theological problems and doctrines were discussed by the Reformed scholastics. It represents the bulk and kernel of the philosophical and theological thought of the period but has been badly neglected by most historians of Reformed theology until now. Studies by Eef Dekker and Aza Goudriaan, however, have tried to rectify this deficit by showing that, in methodological terms, these two scholastic traditions—Catholic and Protestant—resemble one another closely.[28]

SOURCES AND SEMANTICS

Naturally, the diversity and variety within the Reformed tradition, arising from diverse backgrounds and contexts, raises methodological problems of its own. How were the medieval and contemporary scholastic traditions received and employed in the theological discourse of Reformed thought? At this point a new field of research must be brought to bear on the discussion in order to determine the identity of Protestant scholasticism. For this purpose the following tools are required. First, we must study the contemporaneous *florilegia* of patristic and medieval sources, bibliographies, auction catalogues, "study guides," and descriptions of *curricula* from the sixteenth, seventeenth, and eighteenth centuries. They provide a link with the trajectories of theological and philosophical reflection in which Reformed theologians participated. Moreover, they tell us what literature was available, which was read, and which thus helped to forge the linguistic and conceptual worlds within which the Reformed theologians lived and worked.[29]

Secondly, I want to point to the importance of semantic research. Such research focuses primarily on the origin, meaning, and usage of the conceptual apparatus of the scholastic tradition in its context. It relates to the words, concepts, ideas, and doctrines by which Reformed theologians carried on their work, and which gave a specific identity to the Reformed confessions and the ecclesiastical communities oriented on them at the time. It is becoming increasingly clear from such research that the study of the semantic fields of terms and concepts employed in a specific theological argumentative context is a prerequisite for gaining insight into the intentions of the authors. It enables us to think anew about why they organized their texts in a certain way, why they developed a certain vocabulary, and why certain arguments were particularly singled out and emphasized. Posing and answering these preliminary questions help us to understand why, in general, a certain scholastic text possesses its distinctive identity and shape. Because concepts and their context formed a network of mutual influence, scholarship cannot treat Reformed scholasticism as a discrete entity without paying attention to these textual and contextual factors. To this it may be added that during the sixteenth-century fine printed editions of the theological works of Thomas Aquinas, Gregory of Rimini, Henry of Ghent, Pierre D' Ailly, and Thomas of Strasburg, among others, became available[30] and were used by the Reformed scholastics as can be seen in the auction catalogues of their libraries.[31] Furthermore, Johannes Altenstaig's *Vocabularius theologiae* (1517), reissued in 1619 under the title *Lexicon theologicum*, became an important sourcebook for the Reformed scholastics that was frequently quoted, as can be seen in the works of John Owen, Francis Turretin, and Gisbert Voetius.[32] It embodied and reflected the conceptual world of all the participants in scholastic discourse at that time.[33] In studying these works and the specific context in which they were used or questioned by seventeenth-century Reformed authors it is possible to understand why they introduced scholastic concepts into their own theological project.

It will be clear that such a semantic approach requires a much broader conceptualization of the Protestant scholastic tradition than has hitherto been the case. Moreover, through this "resourcing," insights are developed that problematize the older research at several points. Thus terms like "scholasticism," "Aristotelianism," "Thomism," and "Scotism" can no longer be seen as referring to purely static entities. Unqualified references to these "isms" are, historically speaking, inaccurate, because they disregard the contextually determined use of Aristotelian logic or Thomistic and Scotistic tenets during the Renaissance, Reformation, and post-Reformation periods. These are historical phenomena with a long tradition-history.

Methodologically, this implies that researchers ought to take their point of departure in the meaning of "Aristotelianism," "logic," and "scholasticism" as these are encountered in the scholarly writings of sixteenth- and seventeenth-century authors themselves. For example, recent research has pointed out that with regard to the reception of Aristotle by Reformed theologians, one should be careful to distinguish between formal aspects and aspects related to content. Appropriation did occur, but so did disagreement.[34] Aristotle's logic was received from the medieval tradition in a form that was in fact not very Aristotelian, while the Stagirite's concept of God and his views on the eternity of the world were sharply denounced by Reformed theologians. Therefore, we cannot speak of a recrudescence of "Aristotelianism" without any qualification in Reformed theology; rather, we have to examine the modifications of this philosophical tradition in the context of the Reformed debates. This procedure makes clear that only nominally Aristotelian themes had been wedded to the explanation of major doctrinal points of the Reformed tradition.[35] If Aristotelianism is used in order to describe the identity of seventeenth-century Reformed theology, we should be aware of the fact that it is an exceedingly problematic concept. It should be avoided rather than used in an unspecified manner.

Finally, in order to recover the intentions of the Reformed scholastics and what they were doing in quoting an authority (the Bible, Aristotle, Augustine, Aquinas, Scotus) it should be noted that this was not to claim that the text quoted was to be followed without reasoning. Nor was it only an ornament in one's own discourse. Rather the Reformed scholastics cited a text when they considered it to be intrinsically important because of its truth. Such a text did not function "historically" (a notion absent in premodern times), but it was interpreted according to one's own frame of thought. The Reformed theologians did not read their sources of scripture and tradition in a (modern) historical sense, but as "authorities of truth." Neither were they conceived historically, but systematically as a self-evident entity, embodied in texts laden with truth. It would be a mistake, therefore, for us to read the premodern perception of these authoritative texts "historically" in a modern sense. Very illuminating in this respect is Quentin Skinner's comment that seventeenth-century scholars exhibited almost no interest in reconstructing the historical context of the texts they were studying: "On the contrary, they approach them as if they are contemporary documents with an almost wholly unproblematic relevance to their own circumstances."[36] It is, therefore, on historical grounds that we need to make a sharp distinction between the modern idea of history and historical foundation, and the premodern concept of it, as evidenced in Reformed scholasticism.[37]

INTELLECTUAL HISTORY VERSUS SOCIAL HISTORY?

One final issue in the new approach to Protestant (Reformed and Lutheran) scholasticism relates to the institutionalization of the Reformation in the century immediately following it. As already noted, it was an important factor in the development of Protestant scholastic orthodoxy. Social historians such as Heinz Schilling have used the term "confessionalization" to describe the social and political process that occurred during the second half of the sixteenth century, when Protestant religion increasingly began to impose norms and life patterns on everyday and social life.[38] This "confessionalization" by which both Lutheran and Reformed communities defined themselves by explicit and extensive doctrinal formulations represented the inevitable outcome of a quest for a theological self-definition. But these doctrines cannot be studied at the cost of reducing them to social, economic, or political epiphenomena. Social historians must be credited with the insight that abstraction of the social, economic, or political context cannot do full justice to the origin and development of Protestant orthodoxy, including its academic dimension in the form of scholastic theologizing.[39]

In methodological terms this does not mean that I am pleading for intellectual history to be swallowed up by social history. My point is that theological views from the past cannot be obtained in isolation, while at the same time I insist that religious views and theological concepts cannot be reduced to the epiphenomena of political and social power relations hiding under a religious or theological cloak. My ideal is that a fruitful dialogue should emerge between students of the history of theology and practitioners of social history. The remaining fences between the two disciplines need to be torn down, both by recognizing the social context of religious ideas and by recognizing the role of religious ideas in shaping social developments. Historical changes do not occur in the manner of geological shifts but are brought about by thinking and acting subjects: "Ideas have legs." Although I do not believe that history is moved by minds alone, I do believe that preoccupations with material factors and subverbal behavior have obscured the force and relevance of thought and discourse in the complex process of history.

Therefore, my basic assumption underlying my study of Reformed scholasticism is that any interpretation of theological texts has to do justice to the genre, context, and purposes of the text. A historical interpretation requires awareness of the fact that the sixteenth- and seventeenth-century authors might have done theology at various and unexpected points in a way very different from contemporary practice. This obvious statement might seem redundant, but it seems rather "natural" to interpret their texts by our own frame of thought, without consciously investigating *their* way of seeing things, *their* way of dealing with theological sources, *their* methods of treating a subject. Although their ways of seeing things do not immediately appear on the surface of their texts, they are nevertheless crucial for *our* methods of interpreting the phenomenon of Reformed scholasticism in the sixteenth and seventeenth centuries.

NOTES

I would like to thank my colleague Marcel Sarot (Utrecht University) for his friendly comments on this article.

1. For a survey of the older research and the value judgements concerning scholastic orthodoxy contained in it, see Willem J. van Asselt and Eef Dekker, eds., *Reformation and Scholasticism: An Ecumenical Enterprise* (Grand Rapids, Mich.: Baker Academic, 2001), 11–43; Carl R. Trueman and R. S. Clark, eds., *Protestant Scholasticism: Essays in Reassessment* (Carlisle: Paternoster Press,

1999), xi–xix. See also W. J. van Asselt et al., *Inleiding in de gereformeerde scholastiek* (Zoetermeer: Boekencentrum, 1998), 18–30; Richard A. Muller, *After Calvin: Studies in the Development of a Theological Tradition* (Oxford: Oxford University Press, 2003), 25–46, 63–102.

2. Paul Oskar Kristeller, *Renaissance Thought and Its Sources*, ed. Michael Mooney (New York: Columbia University Press, 1979), 105.

3. Q. Skinner, *Visions of Politics*, vol. 1, *Regarding Method* (Cambridge: Cambridge University Press, 2002), 116–19.

4. Carl R. Trueman, "Calvin and Calvinism," in *The Cambridge Companion to John Calvin*, ed. Donald McKim, 225–244 (Cambridge: Cambridge University Press 2004), quotation on 227.

5. H. A. Oberman, *The Harvest of Medieval Theology: Gabriel Biel and Late Medieval Nominalism* (Cambridge, Mass.: Harvard University Press, 1963); H. A. Oberman, *The Dawn of the Reformation: Essays in Late Medieval and Early Reformation Thought* (Edinburgh: T. & T. Clark, 1986); David C. Steinmetz, *Luther in Context*, 2nd ed. (Grand Rapids, Mich.: Baker Academic, 2002); David C. Steinmetz, *Calvin in Context* (Oxford: Oxford University Press, 1995); R. A. Muller, *Post-Reformation Reformed Dogmatics: The Rise and the Development of Reformed Orthodoxy, ca. 1520 to ca. 1725*. vol. 1, *Prolegomena to Theology*, and vol. 2, *Holy Scripture: The Cognitive Foundation of Theology*, 2nd ed. (Grand Rapids, Mich: Baker Academic, 2003).

6. See Antonie Vos, "Reformation and Scholasticism," in *Reformation and Scholasticism*, ed. Van Asselt and Dekker, 99–119; Antoine Vos, *The Philosophy of John Duns Scotus* (Edinburgh: Edinburgh University Press, 2006). See also Andreas Beck, *Gisbertus Voetius (1589–1676): Sein Theologieverständnis und seine Gotteslehre,* Forschungen zur Kirchen- und Dogmengeschichte 92 (Göttingen: Vandenhoeck and Ruprecht, 2007).

7. L. M. de Rijk, *Middeleeuwse wijsbegeerte: Traditie en vernieuwing*, 2nd ed. (Assen: Van Gorcum, 1988), 25.

8. Muller, *Post-Reformation*, vol. 1, 447.

9. See, for example, Calvin G. Normore, "Scholasticism," in *The Cambridge Dictionary of Philosophy*, ed. R. Audi, 716–17 (Cambridge: Cambridge University Press, 1995); David Burrell, "Scholasticism," in *A New Dictionary of Christian Theology*, ed. Alan Richardson and John Bowden, 524–26 (London: SCM Press, 1983); Ulrich G. Leinsle, *Einführung in die scholastische Theologie* (Paderborn: Ferdinand Schöningh, 1995), 5–15; William J. van Asselt, "Scholasticism, Protestant," *The Dictionary of Historical Theology*, ed. Trevor A. Hart, 511–15 (Carlisle: Paternoster, 2000).

10. See, for example, W. J. van Asselt and E. Dekker, eds., *De scholastieke Voetius: Een luisteroefening aan de hand van Voetius' Disputationes Selectae* (Zoetermeer: Boekencentrum, 1995); W. J. van Asselt, "De erfenis van de gereformeerde scholastiek," *Kerk en Theologie* 47, no. 2 (1996): 126-36; W. J. van Asselt, "Studie van de gereformeerde scholastiek: Verleden en toekomst," *Nederlands Theologisch Tijdschrift* 50, no. 4 (1996): 290-312; W. J. van Asselt, *The Federal Theology of Johannes Coccejus (1603-1669)* (Leiden: Brill, 2001), 94-105.

11. H. A. Oberman, *Forerunners of the Reformation: The Shape of Late Medieval Thought Illustrated by Key Documents* (New York: Holt, Rinehart and Winston, 1966), 54-55; H. A. Oberman, *The Harvest of Medieval Theology*, 371-93. For Oberman, the question of authority in the later Middle Ages rests on differing views of tradition. In one view (what he labels "Tradition I"), scripture is identified as the unique source of revealed truth and as the sole norm for Christian doctrine, including its interpretative tradition. In the other view ("Tradition II"), tradition is more than the ongoing churchly interpretation of the biblical revelation: it contains truths handed down orally in the church from the time of the apostles but never placed in written form.

12. Muller, *Post-Reformation*, vol. 2, 51.

13. See Michael A. Mullett, *The Catholic Reformation* (New York: Routledge, 1999), 47-68. See also Robert Scharlemann, *Aquinas and Gerhard: Theological Controversy and Construction in Medieval and Protestant Scholasticism* (New Haven, Conn.: Yale University Press, 1964).

14. Bellarmine combated the Protestants in his monumental work *Disputationes de controversiis christianae fidei adversus huius temporis haereticos*, 3 vols. (Ingolstadt, 1586-1593), a work that was often reprinted and which provoked more than two hundred reactions from Reformed quarters. See Eef Dekker, "An Ecumenical Debate between Reformation and Counter-Reformation? Bellarmine and Ames on liberum arbitrium," in *Reformation and Scholasticism*, ed. van Asselt and Dekker, 141-54 (includes a bibliography on this subject).

15. For more details, see Willem van Asselt, "Scholasticism Protestant and Catholic: Medieval Sources and Methods in Seventeenth-Century Reformed Thought," in *Religious Identity and the Problem of Historical Foundation: The Foundational Character of Authoritative Sources in the History of Christianity and Judaism*, ed. Judith Frishman, Willemien Otten, and Gerard Rouwhorst, 457-70 (Leiden: Brill, 2004).

16. See Charles B. Schmitt, "Towards a Reassessment of Renaissance Aristotelianism," *History of Science* 11, no. 3 (1973): 159-73; C. B. Schmitt, *Aristotle and the Renaissance* (Cambridge, Mass.: Harvard University Press, 1983). See

also J. Platt, *Reformed Thought and Scholasticism: The Arguments for the Existence of God in Dutch Theology, 1575–1650* (Leiden: Brill, 1982); D. C. Steinmetz, "The Scholastic Calvin," in *Protestant Scholasticism*, ed. Trueman and Clark, 16–30; R. A. Muller, *Ad Fontes Argumentorum: The Sources of Reformed Theology in the Seventeenth Century*, inaugural lecture on assuming the post of visiting professor of the Belle van Zuylen Chair at the Faculty of Theology of Utrecht University (Utrecht: Utrechtse Theologische Reeks, 1999).

17. See also Trueman, "Calvin and Calvinism," 236.
18. See Muller, *Post-Reformation*, vol. 1, 53–55.
19. Kristeller, *Renaissance Thought*, 92.
20. See J. Overfield, *Humanism and Scholasticism in Late Medieval Germany* (Princeton, N.J.: Princeton University Press, 1984); M. Gielis, *Scholastiek en Humanisme: De Kritiek van de Leuvense Theoloog Jacobus Latomus op de Erasmiaanse Theologiehervorming* (Tilburg: Tilburg University Press, 1994), 1–5.
21. See Lisa Jardine, "Humanism and the Teaching of Logic," in *The Cambridge History of Later Medieval Philosophy*, ed. Norman Kretzmann, Anthony Kenny, Jan Pinborg, and Eleonore Stump, 796–807 (Cambridge: Cambridge University Press, 1982); Amy Nelson Burnett, "The Educational Roots of Reformed Scholasticism: Dialectic and Scriptural Exegesis in the Sixteenth Century," *Dutch Review of Church History* 84 (2004): 299–317.
22. Erika Rummel, *The Humanist-Scholastic Debate in the Renaissance and Reformation* (Cambridge, Mass.: Harvard University Press, 1998).
23. Kristeller, *Renaissance Thought*, 101.
24. One notable exception is R. A. Muller, *The Unaccommodated Calvin: Studies in the Foundation of a Theological Tradition* (Oxford: Oxford University Press, 2000), 75: "The assumption of a conflict between humanistic rhetoric and scholastic disputation may not apply at all to Calvin's work."
25. B. Hall, "Calvin against the Calvinists," in *John Calvin*, ed. Gervase Duffield, 19–37 (Grand Rapids, Mich.: Eerdmans, 1966).
26. See Muller, *Post-Reformation*, 1:79.
27. See Alister E. McGrath, *The Intellectual Origins of the European Reformation* (Oxford: Basil Blackwell, 1987), 6.
28. E. Dekker, *Rijker dan Midas: Vrijheid, genade en predestinatie in de theologie van Jacobus Arminius (1559–1609)* (Zoetermeer: Boekencentrum, 1993), 157–61; E. Dekker, "Was Arminius a Molinist?" *Sixteenth Century Journal* 27, no. 2 (1996): 337–52; Aza Goudriaan, *Philosophische Gotteserkenntnis bei Suárez und Descartes: im Zusammenhang mit der niederländischen reformierten Theologie und Philosophie des. 17. Jahrhunderts* (Leiden: E. J. Brill, 1999).

29. See Trueman, "Calvin and Calvinism," 227.

30. Thomas Aquinas, *Summa totius theologiae . . . in tres partes ab auctore suo distributa* (Antwerp, 1575, 1585); Gregory of Rimini, *Super Primum et Secundum sententiarum* (Venice, 1521); Henry of Ghent, *Summa quaestionum ordinariarum theologi* (Paris, 1520); Pierre D'Ailly, *Quaestiones super libros sententiarum cum quibusdam in fine adjunctis* (Strasbourg, 1490); Thomas of Strasbourg, *Commentaria in IIII libros Sententiarum* (Venice, 1564).

31. For example, the auction catalogue of Gisbert Voetius's library (sold in two parts): *Pars Prior Bibliothecae Variorum et Insignium Librorum Theologicorum et Miscellaneorum . . . D. Gisberti Voetii*, Ultrajecti, apud Guilielmum Clerck, 1677, and *Pars Posterior Bibliothecae Variorum et Insignium Librorum Theologicorum et Miscellaneorum . . . D. Gisberti Voetii*, Ultrajecti, apud Guilielmum Clerck, 1679. Cf. Sebastian Rehnman, *Divine Discourse: The Theological Methodology of John Owen* (Grand Rapids, Mich.: Baker Academic, 2002), 31–41.

32. See Andreas J. Beck, *Gisbertus Voetius (1589–1676): Sein Theologieverständnis und seine Gotteslehre* (Göttingen: Vandenhoeck und Ruprecht, 2007), 268.

33. Johannes Altenstaig, *Lexicon theologicum quo tanquam clave theologiae fores aperiuntur, et omnium fere terminorum et obscuriorum vocum, quae s. theologiae studiosos facile remorantur, etymologiae, ambiguitates, definitiones, usus, enucleate ob oculos ponuntur, & dilucide explicantur* (Coloniae Agrippinae: sumptibus Petri Henningii, bibliopolae, 1619). The last work contains an alphabetical survey of the most important scholastic definitions derived from the texts of Bonaventure, Thomas Aquinas, Duns Scotus, Gregory of Rimini, Henry of Ghent, Pierre D'Ailly, Thomas of Strasbourg, and others.

34. See D. Sinnema, "Aristotle and Early Reformed Orthodoxy: Moments of Accommodation and Antithesis," in *Christianity and the Classics: The Acceptance of a Heritage*, ed. W. E. Helleman, 119–48 (Lanham Md.: University Press of America, 1990), esp. 123–28.

35. See Richard A. Muller, "Reformation, Orthodoxy, 'Christian Aristotelianism' and the Electicism of Early Modern Philosophy," *Nederlands Archief voor Kerkgeschiedenis/Dutch Review of Church History* 81, no. 3 (2001): 306–25.

36. Quentin Skinner, *Reason and Rhetoric in the Philosophy of Hobbes* (Cambridge: Cambridge University Press, 1996), 40.

37. On the idea of authorities in scholasticism, see de Rijk, *Middeleeuwse wijsbegeerte*, 114–16.

38. Heinz Schilling, "Confessional Europe," in *Handbook of European History, 1400–1600: Late Middle Ages, Renaissance and Reformation*, eds. Thomas A. Brady Jr., Heiko A. Oberman, and James D. Tracy, vol. 2, chap. 21 (Leiden: Brill, 1994–95).

39. Heinrich Richard Schmidt, "Sozialdisziplinierung? Ein Plädoyer für das Ende des Etatismus in der Konfessionalisierungsforschung," *Historische Zeitschrift* 265, no. 3 (1997): 639–82, offers an important critical review of the entire literature on confessionalization.

8 The Changing Shape of Religious Ideas in Enlightened England

JAMES E. BRADLEY

In discussions of enlightened England, it has long been recognized that religion and religious ideas set the nation apart from its European neighbors. The serious religious convictions of major figures like Sir Isaac Newton and John Locke, the Christian antecedents of the Royal Society, and the contributions of Anglican priest and Nonconformist minister alike to science, political and economic theory, and social philosophy have all been cited to show that the "moderate" (or even "conservative") Enlightenment in England must be distinguished from its less religious continental counterparts.[1] At the very minimum, J. G. A. Pocock is certainly correct to say that "because Enlightenment became a post-Christian phenomenon, its origins must be viewed in the context provided by religion."[2] And, since both English universities were essentially arms of the national church, there was, in the words of John Gascoigne, "[a] strong institutional imperative for the clergy to come to terms with secular learning and to seek to demonstrate its moral and theological significance."[3] Equally, the Nonconformist academies of the eighteenth century became productive centers of the new learning and science. Thus the conceptual framework of "enlightenment" in England, however one defines it, is unavoidably associated with a constellation of religious concerns, whether the subject is the origins of science, the rise of heterodoxy, toleration, education, or the more complex concept of secularization.

But it is precisely the nature, or shape, of religious ideas in relation to enlightenment that is contested, and it is this debate over English religion that the present essay addresses in two main parts. First, a survey of the dominant paradigm examines four areas of current research where the prevailing view of religious ideas is now being challenged. Second, an examination of a relatively neglected area of study, the subscription controversy, gives attention to several methodological considerations that may serve to avoid the characteristic weaknesses of the dominant view.

CHALLENGES TO THE DOMINANT PARADIGM

Scholarship before the decade of the 1980s viewed English religion from the Restoration through the end of the eighteenth century largely through a single lens: religious ideas were valued insofar as they were part of a continuous, progressively unfolding, theologically liberal trajectory. The movement of creative Christian thought was seen in terms of a relatively smooth transition from the Cambridge Platonists to the Latitudinarian divines (with a radical offshoot in Deism), moving finally to Unitarianism and enlightened unbelief. Although today the notion of an uninterrupted movement toward modern atheism appears to be unavoidably Whiggish, an earlier, potent teleology seemed to impel each of these groups to progressively give up more of the Christian tradition. Heterodoxy, in the form of Arianism and Socinianism, while still religion, was a halfway house to inevitable secularization and thus a principal component of modernity. This dominant view was first articulated in the nineteenth century by Leslie Stephen in his *History of English Thought* (1876). It was given a lengthened life span by surveys of the period, especially those of G. R. Cragg, and it was further reinforced by scholarly monographs, particularly those that dealt with the so-called "rational" Nonconformists and the Commonwealthman tradition.[4]

Since the 1980s, this dominant view has been challenged in at least four areas of investigation, each of which has taken significant issue with the liberalizing thesis: the Laditudinarians, Georgian literature, Evangelicalism, and, lastly, high-Anglican and Roman Catholic thought. Nontraditional forms of religious thought such as the Deist and Freemason traditions have also contributed to the broad field of study,[5] but here we will examine only those aspects of the debate that address specifically Christian forms of thought that have sought to address and correct, or adjust, the dominant view.

The question of the coherence of the Laditudinarians as a group, and indeed, even the utility of the term itself, has recently received considerable attention.[6] For the sake of convenience, we will adopt the conventional usage here, though there is certainly nothing approximating a monolithic interpretation of this field. Several recent studies (including those of Isabel Rivers and Martin Griffin Jr.) have basically maintained the traditional, older understanding of the theology of the Latitudinarians. According to this view, the men of latitude (such as Benjamin Whichcote, John Tillotson, Edward Stillingfleet, Isaac Barrow, Edward Fowler, John Wilkins, Joseph Glanvill, Gilbert Burnet, Simon Patrick, and Thomas Tennison) argued that true religion was eminently reasonable, and according to Rivers and Griffin, they believed the essence of religion was morality. The differences between natural and revealed religion were minimized, and human nature was seen as characteristically "disposed to act well."[7] Such an understanding of the latitude men was first seriously questioned by H. R. McAdoo in 1965, and the more traditional, Christian character of their theology was clearly set forth in the surveys of Gordon Rupp and John Spurr.[8] In a full-length study of 1992, William Spellman carefully analyzed the latitudinarian views of human nature, sin, and salvation, and concluded that the same divines studied by Rivers and Griffin *were* traditional in their understanding of the limits of human reason. They did understand the serious problem of evil, Christ's divine nature and Atonement, and the character of true worship. While the Latitudinarians emphasized reason and the importance of moral behavior in this life, these emphases were built on a traditional theological foundation. In Spellman's words, their "dogged adherence to an essentially Augustinian picture of human nature" was linked to their innovative efforts to achieve a comprehensive church and to "harness the discoveries of science" to a theocentric and traditionally Christian view of the world.[9] Additional studies by Gerard Reedy, Roger Emerson, and Jeffrey Chamberlain on specific Latitudinarian clergymen similarly found these churchmen traditional in their understanding of the Atonement and positively *opposed* to rationalistic trends in religious thought.[10]

One may find parallels to this latter line of argument in recent work on Isaac Newton and his circle. Newton and Samuel Clarke, for example, are no longer universally viewed as advocates of Arianism. Studies by James Force and Thomas Pfizenmaier have found the religious thought of Newton and Clarke to be much closer to orthodox Trinitarianism than heretofore considered possible.[11] The same, more traditional theology is found in the writings of Benjamin Hoadly in two recent studies. In addition, Brian Young displays significant evidence for the Trinitarianism of the Anglican renegade Francis Blackburne. Remarkably, even the Deists themselves are currently looking more religious—according to Justin Champion—though, to be sure, hardly Christian.[12]

John Gascoigne's monograph on science, religion, and politics at the University of Cambridge concludes with a study of the late eighteenth-century thinkers Thomas Watson, William Paley, and John Hey. Gascoigne adopts the earlier interpretation of the Latitudinarians and judges that the creativity and tolerance of these men was grounded on a heterodox foundation.[13] But if the *rise* of Latitudinarianism in the studies of Spellman and others is now placed on a more traditional theological basis, the idea of a relatively smooth *denouement* of latitudinarian thought at Cambridge is also disputed. Anthony Waterman argues that Watson, Paley, and Hey were at once theologically orthodox and yet at the same time dedicated to rational inquiry and free discourse. Waterman, like Spellman, Reedy, and others, insists that to understand these writers we must take into account the various literary genres that they utilized. "It is true," writes Waterman, "that by comparison with earlier or later generations of Anglican divinity the use of liturgical and mystical language by Paley and his Cambridge contemporaries was slight. But it was not negligible and there is a difference between their didactic writing on the one hand and their homiletic or pastoral writing on the other. In the former the conceptual apparatus is stripped down to the bare minimum to sustain the argument. . . . In the latter sort of writing the traditional dogmas of the Church—incarnation, atonement, trinity—are presented inasmuch and only inasmuch, as they seem to be required by the liturgy and are consistent with Scripture."[14]

A second, related area of study in religious ideas and enlightenment is found in Georgian literature. In an essay on the religious views of five leading eighteenth-century literary figures, Gregory Scholtz argued (much along the lines of G. R. Cragg) that, in his words, the "dominant tendency" of the literature of Georgian Anglicanism was to reduce Christianity to a system of morality built on a crass appeal to self interest.[15] This article of 1989 provoked sharp responses, to my knowledge, unanswered, from two grand old men of eighteenth-century English studies: Donald Greene and Chester Chapin.[16] Addison and Steele, Swift, Johnson, Goldsmith, Young, Smart, Richardson, Fielding, Sterne (the list goes on and on) were, says Greene, "Augustinian" in theology. In fact, Greene writes, "it might be argued that the imaginative literature of no century has been more anti-Pelagian than that of eighteenth-century England."[17]

The debate seems to have touched a nerve, in part because it bears so directly on one's overall conceptualization of what is characteristic about eighteenth-century English thought. Donald Davie addressed similar concerns from the side of the English Nonconformists. In *A Gathered Church* he examined the ways in which Christian thought, and often specifically Calvinist belief, creatively informed the literature of old Dissent.[18] He examined the works of Daniel Defoe, Isaac Watts, Philip Doddridge, and Robert Hall, and then challenged anyone to maintain an image of the Enlightenment as either fundamentally irreligious or heterodox. "The important question here is very obvious," writes Davie, "and it can be posed quite simply: if the Enlightenment is to be understood as a triumph of the secular, infidel intelligence, then how can there be enlisted in its service a body of opinion and sentiment which is explicitly *Christian:* that heterogenous body of Christian belief which, because of developments peculiar to Anglo-American history, gets itself called 'Dissent'?"[19] The "articulated ideology" (E. P. Thompson) of orthodox Christianity means, according to Davie, that there is far more to eighteenth-century English thought than a journey from "unenlightened Belief" to "enlightened Unbelief."

If the eighteenth century was an age of enlightenment, it was also an age of "awakened" religion, and any effort to construe an uninterrupted march to "modernity" must come to terms with the massive international revivals of orthodox Christianity. Hence, on the one hand, Latitudinarian and leading literary figures in recent scholarship are looking more traditionally Christian, but on the other hand, traditional Christian groups are also looking more enlightened, particularly if we have Evangelicals and high-church Anglicans and Roman Catholics in view. Whereas Leslie Stephen construed English Evangelicalism as "the religious reaction" to the Enlightenment and dismissed Wesley as a man deficient in "speculative insight" and Methodism as a movement of "heat without light,"[20] in recent investigations scholars have drawn attention to the parallels between enlightenment motifs and Wesley's emphasis on free will, universal salvation, and tolerance. Already in the 1970s Bernard Semmel and W. R. Ward toyed with the implicit connections between enlightenment and eighteenth-century religious revivals.[21] Wesley's indebtedness to Locke was then sketched in a formative article by Frederick Dreyer, who took Wesley seriously as a thinker of the Enlightenment, and this line of research was immediately followed by Richard Brantley's major study on Lockean influences on Wesley's thought.[22]

And if significant evidence was accumulating for the influence of enlightenment on Wesley, there was also growing evidence for the influence of Wesley on enlightenment. Ward thought that Methodism had "done the work of enlightenment as much as resisted it," and Brantley concluded that by spreading the message of Lockean psychology, Wesley helped to assure "both depth and breadth in the Anglo-American Enlightenment."[23] Expanding the thesis beyond the confines of Wesley's own thought, David Bebbington has argued that many Evangelicals besides Wesley accepted the characteristic ideas of the Enlightenment. Evangelicalism "was itself an expression of the age of reason" in that Evangelicals owned and disseminated the traits of optimism, moderation in doctrine, pragmatism, and devotion to experiment and investigation.[24]

In the last two decades, a series of important studies has appeared on the topic of high-church Anglicanism, and several of these studies bear directly on the question of religious ideas and enlightened England. F. C. Mather's long-awaited book on Samuel Horsley, *High Church Prophet,* appeared in 1992, and it should be required reading for anyone interested in these matters. It is well to remember that Horsley's scientific investigations, his edition of Newton's works, and his brief service as secretary of the Royal Society all suggest that historians have made too facile a causal connection between Latitudinarianism and science.[25] The same associations between high-church thinkers and science were studied in an article by Anita Guerrini entitled "The Tory Newtonians: Gregory Pitcairne and Their Circle."[26] Guerrini's high-Anglican Newtonians in Edinburgh and Oxford offer evidence against any notion that eighteenth-century science was uniquely associated with Latitudinarianism.

English Roman Catholics have also been studied in relation to enlightened England. In Robert Hole's *Pulpit, Politics, and Public Order in England,* Christian thought is deftly placed in the context of politics and society, philosophical and theological developments, and the various denominations' concern for toleration and civil rights. Hole makes a convincing case that at least some eighteenth-century Catholic thinkers (Joseph Berrington, for example), while orthodox in theological terms, were radically opposed to the government's policies during the French Revolution and its aftermath. Hole is suspicious of recent "revisionists" who see a causal nexus between heresy and radicalism; Catholics were, after all, orthodox, and yet according to Hole, they wished to "subvert" the existing constitution as surely as any "infidel."[27]

Broadly speaking, then, we are now seeing so much traditional religion in what was heretofore considered enlightened, heterodox thought, and so much "enlightenment" in people who to this point were considered to be purely religious figures, that the dominant conception would seem to be in need of serious recasting. One finds so much religion in eighteenth-century England that in a recent issue of the journal *Albion* Jeremy Black gently chides the late Roy Porter for the lack of attention he gave to religion in his new survey of the British Enlightenment. And as if to indicate how embarrassingly religious the century seems to have become, Black felt it important to explain to his readers that while he was appealing for more attention to religion, he himself is not a "believer."[28]

But despite the scholarship outlined here, the older dominant paradigm of Leslie Stephen and G. R. Cragg prevails in the field of political and religious thought. Certainly the view is still dominant in part because there is some truth in it; for example, many of the most outspoken and able advocates of toleration in the latter half of the eighteenth century were Arian, Socinian, or Unitarian in belief. So, on the one hand, a great deal of understandable attention has been given to Richard Price, Joseph Priestley, and their colleagues. Indeed, the general interest in "rational" or heterodox Nonconformity is sustained programmatically by the journal *Enlightenment and Dissent*.[29] On the other hand, the challenges to the prevailing view sketched in this essay are piecemeal and they do not at this stage, even taken together, provide an overarching or compelling alternative narrative.

Secondly, the links between heterodoxy and enlightenment (or something like it) have been rearticulated of late by several leading historians, and these views *are* cast in the form of overarching narratives. J. C. D. Clark, for example, argues that England is an *ancien regime* state *sans* enlightenment. By setting aside the world of "secular bourgeois thought" Clark rejects the utility of "enlightenment" as a conceptual tool.[30] His conclusion is based principally on two arguments. First, both the Anglican-monarchical and the heretical-subversive traditions were profoundly religious (in this view, it must be observed, enlightenment is by definition secular). Second, and more importantly, Clark's thesis hinges on construing English history in terms of a single, continuous dominant tradition, and thus, while the alternative radical (enlightenment, if you will) tradition is examined, it is, in Clark's view, largely impotent until 1828–1832. The radical, heterodox cause was formulated early, says Clark, but it achieved significant victories only in 1828–1832. Why was this? Clark argues that the radical program was chiefly the cause of a small minority; in the face of hegemonic Anglicanism, it was stymied by a series of failures, and then finally, through the progressive weakening of the national church's theological underpinnings, the Anglican dike gave way.[31] In the second edition of *English Society* Clark still contends that Christological heterodoxy is the main, if not the sole, "matrix of ideological innovation."[32]

J. G. A. Pocock has argued that enlightenment in England was more religious than on the continent, yet he has come to the same conclusion on heterodoxy as Clark. Pocock wishes to underscore, in his words, "the extent to which all discourse of toleration, liberty, and enlightenment was a polemic against the orthodox theology of Christ's divinity, against the Trinity and the Incarnation." This view of the centrality of heterodoxy is important because, says Pocock, it "explains so much in the political, philosophical, theological, and historical controversies of the long eighteenth century."[33] More recently, in his study of Edward Gibbon, called *Barbarism and Religion,* Pocock characterizes enlightenment as "the Anti-Nicene consequences of a subordination of spiritual to civil authority."[34]

Recently B. W. Young has helped stanch the secularizing interpretation of eighteenth-century England by looking closely at the contributions of people like Daniel Waterland and William Warburton. He rightly insists on the deeply religious character of most eighteenth-century debates, and he also rightly, if provocatively, argues that in the eighteenth century Warburton was important, David Hume, unimportant. But Young, too, retains the older liberalizing thesis regarding heterodoxy. He accedes to the idea of a move from Latitudinarianism to Unitarianism at the end of the eighteenth century, and falls back explicitly on Leslie Stephen's contention that the intellectual party of the Church of England was "Socinian in everything but name."[35]

The writings of Clark, Pocock, and Young have done much to reaffirm the importance of Anglicanism for eighteenth-century England, and they have correctly challenged the notion of an early and pervasive secularization of English thought. Few historians have been as insistent on challenging older, anachronistic assumptions as these three scholars. Religion in its heterodox expressions, however, is given the task of explaining change at a wide variety of levels, including radical politics and toleration, and while the importance of Arianism and Unitarianism may not be doubted, their influence as an explanatory device has arguably been exaggerated. The second part of this essay will gently dissent from Clark's contention that heterodoxy was the "main matrix" of innovation and Pocock's parallel argument that "all discourse of toleration, liberty, and enlightenment" can be traced to heresy. We will investigate the single leading issue of subscription to orthodox creeds as a microcosm of the larger discussion over religion in the English Enlightenment, and since the controversy over subscription centered around the issue of Trinitarian orthodoxy in relation to the state and public order, it goes to the heart of the reputed explanatory salience of heterodoxy. This abbreviated sketch will attempt to take into account the contributions of Trinitarian thinkers, principally in the Nonconformist tradition (though the project will eventually be broadened to include low-church Anglicans as well). By addressing a single controversy, we aim to build into it some methodological safeguards that will help to sidestep some of the problems of past investigations.

THE SUBSCRIPTION CONTROVERSY

The anti-subscription movement, which sought freedom of conscience from the necessity of subscribing to human creeds and confessions, is generally construed as one aspect of enlightened thought. Since the creeds were themselves the very definition of "orthodoxy," the movement is widely viewed as one of the leading expressions of the growing appeal of heterodoxy. The standard scholarly accounts of both the Anglican and the Nonconformist movements understand the main motivation to be a progressive and rapidly expanding theological heterodoxy. Grayson Ditchfield, for example, attributes the Dissenters' movement against subscribing to the Thirty-nine Articles to "a growing theological heterodoxy" and a more confident sense of the Dissenters' legal status, while John Stephens puts all of the emphasis on heterodoxy.[36] To begin with, in order to address what seems to be an almost unavoidable teleology, any study of subscription needs to be explicitly comparative, and comparative in several ways. At a minimum, and provisionally, I propose a comparison across a broader chronological sweep than previous studies and recommend an approach that would also entail looking at authors who held different theological views.[37]

Subscription as a divisive issue emerged in the early eighteenth century, and it came to a head first among the Nonconformists. The immediate cause among both Anglicans and Nonconformists was the publication of purportedly Arian writings. Samuel Clarke, an Anglican, indirectly contributed to the debate, but it was the writings of the Dissenter James Peirce that provoked the real first crisis over subscription among the Nonconformists. At Salter's Hall Chapel in London in 1719, in a large gathering of over one hundred Nonconformist ministers, the majority (a narrow majority, to be sure) refused to subscribe their names to a document affirming belief in the Trinity, refusing, they said, not because they did not believe in the Trinity but because the act of subscribing to any human formulation of the truth would unduly bind their consciences. This act of resistance to subscription is still occasionally interpreted as evidence of the majority's sympathy for Arianism, but since the early-twentieth-century study by F. J. Powicke, the orthodoxy of the majority is undisputed.[38]

Among Nonconformists, the issue of subscribing to the Thirty-nine Articles was raised in the 1730s by Samuel Chandler, and then it was brought back to life again in 1757, this time by the Anglican William Powell, and in 1767, famously, by the publication of Francis Blackburne's *The Confessional*. The controversy over subscription among both Anglicans and Nonconformists reached the height of intensity in the period 1772–1773, with a final episode in 1779 that led to a qualified success for the Nonconformists. Subscription was particularly onerous to non-Trinitarian Anglican clergy and to all Nonconformists. In order to benefit from the provisions of the Act of Toleration of 1689, Nonconformist ministers (Presbyterians, Congregationalists, and Baptists) were required to take the oaths of allegiance and supremacy and subscribe to the declaration against popery and to the Thirty-nine Articles.[39] If Dissenting ministers failed to subscribe, they were vulnerable to severe penalties in the form of fines and even imprisonment. Dissenting tutors and schoolmasters were a distinct category from ministers, and strictly speaking, they did not fall under the protection offered by the Act of Toleration. To my knowledge the controversy has not yet been studied extensively, with all sides of the debate taken into account. Such a chronologically extended and denominationally diverse study would allow comparisons across time to identify changes in argument and discern potentially secularizing or theologically liberalizing trends. A comparative approach should allow us to settle the question whether arguments and sanctions for arguments grew more heterodox over time.

How then did leading contemporaries view this issue, and does viewing the matter through the eyes of the participants shed any light on the reigning paradigm of religion in the Enlightenment? Andrew Kippis, a leading anti-subscriptionist who was himself "inclined toward Socinianism" (DNB), was the first to recommend a comparative approach to the issue, and instead of finding an increasing heterodoxy over time, he reported a greater reliance on specifically orthodox Christology. Kippis compared the movement of the 1770s with that of the first decades of the century, and observed that at Salter's Hall in 1719 there was a narrow majority of fifty-seven ministers who opposed subscription, compared to fifty-three who favored it. All fifty-seven of the former were believers "and most of them zealous asserters of the commonly received opinions with regard to the Trinity." But now, writing in the 1770s, Kippis observed, many more Dissenters than a bare majority understood the enlarged principles of toleration. The present principles of the Dissenters, according to Kippis, stood on enlarged grounds, "and not upon scruples relative to particular articles or doctrines."

But what, precisely, were these larger grounds? "Mr. Locke's admirable Letters on Toleration," wrote Kippis, "had, no doubt, a considerable effect on the minds of thoughtful and philosophical persons. But the circumstances which much contributed to open the eyes of Dissenting Ministers, was Dr. Calamy's Introduction to the second volume of his Defense of Moderate Nonconformity [of 1703–1705]." From Calamy forward the debate between the Church of England and the Dissenters was "placed, in part, on a new footing." "It is an undoubted fact, that his [Calamy's] arguments were approved of by Mr. Locke; and Bishop Hoadly himself appears to have been enlightened by them. It is certain, at least, that he availed himself of the same method of reasoning in his subsequent writings." The "new footing" advanced by Edmund Calamy was not heterodoxy, according to Kippis, but the pivotal idea of the sole authority of Christ over his church, with the ancillary arguments of the right of private judgement and the sufficiency of scripture.[40]

Kippis's comparative approach and his thesis about the leading arguments can actually be tested by appealing to *The English Short Title Catalog*. By using the catalog, it is possible to determine the precise parameters of the debate on the Nonconformist side by identifying every treatise that was published on the subject from 1772 to 1779. The short title catalog also allows us to identify the ordination services and sermons of the authors who wrote on subscription, and it then becomes possible to establish the precise theological persuasion of the authors of these pamphlets.[41] Altogether, thirty-seven treatises were written on the subject by Nonconformists. Fifteen can be identified as traditional and

Trinitarian in theology, sixteen are by Arian or Socinian authors, three argue against dropping subscription, and the theological orientation of the remaining three cannot at present be determined.[42] Hence, there were almost as many treatises written against subscription by orthodox Trinitarians as by non-Trinitarians. Therefore, on the basis of just the number of pamphlet publications, we can safely conclude that the heterodox tradition was not dominant. In this controversy heterodox authors contributed about half of the whole, and yet in the secondary literature on the controversy, they are consistently credited with possessing the "dominant" view.[43] It is true, however, that the number of heterodox authors who wrote against subscription relative to the total number of Nonconformists is disproportionately large (that is, the heterodox make up, at best, only ten percent of the total number of Nonconformist ministers in London, and hence they were more forward in the debate than the orthodox authors). Given the penalties that heterodox believers endured under the Blasphemy Act of 1698, their disproportionate numbers are entirely congruent with what we would expect to find.

The movement against subscription, however, was largely unified. Virtually all Dissenters, both heterodox and orthodox, and representative of the Presbyterian, Congregational, and Baptist denominations, were united in their opposition to subscription and in their defense of an expanded toleration. Calvinist Samuel Stennett observed that Dissenting ministers definitely disagreed on "the peculiar doctrines of Christianity," but, he added, they were united by a general regard "to the interests of religious liberty." Stennett, who was a leader in the application to Parliament, explicitly argued that the movement did not originate in a zeal for the principles of Arians or Unitarians, but in a concern for "the interests of liberty."[44] Moreover, the arguments were the same regardless of the author's theological views: the views of the heterodox and the orthodox for abolishing subscription are indistinguishable. All Dissenters grounded their arguments for relief from subscription in what can only be called a "high" Christology. The key argument in this debate over toleration was about the location of Christ's authority, but it did not hinge, strictly speaking, on a heterodox or an orthodox view of Christ. Arian Joseph Cornish observed: "our allegiance to Christ, the only King in his Church, justifies, yea obliges us to dissent from it [the Church of England]." The claim of the Thirty-nine Articles to authority in religious matters "is a bold usurpation upon the office of Christ, the only king in his church," for such a power "belongs only to the head, which is Christ."[45] The argument was over the nature of Christ's authority and where it was located, and the debate hinged ultimately on the question of the legitimacy of separate, minority ecclesiastical polities. In short, as the Arian Caleb Fleming argued, "the rights of private judgment are the same, whether they [defenders of liberty] be Calvinists or Arminians, whether Athanasians, Arians, or Nazarenes."[46] It is therefore pivotal to distinguish between the private theological conviction of individual ministers and the uniform public Christology that Dissenters of all persuasions deployed against the establishment. The Dissenters' public Christology in its political expression was uniform and orthodox, and it functioned identically in the mouths of Arians and Trinitarians. Even if Christ's authority was privately doubted by some, the public appeal to his Lordship over conscience and the church speaks to the abiding salience of religious argument in the late eighteenth century.

The unity between orthodox and heterodox is found not only in the arguments they advanced, but in the fact that during the controversy itself the orthodox authors appealed to the heterodox and vice versa. For example, the Socinian Joshua Toulmin cited the Trinitarian Samuel Stennett and the Calvinists John Fell and Edward Hitchin in his footnotes as colleagues and like-minded advocates.[47] Finally, all groups also appealed to the same sources: the anti-Trinitarian appeal, just like the Trinitarian, drew on the same texts of Scripture, especially the passage made famous by Benjamin Hoadly, "My Kingdom is not of this world" (John 18:36).[48] Both groups refer their readers to the same secondary authorities, most frequently to John Locke and Benjamin Hoadly, with the greater deference and larger number of citations directed to Hoadly.[49] It follows, then, that in the debate over subscription, the distinction between heterodox and orthodox authors was not as important as has been supposed, and hence, among Nonconformists, heterodoxy alone certainly does not account for the movement.

To find this much emphasis on traditional religion in the form of an appeal to biblical texts and the authority of Christ in defense of universal toleration seems to call into question the assumption of an early secularization and a concomitant decrease in the importance of traditional religion. In this case, modernity cannot be equated with a decline in religious argumentation. To be sure, traditional doctrine is here being used in very untraditional ways, in that the authors aim to secularize the public and political spheres. But it is still essentially a religious consciousness that shifts ultimate questions to the personal and private realm and seeks to banish efforts to influence the conscience from the public sphere, at least insofar as governments might elect to use coercive force.

If heterodoxy does not have the explanatory force that has been attributed to it, what does account for the anti-subscription movement among Dissenters? This question leads us to a second methodological matter related to the problem of teleology, namely, the remoteness and abstraction of political and religious theory in most past accounts. Part of the reason that religion and religious ideas have been construed in a progressively liberal and secular direction is that the level of abstraction in intellectual history is often too great and tends to be suspended above local events and practices. In this respect it is noteworthy that most recent accounts of religion in early modern England that have challenged the theory of rapid and pervasive secularization have constructed their arguments on a foundation of local history.[50] Recent writings that privilege the causal force of heterodoxy seem to assume a kind of disembodied discourse that evolves at an elevated level, but at altitudes so high that they fail to touch the local community consciousness of the actual inhabitants of eighteenth-century England. The study of canonical authors and the purported shape of intellectual developments in an increasingly heterodox direction presents one picture; religious life in the context of local history often presents a very different picture. The minority social status of local congregations, reinforced in their separate and oppositionist identity by various intermittent legal wrangles, must be taken into account.

We thus need to find ways to bring congregational and local concerns into dialogue with high religious claims if we hope to understand the genuine "tendency" of religious and political thought. In other words, if we are to truly see things "their way," we must adopt an angle of vision that is wide enough to include local history and practice. The potential for a more rigorous local and statistical approach to the study of subscription exists in the form of a sizable, nationwide petition of Nonconformist ministers in favor of abolishing subscription. Circulated in 1772–1773 to nearly a thousand congregations, this petition provides us with the names of 740 pastors of Nonconformist chapels in England, arranged by county and congregation. Even heterodox authors concede that the vast majority of these ministers were orthodox.[51] Possibly the further analysis of names may allow us to make links between published pamphlets and local congregations and circumstances. The petition can also help with quantifying the heterodox/orthodox issue and put the question of the shape of religion in relation to enlightenment on a more empirical basis.

The 1772 petition from the provinces shows ministers and their congregations all across England wishing for changes in the law. Using this refocused local angle of vision, we may ask what accounts for the widespread and unified interest in toleration among Nonconformists? The sense of grievance that lay behind the movement for an expanded toleration was grounded in a much wider range of concerns than merely the subscription of ministers. The religious rituals of the Nonconformists clearly functioned to reaffirm their ideals of what was honorable and to sustain their group identity over against the competing ideals of the majority culture, and the fact that the latter was sustained by the superior power and authority of the majority, and competing, religion simply reinforced the Nonconformist's self-ascription of honor and virtue. The language of the subscription controversy is a case in point. The Dissenters strengthened their alternative world view in the language of the controversy itself. But behind and beyond the controversy was the everyday life of Nonconformists where they reasserted their commitment to these verbally constructed alternative worldviews by holding each other responsible to them through their minority religious practices, particularly at key life passages such as birth and infant baptism (and for Baptists, adult baptism), faithfully maintaining nonparochial birth and baptismal registers, weekly worship in separate chapels, ordinations (and, occasionally, dismissals) of pastors, and, finally, burial services in the grounds outside the parish boundaries. The worry over legal prosecution by overzealous Anglicans was ever present in the form of a threat, and the threat was intermittently and powerfully reinforced on some occasions in actuality. Here we will examine two practices that were clearly embedded in the local community, namely, ordination and ongoing legal prosecutions, as illustrative of the larger problem.

In the ordination of Dissenting ministers, we find a congregational and hence social and very specific local ritual that reinforced the principles of the Dissenters in relation to religious freedom. Dissenters were careful to distinguish between a confession of faith at an ordination, on the one hand, and compulsory subscription to the doctrine of the established church, "enforced by pains and penalties," on the other.[52] Joseph Jenkins was one of the Trinitarian authors who wrote against subscription; at his ordination we find the confession, made before the congregation: "I believe that Christ is alone king in his church; and that to him only of right belongs the ordering of every circumstance, relative to his worship and the discipline of his house." The Dissenting critique of the national church is here just below the surface. At the ordination of Samuel Wilton, another Trinitarian Dissenter who wrote against subscription, we have the confession that Christ is the "supreme law-giver and King in his Church."[53] Just as the choice of ministers by the congregation was an important ritual of self-government,[54] the ordination that explicitly entailed a denial of the authority of the established church was an important declaration of independence. Occasionally the defiance of the ordination ceremony was put even more forcefully: one Dissenting minister declared, "I can assure you, brother, I neither at ordination nor institution was forced to *bow my knees* before a Lord Bishop, or any other ecclesiastical superior."[55] This is the practical, local, and congregational setting in which at least one impetus to enlightenment and toleration was hammered into a formidable shape. Here an idea was imbedded in a practice, and the practice in turn reinforced and even interpreted the ideal.

A second illustration of the importance of the local setting for understanding religion in the Enlightenment is found in the practical dilemma that people in a minority culture faced on a daily basis. The prominent London ministers who wrote on behalf of such causes as the anti-subscription campaign were often involved as liaisons between local ministers and the central, London-based committee of the Dissenting Deputies, thus forging a link between national and local concerns.[56] In the five-year period leading up to the subscription campaign, the Dissenting Deputies heard eighteen cases from the local level, some taken all the way to the Court of King's Bench, two at the parliamentary level, and one from the American colonies. Of the eighteen, five had to do with the recovery of Dissenting property, principally meeting houses; three were disputes over mortuary fees and Anglican denial of burial to deceased Nonconformists in the parish churchyard; three related to the refusal to register meeting houses; two each with the taxing of meeting houses and the problems of school masters; and one each for an illegal toll on a thoroughfare to the meeting house, a refusal to marry a Baptist couple, and a riot provoked by non-Dissenters.[57] The established church collected fees from parishioners at major life passages, such as at births (in churching mothers who had recently given birth), weddings, and burials, and so it is little wonder that conflict arose precisely at the points of those life passages. But these were also those precise points at which one's religious identity was affirmed (or denied), and hence the conflict took on precise and powerfully symbolic meaning for a religious minority.

Two cases involving Dissenting schoolmasters in the period leading up to the subscription controversy illustrate the ways in which local congregational concerns became vectors of the Enlightenment. A Rev. Mr. Porter appealed to the secretary and attended the committee "in behalf of one Mr. Andrews of Royston who was cited to appear to the Visitation to be held next Tuesday at Bishop Stortford to exhibit the Licence or to take out a licence for being a Schoolmaster, and praying for advice & assistance of this committee." Even though the advice might have been friendly, and the law was clear that he had to be licenced, the request reflects uncertainty and apprehension. The committee recommended that Mr. Andrews appear at the visitation, and in their words "tell them he is a Protestant Dissenter, and must leave it to them to do as they please."[58] Here, apprehension is followed by a kind of resignation. A second case from the city of Coventry shows the ambivalence of the situation of the Dissenters' quasi-legal status. On the one hand, Dissenters were so numerous and so powerful in the borough politics of Coventry that they held the majority of the seats on the corporation and clearly dominated it. On the other hand, they were in an uncertain legal situation, as illustrated in a letter from Dr. Thomas Gibbons, one of the principal Trinitarian leaders in the subscription controversy. The minutes record a letter received from Dr. Gibbons relating to a schoolmaster near Coventry, desiring the opinion of the committee "whether the corporation in whose gift it is, might present a Dissenter."[59] Evidently the participants were thinking ahead about the appearance of such a move in the eyes of their Anglican neighbors and the possible legal consequences of a body corporate virtually appointing a Dissenting schoolmaster.

The case of the Coventry schoolmaster illustrates the ambivalent position of the Dissenters in eighteenth-century England. Protected by the Act of Toleration if they carefully fulfilled all the stipulations of registering their meeting houses and qualifying themselves before the Justices of the Peace, they lived with the constant perception of being discriminated against. Their agitation for an expanded toleration thus had two crucial and equally important components: a theoretical or theological component and a local, practical, and experiential component. The Dissenters' ideas, therefore, are most helpfully understood in the dual context of the local meeting and the local Anglican majority culture.

The importance of minority group experience in the movement toward greater religious toleration was acknowledged as early as the late eighteenth century. In 1791 the Baptist Robert Hall came to the remarkably modern sounding conclusion that the zeal of the Unitarians for freedom "cannot be imputed to any alliance between their religious and political opinions but to the conduct natural to a minority."[60] In his study of dissident religion, Max Weber reached a similar conclusion for the importance of minorities, but one which also made room for the role of doctrine. "As with toleration, so it is with the modern 'liberal' idea," writes Weber. "The religious repudiation of all human authority as idolatry of the flesh ... as it appears most strongly in the Quakers and in mitigated form in all ascetic sects, this hostility to all constituted authority from positive religious motives was the historically decisive psychological basis to freedom in the Puritan countries. No matter how high one may want to rank the historical significance of the Enlightenment, its ideals of liberty were not anchored in such positive motives, which alone would secure their persistence."[61]

Issues of social location and the self-interest of minority religious groups need to be brought into play with religious principle, and this requires finding ways to bring congregational and local concerns into dialogue with high religious claims. This survey of the subscription controversy illustrates the heightened difficulty of attributing causal force directly to heterodox ideas, and it indirectly challenges the notion that heterodoxy was a halfway house to secularization. On the one hand, Christology was important, though this essay has shown that it was a high Christology and that it functioned in political and enlightened thought through its connection with local ecclesiastical polity. In other words, the doctrine of Christ among Nonconformists, both among orthodox and heterodox, functioned to reinforce the legitimacy of a separated, free-church congregational life. Local congregational life in turn reinforced the original idea through a range of practices as diverse as Nonconformist ordinations in life and the internment of Nonconformist dead in graveyards where in death itself, in a kind of ultimate insult, Dissenters were separated from the parish church. So ideas, in this view, became embedded in congregational practice, and it is the idea-laden practice (or the practice-laden idea) that possessed social and political salience and contributed finally, if indirectly, to the English Enlightenment.

NOTES

1. Roy Porter, "The Enlightenment in England," in *The Enlightenment in National Context,* ed. Roy Porter and Mikulas Teich, 1–18 (Cambridge: Cambridge University Press, 1981); John Spurr, *The Restoration Church of England, 1646–1689* (New Haven, Conn.: Yale University Press, 1991), 385; Henry F. May, *The Enlightenment in America* (New York: Oxford University Press, 1976), 3–101, on the "moderate" English enlightenment and enlightenment *as* religion. For a broad ranging discussion of recent interpretations, see Jonathan Sheehan, "Enlightenment, Religion, and the Enigma of Secularization: A Review Essay," *American Historical Review* 108, no. 4 (2003): 1061–80.

2. John G. A. Pocock, "Clergy and Commerce: The Conservative Enlightenment in England," in *L'Età Dei Lumi, Studi Storici sul Settecento Europeo in Onore Di Franco Venturi,* vol. 1, ed. R. Ajello, E. Contese, V. Prano, 523–62 (Naples: Casa Editrice Jovene, 1985), 530.

3. John Gascoigne, *Cambridge in the Age of Enlightenment: Science, Religion and Politics from the Restoration to the French Revolution* (Cambridge: Cambridge University Press, 1989), 305.

4. Sir Leslie Stephen, *History of English Thought in the Eighteenth Century*, 3rd ed. (1902; New York: Harbinger, 1962), vol. 1, 76–77; Gerald R. Cragg, *From Puritanism to the Age of Reason* (Cambridge: Cambridge University Press, 1950); Gerald R. Cragg, *The Church in an Age of Reason* (London: Pelican, 1980); Anthony Lincoln, *Some Political and Social Ideas of English Dissent, 1763–1800* (Cambridge: Cambridge University Press, 1738), 30; Caroline Robbins, *The Eighteenth Century Commonwealthman* (Cambridge, Mass.: Harvard University Press, 1959), 335–56.

5. On the Deists, the studies of Stephen H. Daniel, Richard E. Sullivan, and J. A. I. Champion have had to be passed over. Similarly, the recent work on Freemasons by Margaret Jacob, Philip Jenkins, and John Money should be investigated in any thorough survey of religion and enlightenment.

6. Gascoigne, *Cambridge*, 4–6, and 40–51, 82–94; John Spurr, "Latitudinarianism and the Restoration Church," *The Historical Journal* 31, no. 1 (1988): 61–82.

7. Isabel Rivers, *Reason, Grace, and Sentiment: A Study of the Language of Religion and Ethics in England, 1660–1780* (Cambridge: Cambridge University Press, 1991), vol. 1, 37, 46, 67, 69–70, 73, 77, 79, 84, 87; Martin I. J. Griffin Jr., *Latitudinarianism in the Seventeenth-Century Church of England* (Leiden: E. J. Brill, 1992), 106, 133, 135.

8. H. R. McAdoo, *The Spirit of Anglicanism: A Survey of Anglican Theological Method in the Seventeenth Century* (London: Adam and Charles Black, 1965): "Their theology was orthodox and their method liberal," 158; Gordon Rupp, *Religion in England, 1688–1791* (Oxford: Clarendon Press, 1986), 29–39; John Spurr, *The Restoration Church*, 382–91. See also Donald Greene, "Latitudinarianism and Sensibility: The Genealogy of the 'Man of Feeling' Reconsidered," *Modern Philology* 75, no. 2 (1977): 154–83, at 177.

9. W. M. Spellman, *The Latitudinarians and the Church of England, 1660–1700* (Athens: University of Georgia Press, 1992), 3, 5, 6, 9.

10. Gerard Reedy, *Robert South (1634–1716): An Introduction to His Life and Sermons* (Cambridge: Cambridge University Press, 1992), examines Burnet, Stillingfleet, and Tillotson, in passing, 124, 150; Roger Emerson, "Latitudinarianism and the English Deists," in *Deism, Masonry, and the Enlightenment*, ed. J. A. Leo Lemay, 19–48 (Newark: University of Delaware Press, 1987); Jeffrey S. Chamberlain, "The Limits of Moderation in a Latitudinarian Parson, or High Church Zeal in a Low Churchman Discover'd," in *The Margins of Orthodoxy: Heterodox Writing and Cultural Response, 1660–1750*, ed. Roger D. Lund, 195–215 (Cambridge: Cambridge University Press, 1995).

11. James E. Force, "The Newtonians and Deism," in *Essays on the Context, Nature, and Influence of Isaac Newton's Theology,* ed. James E. Force and Richard H. Popkin, 43–76 (Dordrecht: Kluwer Academic Publishers, 1990); Thomas C. Pfizenmaier, "Was Isaac Newton an Arian?" *Journal of the History of Ideas* 58, no. 1 (1997): 57–80; and Thomas C. Pfizenmaier, *The Trinitarian Theology of Dr. Samuel Clarke (1675–1729): Context, Sources, and Controversy* (Leiden: E. J. Brill, 1997).

12. William Gibson, *Enlightenment Prelate: Benjamin Hoadly, 1676–1761* (Cambridge: James Clarke & Co, 2004); Guglielmo Sana, "How Heterodox was Benjamin Hoadly?" in *Religious Identities in Britain, 1660–1832,* ed. William Gibson and Robert G. Ingram, 61–79 (Aldershot: Ashgate, 2005); B. W. Young, *Religion and Enlightenment in Eighteenth-Century England: Theological Debate from Locke to Burke* (Oxford: Clarendon Press, 1998), 52; J. H. I. Champion, *The Pillars of Priestcraft Shaken: The Church of England and Its Enemies, 1660–1730* (Cambridge: Cambridge University Press, 1992).

13. Gascoigne, *Cambridge,* 239.

14. A. M. C. Waterman, "A Cambridge 'Via Media' in Late Georgian Anglicanism," *Journal of Ecclesiastical History* 42, no. 3 (1991): 419–36, at 428–29.

15. Gregory F. Scholtz, "Anglicanism in the Age of Johnson: The Doctrine of Conditional Salvation," *Eighteenth-Century Studies* 22, no. 2 (1988–89): 182–207, at 183, 188, 190, 200.

16. Donald Greene, "How 'Degraded' was Eighteenth-Century Anglicanism?" *Eighteenth-Century Studies* 24, no. 1 (1990): 93–108, and Scholtz, "Reply," in the same volume, 109–11; Chester Chapin, "The Inseparability of Faith and Works in Eighteenth-Century Anglican Thought: Reflections on a Recent Debate," *The Age of Johnson: A Scholarly Annual* 6 (1994): 283–320.

17. Greene, "How Degraded," 104. See also, Greene, "Latitudinarianism," 165, 167–68, and Donald Greene, "Augustinianism and Empiricism: A Note on Eighteenth-Century English Intellectual History," *Eighteenth-Century Studies* 1, no. 1 (1967): 33–68, at 39–41.

18. Donald Davie, *A Gathered Church: The Literature of the English Dissenting Interest, 1700–1930* (New York: Oxford University Press, 1978), 17, 19–54.

19. Donald Davie, *Dissentient Voice: Enlightenment and Christian Dissent* (Notre Dame, Ind.: University of Notre Dame Press, 1982), 23–24.

20. Stephen, *History of English Thought,* vol. 2, 348, 360–61.

21. Bernard Semmel, *The Methodist Revolution* (New York: Basic Books, 1973), 87–96; W. R. Ward, "The Relations of Enlightenment and Religious Revival in Central Europe and in the English-Speaking World," in *Reform and Reformation: England and the Continent, c1500–c1750,* ed. Derek Baker, 281–305 (Oxford: Basil Blackwell, 1979), 285.

22. Frederick Dreyer, "Faith and Experience in the Thought of John Wesley," *The American Historical Review* 88, no. 1 (1983): 12–30, at 25–26; Richard E. Brantley, *Locke, Wesley, and the Method of English Romanticism* (Gainesville: University Presses of Florida, 1984), 2, 4–5.

23. Ward, "The Relations of Enlightenment," 300. Brantley, *Locke, Wesley, and the Method*, 17, 18, and 103–28.

24. David Bebbington, *Evangelicalism in Modern Britain: A History from the 1730s to the 1980s* (London: Routledge, 1989), 53, 57–74. David Hempton provides an up-to-date overview in *Methodism: Empire of the Spirit* (New Haven, Conn.: Yale University Press, 2005), chap. 2, "Enlightenment and Enthusiasm," 32–54.

25. F. C. Mather, *High Church Prophet: Bishop Samuel Horsley (1733–1806) and the Caroline Tradition in the Later Georgian Church* (Oxford: Clarendon Press, 1992), see chap. 3, "Man of Science and Liberality," a deliberate allusion to Horsley's breadth, no doubt intended to challenge preconceptions.

26. Anita Guerrini, "The Tory Newtonians: Gregory Pitcairne and Their Circle," *Journal of British Studies* 25, no. 3 (1986): 288–311.

27. Robert Hole, *Pulpits, Politics, and Public Order in England, 1760–1832* (Cambridge: Cambridge University Press, 1989), 269, 146.

28. Jeremy Black, "Eighteenth-Century English Politics: Recent Work," *Albion* 35, no. 1 (2003): 25–52, at 34, commenting on Roy Porter, *The Creation of the Modern World: The Untold Story of the British Enlightenment* (New York and London: W. W. Norton, 2000).

29. On heterodox Dissent and political radicalism, see also Knud Haakonssen, ed., *Enlightenment and Religion: Rational Dissent in Eighteenth-Century Britain* (Cambridge: Cambridge University Press, 1996).

30. J. C. D. Clark, *Revolution and Rebellion* (Cambridge: Cambridge University Press, 1986), 110, and generally, 104–11.

31. J. C. D. Clark, *English Society, 1688–1832: Ideology, Social Structure, and Political Practice during the Ancien Regime* (Cambridge: Cambridge University Press, 1985), 278, 280. These are complex matters that require much further discussion than a short survey will allow; some elaboration of this last point, however is required. Clark sees Anglicanism as largely triumphant in the eighteenth century and gives little attention to the reality of "insubordination and disrespect" (*English Society*, 104). But Clark leaves lingering impressions of genuine change at points that are revealing. He observes that Anglicans like John Gordon, George Horne, and William Jones espoused their views in response to their *perception* of rapid social and political change (prosperity, growing literacy, increased leisure, self-interest; 214, 225, 227), and he does acknowledge in passing that the revolutionary periods elicited a "frenzied tone" from

the defenders of the Establishment (227, 230). Why, we might ask, was the tone frenzied? But these hints remain largely unexamined, and the importance of radicalism and low-church and latitudinarian Anglicanism during the eighteenth century (229, 247, 279, 289) is generally minimized.

32. J. C. D. Clark, *English Society, 1660–1832: Religion, Ideology and Politics during the Ancien Regime,* 2nd ed. (Cambridge: Cambridge University Press, 2000), 319, 368. The assumption of the Enlightenment as necessarily secular is maintained in Clark's recent essay, "Providence, Predestination and Progress, or Did the Enlightenment Fail?" *Albion* 35, no. 4 (2003): 559–89.

33. J. G. A. Pocock, "Within the Margins: The Definitions of Orthodoxy," in *The Margins of Orthodoxy,* ed. Lund, 33–53, at 36, 50, 51.

34. J. G. A. Pocock, *Barbarism and Religion: The Enlightenment of Edward Gibbon, 1737–1764* (Cambridge: Cambridge University Press, 1999), vol. 1, 297–98, and see also 8–9, 53–55, 60, 62–63, 73, 295.

35. Young, *Religion and Enlightenment,* 53.

36. For the Anglican side of the controversy, see Young, *Religion and Enlightenment,* chap. 2. For the Dissenting side, see G. M. Ditchfield, "The Subscription Issue in British Parliamentary Politics, 1772–79," *Parliamentary History* 7, no. 1 (1988): 45–80, esp. 52–53. Ditchfield places liberal Anglicans and heterodox Dissenters together on one side, and high-church Anglicans and Trinitarian Dissenters opposing them on the other, 57–59, 62, 76, note 74. Similarly, John Stephens thinks the Calvinist Trinitarians were opponents of the movement. He observes, "the orthodox were afraid that the modifications of the existing law could lead to the spread of heresy"; John Stephens, "The London Ministers and Subscription, 1772–1779," *Enlightenment and Dissent* 1 (1982): 42–71, at 43.

37. Ideally, these comparisons should cross denominational and national boundaries, extending to Ireland and possibly even to the continent, particularly the Netherlands and Switzerland. Colin Kidd has provided a provisional sketch of an international phenomenon: "Scotland's invisible Enlightenment: Subscription and Heterodoxy in the Eighteenth-century Kirk," *Records of the Scottish Church History Society* 30 (2000): 28–59, at 28–32.

38. F. J. Powicke, "The Salter's Hall Controversy," *Transactions of the Congregational Historical Society* 7 (1916–1918): 110–24. Following a minute account of the theology of the participants, Powicke concludes that the "real issue," was "liberty of interpretation" rather than orthodoxy (123).

39. Excepting Articles 34, 35, 36, and parts of 20, with the Baptists exempt from parts of 27.

40. Andrew Kippis, *A Vindication of the Protestant Dissenting Ministers, with Regard to Their Late Application to Parliament* (London, 1772), 29, 32, 36–37.

41. For example, on the Trinitarian orthodoxy of Samuel Wilton, see Philip Furneaux, *A Sermon Preached at the Ordination of Mr. Samuel Wilton* (London, 1766), 45, 47, 52. Occasionally, within the treatises on toleration themselves, we also find orthodox confessions of faith, for example, with Samuel Wilton. "To prevent any groundless suspicions, I think it proper here to premise, that upon the authority of divine revelation, I most firmly believe the true and proper Deity of the Son and Spirit, as essentially partakers of the Divine nature. The doctrine of the Trinity, I receive as the doctrine of Scripture"; Samuel Wilton, *A Review of Some of the Articles of the Church of England, to Which a Subscription is Required of Protestant Dissenting Ministers* (London, 1774), 87.

42. On the Arian or Socinian side there are, with the number of treatises (if greater than one) in parentheses: Joseph Cornish (2), Caleb Fleming, Joseph Fownes, Philip Furneaux, William Hazlitt, Andrew Kippis, John Palmer (2), Joseph Priestley, Ebenzer Radcliff (2), Joshua Toulmin, Joseph Towers, Micaiah Towgood, and David Williams. On the firmly Trinitarian side there was John Beatson, Charles Case, Benjamin Fawcett, John Fell (3), Thomas Gibbons, Joseph Jenkins, John Macgowan, James Murray, Robert Robinson, Samuel Stennett, Benjamin Wallin, and Samuel Wilton (2).

43. Ditchfield, "The Subscription Issue," refers to only three Trinitarian Dissenters (Hitchin, Stennett, and Wilton), but he does not know that Stennett and Wilton were Trinitarians and opposed subscription (54, 47). Stephens, "The London Ministers," cites the works of Stennett, Gibbons, Fell, and Wilton, but does not make the connection between the fact that they are Trinitarian and oppose subscription (44–46, 50).

44. Samuel Stennett, *A Free and Dispassionate Account of the Late Application of the Protestant Dissenting Ministers to Parliament: In a Letter to a Friend* (London, 1772), 12, 42; Wilton, *A Review of Some of the Articles*, 2. Wilton says that "it seems to have been generally, but as I hope to show, very erroneously concluded, that none but *Socinians, Arians,* and *Arminians,* can have objection to the doctrines of those articles, which we are required to subscribe"; Wilton, *A Review of Some of the Articles*, 3.

45. Joseph Cornish, *A Serious and Earnest Address to Protestant Dissenters Representing the Many and Important Principles, on Which Their Dissent from the Establishment Is Grounded* (London, 1772), 20, 17.

46. Caleb Fleming, *Religion Not the Magistrate's Province* (London, 1773), iii–iv.

47. Joshua Toulmin, *Two Letters on the Late Applications to Parliament by the Protestant Dissenting Ministers* (London, 1774), 42, 83; Philip Furneaux, *An Essay on Toleration: with a Particular View to the Late Application of the Protestant Dissenting Ministers to Parliament* (London, 1773), 1, also cites Stennett approvingly.

48. Also, "One is your master even Christ" (Matthew 23:8) and "Stand fast therefore in the liberty wherewith Christ had made us free" (Galatians 5:1). Joseph Cornish, *A Serious and Earnest Address*, title page, 10, 17, 19, 20, 24, 26; Joshua Toulmin, *Two Letters*, 1–3, 28–29, 48.

49. Caleb Fleming appeals to Hoadly (10–11, 48, 50, 60–61) and Locke (19, 35) in *Religion Not the Magistrate's Province*; so does Kippis, *A Vindication*, 1, 36–37. Israel Mauduit appeals to both Hoadly and Locke in *The Case of the Dissenting Ministers: Addressed to the Lords Spiritual and Temporal* (London, 1772), 1, 16–17; as does the orthodox Dissenter John Fell, *The Justice and Utility of the Penal Laws for the Direction of Conscience* (London, 1774), 7, 10, 46, 51–52; Benjamin Fawcett, Trinitarian, is one of the few to appeal to Locke and not Hoadly, *The Encouraging Prospect that Religion Will Be Enlarged* (Shrewsbury, 1773), 20. The heterodox Radcliff cites Hoadly at greatest length, in *Two Letters, Addressed to the Right Rev. Prelates, Who a Second Time Rejected the Dissenters' Bill* (London, 1772), 109–16, as well as Tillotson, in *A Sermon Preached to a Congregation of Protestant Dissenters, at Crutched Friars* (London, 1772), 32, but not Locke.

50. I am thinking, for example, of the studies of Albion Urdank on Nailsworth, and Mark Smith on Oldham and Saddleworth.

51. In 1772 Richard Price said he could name only eleven "preachers of Christianity on the rational plan" in London, quoted in Verner W. Crane, "The Club of Honest Whigs: Friends of Science and Liberty," *William and Mary Quarterly*, 3rd ser., 23, no. 2 (1966): 210–33 at 217; this was a tiny minority of the sixty-five Nonconformist ministers in London who signed the petition of 1772. Fawcett refers to the "calvinistical" orientation of the 850 (including both England and Wales) petitioners of 1772, *The Encouraging Prospect*, 9, and adds: "Though the generality of petitioning Dissenting ministers are calvinistical, yet they cannot consider their petition as any encouragement to doctrinal error."

52. Joseph Jenkins, *A Confession of Faith, delivered at the Ordination of Joseph Jenkins* (Shrewsbury, 1773), 3; Cornish, *A Serious and Earnest Address*, 9; Fawcett, *The Encouraging Prospect*, 11.

53. Jenkins, *A Confession of Faith*, 18; Philip Furneaux, *A Sermon Preached at the Ordination of Mr. Samuel Wilton*, 52.

54. Fawcett, *The Encouraging Prospect*, 11.

55. "A Dissenting Minister," *An Apology, and a Shield for Protestant Dissenters, in these Times of Instability and Misrepresentation: Four Letters to the Rev Mr. Newton* (London, 1784), 195.

56. Dissenting Deputies Minute book, Guildhall Library MS 3083-II, London. All subsequent references are to this manuscript. Dr. Stennett, October 11, 1771, 105; Dr. Gibbons, October 20, 1769, 54; July 31, 1770, 74; Dr. Price, December 18, 1771, 114.

57. This summary excludes all purely intramural disputes between Dissenters, which were typically about legacies. Based on a five-year survey of Dissenting Deputies Minutes, January 13, 1768 (21) to December 9, 1772 (145).

58. May 11, 1770, 67–68; July 31, 1770, 77.

59. July 31, 1770, 74. The Committee is uncertain. They wrote to Rev. Dr. Ashworth regarding it, October 12, 1770, 79, but no answer was ever recorded.

60. Robert Hall, *Christianity Consistent with the Love of Freedom* (London, 1791), 16–17.

61. Quoted in Guenther Roth's introduction to *Weber's Protestant Ethic: Origins, Evidence, Contexts*, ed. Hartmut Lehmann and Guenther Roth (Cambridge: Cambridge University Press, 1995), 21.

9 British Methodological Pointers for Writing a History of Theology in America

MARK A. NOLL

Comparing the contemporary state of Christianity in the United States to its state in the United Kingdom leads to a number of anomalies, not least concerning efforts at writing the history of religious ideas. For adherence to Christian churches and maintenance of traditional Christian practices during the last two generations, levels of participation have been much higher in the United States. But for providing insightful guidance concerning how to interpret the history of Christian ideas, as well as for offering sturdy examples that actually make such interpretations, the United Kingdom has gone much further. To be sure, this situation arises partly through inadvertence, since on one level the British contribution to better historical understanding of Christian ideas over time has come from the labors of historians of political thought whose interests in Christianity are usually incidental. On a second level, however, the British contribution to better historical understanding of Christian ideas over time is direct and intentional because it arises from self-consciously Christian historians of the missionary transmission of Christianity and its development in previously non-Christian settings.

What I would like to do in this chapter is, first, sketch the standpoint and methods of the British historians of political thought whose work provides unusually helpful pointers for those who want to study the development of religious thought. Second, I would like to describe several exemplary studies that by more or less following such methods have produced unusually effective historical results. Third, as a theological footnote, the paper ends by turning to the second group of British historians who not only study the cross-cultural transmission of Christianity but also offer theological reasons for interpreting that history the way they do. Among other benefits, their interpretations provide a reason for thinking that the standpoint and methods of the political historians may be put to use in ways that complement, rather than undercut, the Christian content of the religious ideas under consideration.

The paper must by its nature be more self-referential than is usually wise because it offers an opportunity to explain the point of view I employed in writing a book, *America's God, from Jonathan Edwards to Abraham Lincoln*,[1] which tried to describe the development of Christian theology in North America from the early eighteenth century to the mid-nineteenth century. It is also pertinent to note at the outset that my account of "British" historians depends on the widest possible flexibility for the category, "British," because it includes several historians born in the commonwealth or trained in Britain who in fact have mostly practiced their trade in the United States.

CONTEXTS, "NORMATIVE LANGUAGES," AND THE HISTORY OF THOUGHT

When writing a history of theology in America, I found great methodological help in British historians of political thought who combined two mandates as guides for their own work. The first mandate is that, for a genuine *history* of ideas, it is imperative to study those ideas in contexts provided by the social, cultural, intellectual, religious, and political circumstances of the time in which the ideas were first expressed. Political treatises may or may not make timeless contributions to describing the universal human condition, but they definitely reflect, or respond to, or interact with, the immediate environments that existed when they were written. This stress on the social contexts in which political ideas are expressed has been a major contribution of Quentin Skinner. Thus, in a recent recapitulation, Skinner has insisted that "intellectual historians will do well to focus not merely or even mainly on a canon of so-called classic texts, but rather on the place occupied by such texts in broader traditions and frameworks of thought."[2]

The second mandate is that for intellectual history it is highly useful to identify the clusters of widely shared concepts, assumptions about states of affairs, and taken-for-granted convictions that within any given society function like languages. These clusters, or languages, may or may not reflect universal or ultimate reality, but in their interactions with each other they do provide concrete information that historians can research to discover connections, influences, borrowings, and changes over time in the history of ideas. This way of defining conceptual languages has been a major contribution of J. G. A. Pocock. In one account of this approach from 1985, Pocock described these conceptual clusters as "in strict fact . . . sublanguages, idioms, and rhetorics, rather than languages in the ethnic sense . . . modes of discourse stable enough to be available for the use of more than one discussant and to present the character of games defined by a structure of rules for more than one player." The point in isolating such languages, or sublanguages, is to allow historians to see where "each will present information selectively as relevant to the conduct and character of politics, and it will encourage the definition of political problems and values in certain ways and not in others." In this view, the job of a historian is to read widely enough in the literature of a period to "recognize the diverse idioms of political discourse as they were available in the culture and at the time" being studied and so "to know what they would ordinarily have enabled that text's author to propound or 'say.'" According to Pocock, by following this approach, historians will gain confidence that research is leading to a surer grasp of what was happening in the past by showing, "(a) that diverse authors employed the same idiom and performed diverse and even contrary utterances in it, (b) that the idiom recurs in texts and contexts varying from those in which it was at first detected, and (c) that authors expressed in words their consciousness that they were employing such an idiom and developed critical and second-order languages to comment on and regulate their employment of it."[3]

For my purposes, the emphasis on contexts in which theology was written and on clusters of ideas functioning as relatively discrete languages provided helpful guidance for recording and then interpreting the shifts over time that took place within theological traditions. Of particular assistance was the contention that patterns of speech reveal the competing value systems within a society. These value systems are, again in Pocock's phrase, "for the most part sub-languages: idioms, rhetorics, ways of talking about politics, distinguishable language games of which each may have its own vocabulary, rules, preconditions and implications, tone and style." Pocock and Skinner recognize that public actors use whatever concepts or linguistic conventions exist in a given culture to move others (or persuade themselves) to take an action or accept an opinion. But they also insist that these inheritable "languages" control to some extent the perceptions and possible arguments of writers or speakers who put them to use. Skinner has described the relationship of "languages" to arguments like this: "it is evident that the nature and limits of the normative vocabulary available at any given time will also help to determine the ways in which particular questions come to be singled out and discussed. . . . [T]he problem facing an agent who wishes to legitimate what he is doing at the same time as gaining what he wants cannot simply be the instrumental problem of tailoring his normative language in order to fit his projects. It must in part be the problem of tailoring his projects in order to fit the available normative language."[4]

A particular virtue of this approach for my purposes is its ability to show how perceived realities in one sphere of existence come to influence perceived realities in other spheres. Pocock, for example, claims that in the normal course of historical development, "languages of the subpolitical activities *migrate* into the political speech" and so carry meaning from those other spheres into politics. Another virtue is awareness of the complexity at work in the use of multivalent terms because of, again in Pocock's phrase, "the inconclusive *contests for hegemony* that go on, and the complex dialectics to which they give rise, between languages which compete, and argue, with one another."[5]

An illustration of the way in which these theoretical assertions helped my efforts can be provided by an assessment of the theological writings of the Connecticut theologian Nathaniel W. Taylor during the 1820s.[6] In his position as the first professor of theology at the Yale Divinity School, Taylor's most pressing "project" was to provide a theological rationale for revival. In setting about this effort, Taylor employed several conceptual sublanguages, some that were distinctly theological and some that were borrowed from other realms of discourse beside theology. Taylor had inherited one "normative language" from New England Puritanism and especially from Jonathan Edwards, who had done so much to renovate Puritan Calvinism in the intellectual contexts of the mid-eighteenth century. This theological idiom stressed the sovereignty of God over all aspects of life, including revival.

Taylor in the 1820s, however, was living in a situation quite different from what Edwards had experienced about a century before. In Taylor's New England the Congregational churches had reluctantly given up the Puritans' church-state establishment and were now floundering as they struggled to get along with nearly complete freedom of religion. Taylor's promotion of revival was, thus, aimed not simply at converting the lost but also at reviving the Congregational churches. In that contemporary context, a "vocabulary" of republican political principle had also become "normative," especially because of its authority in justifying the War for Independence and then for providing norms to reconstitute American political life. The separation of church and state in New England had taken place, in part, when that republican vocabulary was applied to the ancient privileges of Puritan churches and, in part, when an influx of non-Congregationalists made it increasingly impractical to enforce the old Puritan establishments. With the demise of New England's historic church-state connections and also the demise of New England's traditional deference to learned ministers, a second, newer vocabulary had also acquired normative power. It was a vocabulary of common sense moral reasoning that relied for its authority on what all right-thinking humans could simply take for granted as true. This vocabulary, although at first imported from Scotland, had become normative in the United States because it provided what looked like a scientific rationale (and, therefore, a rationale not dependent on place, learned prescription, history, or tradition) for republican political innovations and also because older vocabularies of intellectual authority, which *had* relied on place, learned prescription, history, and tradition, were so thoroughly discredited by the politics of the American revolution.

When Taylor—as in a famous sermon at Yale in September 1828 entitled "Concio ad Clerum"—articulated the theological reflections that he hoped would promote an active Christian revivalism, he put to use all of the main "normative languages" at his disposal, including a vocabulary of ancient Puritan theology, but also the newer vocabularies of republican political principle and common sense moral reasoning. From our historical distance, it is apparent that he was "tailoring" his project—which was to define a theology that would inspire his listeners to become active evangelists—so as to exploit the force of his era's normative languages. In other words, he used what had become the powerful assumptions of republican politics and common sense moral reasoning to promote revivalism. Yet—and this is a critical point—as he did so the values latent in those vocabularies came to influence his theological values. So, this sermon did maintain something of the ancient Puritan theology by describing "the providential government of God as the basis of submission, confidence, and joy, under all the evils that befall his dependent creatures." But the sermon relied even more heavily on language taking its force from republican values, especially the republican value of freedom: "*Nature*" may still be the occasion of sin, but sin is always "a free act." Again, "Nor is sin [for any person], although a consequence of Adam's sin, in such a sense its consequence, as not to be a free voluntary act of his own. He sins freely, voluntarily." The sermon also made full use of the normative vocabulary carried over from common sense moral reasoning: "This preference then of some private interest, object or end, rather than God, common sense decides to be the sin of all that we call sinful action." In defining sin as free action that anyone can resist at any time upon the exertion of free will, Taylor said simply, "I appeal to human consciousness."[7]

The result of employing these different normative vocabularies was, in Pocock's phrase, a "contest for hegemony." In Taylor's case the contest was decided in favor of modern convictions. In his sermon he redefined critical doctrines from his Puritan past in order to conform to the new intellectual assumptions of his age. Thus, human free will was primarily a function of choice instead of character; and the nature of sinfulness was not primarily a generically human inheritance from Adam and Eve, but a product of personal sinning.

By paying attention to the form of words in Taylor's sermon, it is indeed possible to observe a "complex dialectic" at work in which the older language of Puritanism was "competing" or "arguing" with the newer vocabularies of republican political principle and common sense morality. Something of the older language is still visible, and so historians may conclude that Taylor retained something of the older Puritan view about the sole sovereignty of God. But for the most part the sermon puts to use the newer normative vocabularies of American political and intellectual experience to argue for the sovereignty of human beings over their own moral choices.

The advantage to be gained by studying Taylor's sermon with the methods of Skinner and Pocock lies in the scope they open up for research. For example, by comparing the actual phrases that Taylor relied upon to bear the force of his argument with the phrases that Edwards had used as lynchpins of his arguments about similar topics—and then by comparing the phrases of both theologians to phrases that had come into wide popular usage as a direct result of the American Revolution—several conclusions can be drawn. First, it is clear that change had taken place between Edwards and Taylor concerning how to understand the relationship between divine sovereignty and human responsibility. It is also clear that, when speaking about theological topics, Taylor's vocabulary included more words and concepts that owed their authority to the force they had gained by use in political debates than had been the case with Edwards. (Edwards's vocabulary, it is important to note, was not apolitical, but the political overtones in the phrases that Edwards used were relatively subdued by comparison to the weight of traditional theological overtones that pervaded his standard vocabulary.) Finally, it is clear that the newer normative vocabularies of republican politics and common sense moral reasoning became especially prominent for Taylor at those points in his sermon where he framed conclusions that differed most dramatically from what Edwards had held. By being alert to the circumstances in which Taylor preached (especially the altered relation of churches to society) and to how he put to use the normative vocabularies available to him (especially for promoting revival), we are in position to write *an intellectual and social history* of theology as it was developing in his time. By attending closely to the conceptual languages employed and how those languages were changing over time, we discover a great deal about the course of theological development.

What, of course, we are not able to say is whether Taylor's theology was correct or not, whether it reflected the way things truly stand between God and humanity. In addition, even if we can be confident that close attention to contexts and normative vocabularies gives us reasonable confidence in how the history of theological ideas had developed, we are not necessarily in position to understand or interpret the whole of this intellectual history. Besides the play of conceptual languages over against each other—in this case, Puritan, republican, and common sense—it is also possible that material factors, personal factors, or factors relating to Taylor's peculiar interests contributed to his theological expressions as well. If, however, we cannot arrive at definitive judgments about the correctness of N. W. Taylor's theology by following the methods of Skinner and Pocock, and if we cannot claim to have written an exhaustive history of Taylor's theology, we can make a pretty good claim to have understood correctly some aspects of the actual theological development to which Taylor contributed.

The main point in recommending Skinner and Pocock as methodological guides for writing the history of religious ideas is not to claim that their proposals are the only ones that facilitate historical understanding. Much the same methodological guidance is available from other perspectives where attention is focused on the interplay of contexts and ideas over times. As an example of other strategies, the work of the Princeton sociologist, Robert Wuthnow, can be cited. In particular, Wuthnow's definition of "ideology" opens up a similar doorway to the understanding of ideas in time. Wuthnow has defined ideology "as a set of utterances (verbal or written)" that "serve particularly well as methods of defining and communicating the nature of moral obligations." For Wuthnow, ideology is not primarily linguistic rationalization for more basic social, economic, or power relationships, but "a constitutive feature of social order itself," requiring "social resources to be produced and maintained," defining "moral obligations that influence the distribution of social resources," and becoming "institutionalized in organizations, in professional roles, in collective rituals, and in relation with the state." Wuthnow's "structural approach," in other words, does not account for ideology "in terms of its subjective appeal," but "emphasizes the embeddedness of ideology in social arrangements."[8] The result is a conception of ideology less as verbal legitimization for the ordering of social or economic power than as a construct, complexly active and passive at the same time, that comprehends both independent intellectual convictions and socially dependent assumptions and beliefs.

The utility of Skinner and Pocock for writing a history of theology lies not in their unique wisdom, but rather in the particularly helpful insight they provide for efforts at describing change in thought over time. Their insights also show how such histories can be constructed through diligent research into what people actually wrote, as well as through empirically testable interpretations about how those writings related to the situations in which they were written. Such an approach to the history of political discourse seemed to me equally useful for writing the history of theology in America because in early America the interplay between religious ideas and surrounding society was so often a process of actors "tailoring," or promoting, projects through the use of vocabularies enjoying power in the culture at large, even if those vocabularies had not originated in the sphere where they were being applied. In addition, this process of tailoring also involved what Pocock calls "migration." As participants tailored political or intellectual projects to fit a normative religious vocabulary, or tailored religious purposes to fit normative philosophical or political vocabularies, meanings from the religious sphere came to infuse politics, and—from the other direction—valences of politics and philosophy came to inform religious life. The latter move, as languages migrated from the broader culture into the churches, holds the key to much theological history in this period.

With this understanding of language it is possible to recognize the way in which different spheres of life played upon each other while still treating religious utterances as primarily about religion and political utterances as primarily about politics.[9] This multivalence provides for a fuller account of religion and politics than efforts at interpreting politics as religion, the more common practice of collapsing religion into politics, or the equally common attempt at portraying both religion and politics as epiphenomenal expressions of more fundamental realities.[10]

Whether I have read these British guides correctly or not, they encouraged me to undertake my work with the belief that written and spoken words could be studied fruitfully as making up conceptual "languages," that such languages corresponded, at least potentially, with real states of being, and that when languages bled into one another, they were reflecting interactions among the value systems to which the languages refer.[11]

EXEMPLARS

The guidance that Skinner and Pocock provide for how to carry out a history of political thought can rightly be regarded as a depiction of what quite a few historians have long been doing as well as an encouragement to open fresh terrain for fresh research. A self-consciously methodological vocabulary that explains how to treat ideas in relationship to each other, and ideas in relationship to their contexts, is not the critical issue, but rather the carrying out of research that actually shows how ideas relate to each and to their contexts. If historians have done this work more or less intuitively, nonetheless many have done it very well.

Thus, when I set out to write a history of theology in the early United States, I knew I could follow paths that had long since been pioneered by others. And not all of these pioneers were British.

Of many helpful predecessors, the most useful were those whose close attention to the moral freight of individual words was combined with careful observation of discourse patterns and sensitive examination of the social constraints working upon language. As an example, one of the ablest nineteenth-century summaries of English religious thought was published in 1860 by the Oxford don Mark Pattison. Its perceptive account drew heavily upon sermons—"the surest index of the prevailing religious feeling of their age"—since Pattison felt that pulpit discourses were "as necessarily bound to the preconceived notions as to the language of those whom they have to exhort."[12] The historian of early America, Edmund S. Morgan, has long exemplified a similar discernment. Morgan, for example, once ably summarized the process of "[c]hange in Christian thought" by also focusing on the use of words, the general evolution of ideas over time, and the situations in which words and ideas were employed. Shifts in religious thought, as he put it, have "usually been a matter of emphasis, of giving certain ideas a greater weight than was previously accorded them or of carrying one idea to its logical conclusion at the expense of another." But besides observing the relationship of words to each other, Morgan also has dealt shrewdly with the relation of ideas to surrounding circumstances: "a change brought about by other forces—by war or rebellion, growth or decline—may be justified and rationalized simply by a rearrangement of old ideas."[13] The potential for history written by paying attention to such matters is well illustrated by Morgan's own interpretation of the explosive combination created when the conceptual language of republicanism met the social realities of race in *American Slavery, American Freedom: The Ordeal of Colonial Virginia*;[14] or by his splendid account of how political convictions from Britain evolved in the environment of American circumstances in *Inventing the People: The Rise of Popular Sovereignty in England and America*.[15]

Other historians of intellectual culture have repeatedly demonstrated how illuminating it can be to chart the eddies, shoals, currents, and erosion patterns observable in the formal discourse of an era. Several examples are especially pertinent to the development of American theology. Bernard Bailyn has shown how the language of political liberty acted as a "contagion" in other spheres of American life during the generation after the Revolution.[16] John Murrin has helpfully depicted six competing "value systems" (or normative vocabularies) that came to bear as newly independent Americans attempted to define the society they had created.[17] And Nathan Hatch has provided a careful account of the "blurring of worlds" that occurred in American religion at the start of the nineteenth century when previously marginalized outsiders thrust themselves into the public by mingling "diverse, even contradictory sources, erasing distinctions that the polite culture of the eighteenth century had struggled to keep separate."[18] The work of such historians opened pathways for others in part because of the subjects they treated, but even more for how they treated these subjects.

Three exemplars are worth more extended attention because of how well they have actually done for the history of religious thought what Skinner and Pocock describe as possible for the history of political thought. The first is Boyd Hilton's *The Age of Atonement: The Influence of Evangelicalism on Social and Economic Thought, 1785–1865,* with its account of the intermingling of theology and political economy. Although Hilton did not set out to write a history of religious thought as such, the components of a superb history of theology were present in his work, including an account of intellectual change over time, of ideas in relationship with other ideas, and of ideas in relationship to their social settings. Hilton's main purpose was to describe how in the early nineteenth century a particular kind of moderate evangelical theology offered particularly strong support for a particular view of market economics. This moderate evangelical theology became influential partly because it was advocated by important leaders like the reformer William Wilberforce, the theological statesman Thomas Chalmers, and the capable administrator John Bird Sumner, who eventually became Archbishop of Canterbury. Even more, it became influential because its picture of how God's providence ruled over the worlds of personal religion and church order seemed to offer also a compelling account of how God ruled over the world of markets, population growth, and economic competition. It was "the age of atonement" because the moderate evangelical view of law, sin, grace, redemption, and holiness was presented so persuasively on its own terms and because those terms also seemed to explain so much about the workings of the material world. The "centerpiece" of this theology, according to Hilton, was "an 'economy of redemption' in which souls were bought in the cheapest market and sold in the dearest." For broader historical purposes, the flow of authority between parallel languages was the key—between, for example, God's law as a practical condemnation of sinfulness and bankruptcy as a practical rebuke for speculation, between common sense as applied to personal moral choices and common sense applied to the working of markets, between the atonement of Christ as demonstrating God's government of the moral universe and the workings of laissez-faire political economy as demonstrating God's government of the social universe. Hilton's summary highlights these parallel interactions as the key to understanding the era:

> Links between economic and theological thought mostly took place below the surface of consciousness, and usually have to be adduced,

with caution, from linguistic parallels (such as Chalmer's description of the earth as a "theatre of . . . competition"). The fact remains that the dominant mode of economic thought in the first half of the nineteenth century looked to religion as a powerful sanction, while religion itself, coloured as it was by moderate evangelicalism, resembled nothing so much as a type of spiritual capitalism in which, as Miss Cobbe put it, sinners acquired "a saving interest in the Blood of Jesus."[19]

The persuasiveness of Hilton's account lies primarily in his ability to link alternative theological positions to alternative understandings of political economy. Thus, in the early nineteenth century a more radical evangelicalism, which looked for the in-breaking of God's special providence in miracles and a premillennial return of Christ, supported economic principles more attuned to governmental interventions. Later, by mid-century, according to Hilton, "the age of atonement" gave way to "the age of incarnation." In this development, a shift of theological emphasis from God as static moral governor to God as expressive metaphysical actor corresponded to a shift in economic emphasis illustrated by the introduction of limited liability to mitigate the calamity of bankruptcy. By suggesting that the shift in theological emphasis, as also in economic emphasis, had something to do with both the rising power of the idea of evolution and the dramatic tragedy of the Irish famine, Hilton keeps his history focused on the interaction of ideas with other ideas and the social contexts of the era. Aspects of Hilton's argument have been helpfully critiqued, as when David Bebbington questioned whether Hilton rightly grasped evangelical teaching on the assurance of salvation. But Bebbington himself underscored the great power of Hilton's analysis by using terms similar to Pocock's in praising Hilton for being able "to disentangle the various strands of churchmanship and their associated social theories."[20]

My second example of intellectual history that did instinctively what Skinner and Pocock have outlined as possible for the history of political thought comes from Daniel Walker Howe. In writing about American political developments in the same era as Hilton's "age of atonement" Howe shared Hilton's sensitivity to the interplay of ideas and their settings.²¹ In a perceptive analysis that has stood the test of time, Howe's *Political Culture of the American Whigs* (1979) showed how the moderate Calvinism of the 1830s, especially the New Haven Theology as encompassing the activism of Lyman Beecher and the ratiocination of N. W. Taylor, paralleled the main emphases of the Whig Party that emerged as the main opposition to Andrew Jackson and the Democrats during the "second party system" from roughly 1830 to 1855. In Howe's depiction, the ultimate goal of these evangelical Calvinists was "to win souls for Christ," but along the way their efforts also helped "to create a modern capitalist social order." What Howe accurately described was the mix of elements that went into much of the era's Calvinist theology as well as its Whig political ideology: self-realization linked to care for community, personal liberty coordinated with self-discipline, "moral responsibility" existing alongside "moral conditioning"—in a word, "the balancing of freedom and control."²² Howe also showed how central to the Whig worldview were the instincts of republican political analysis and the intellectual tools of Scottish common sense philosophy.²³ In speaking specifically about the theological contribution of N. W. Taylor, Howe made the important suggestion that its objective was "to blend the activist, voluntaristic, ambitious, fluid attitudes of nineteenth-century America with the religious doctrines of the Reformation." In other words, "this meant formulating into a religious ideology the culture associated with Whiggery."²⁴

Subsequent scholarship has underscored the wisdom of Howe's analysis. Although it is still possible to debate the exact character of the connections—were New Haven theologians, for instance, interacting purposively with a political agenda or, alternatively, promoting ideas that paralleled Whig ideology as a byproduct of their more specific religious commitments?—it is increasingly clear that the ideology of the Whig Party and the worldview of many Calvinists shared a very great deal in common.²⁵ Those commonalities were highlighted, for example, in Richard Carwardine's magisterial account of antebellum religion and politics when he wrote that, where "the exponents of the new revivalism respected no lines of division between an individual's responsibilities to himself, his church, and the wider world, and recognized the importance of political engagement," the Whig Party "too, sought to harness the activist, optimistic energies of America, believing that government had a positive, participatory role to play in the development of the country's economy and in the creation of a morally well-ordered society."[26] Allen Guelzo's compelling intellectual biography of Abraham Lincoln makes much the same point when he observes that Lincoln, though himself never the member of a church, nonetheless as a dedicated Whig shared a natural "alliance with middle-class Protestant evangelicals." That alliance grew particularly from common commitments to rigorous personal morality, scrupulous self-honesty, active self-improvement, and resolute resistance to the arbitrary exercise of power.[27] Richard Carwardine has well summarized the congruence of evangelical Calvinism and Whig ideology: "If the typical Presbygationalist was a sort of spiritual engineer, the representative Whig favored a form of socioeconomic engineering."[28] What Howe, first, and then Carwardine and Guelzo have done is to describe normative languages of great social significance, to chart the struggles these normative languages entered into with other conceptual clusters, and then to assess what happened as these normative languages migrated in response to other normative languages or to answer new questions arising from altered social circumstances.

My last example of a historian who makes excellent use of the substance, though not the vocabulary, of approaches to the history of political thought outlined by Skinner and Pocock is the Canadian Marguerite Van Die. Her book, *Religion, Family, and Community in Victorian Canada: The Colbys of Carrolcraft*, traces the religious, economic, and domestic fortunes of an English-speaking family in Quebec's Eastern Townships over the last two-thirds of the nineteenth century. The book interprets a tremendous array of primary sources against the background of pertinent academic literature from four scholarly domains (Anglo- and Francophone Canada, United States, United Kingdom). It is a model study for integrating the story of one extended family and interrelated issues of broad national or regional history.[29]

Van Die's main argument is that most interpretations of religion in Victorian Canada have been, not so much incorrect, as misdirected. When historians have tried to interpret religion as a function of other developments (like the coming of commercial industrial capitalism), or as an entity in itself (as explainable only by the dynamics of evangelical revival or intellectual wrestling with new learning), or as wrapped up in a process of accommodation to rapid changes in economy and society, or as entering into a new synergism with self-conscious domestic concerns, they are in fact viewing aspects of the situation correctly. But by failing to chart what Van Die calls "the close fit . . . between socio-economic situations, the family, and Protestant religion," and by failing to note how these very interconnections supplied "meaning and form" to contemporary life, historians fail to grasp both the character of "lived religion" and its significance for broader interpretations. Van Die's attention to the warp and woof of situations—centered on the home but reaching out to encompass many other spheres—undergirds her compelling interpretations of the changing character of Victorian Methodism, the evolving relationship of Protestantism and Catholicism to politics, the moral (as well as practical) transformation of Canadian economic life, the tangled (often ironic) connections between liberal political principles and liberal evangelical religion, and much more.

The secret of Van Die's success lies, first, in the clarity with which she defines the normative languages that the Colby family put to use in describing their own lives; second, in the detailed account of how over the course of three generations these languages interacted with each other and with the conditions of the family's domestic setting; and, third, in the persuasive interpretation of how themes from various spheres migrated across cultural borders to influence the expression of normative languages in other spheres. Like Boyd Hilton, Marguerite Van Die did not set out primarily to write a history of theology. But because of her patient attention to how the Colbys put words to use in talking about their own lives, she provides a compelling account of how nineteenth-century Canadian Methodist theology moved from convictions similar to what Hilton describes as an atonement theology to what he calls an incarnational theology.

As the examples from Hilton, Howe, and Van Die suggest, it is not necessary to use the vocabulary suggested by Skinner and Pocock in order to write forceful histories that interpret intellectual developments with reference to the interplay of normative languages and the contexts in which ideas exist. Rather, what is most important is the ability to write a persuasive history growing out of extensive research into both written records and the settings in which those records were made. Such histories provide real insight into how people and their actions actually functioned in past times, as opposed to other historical approaches that sometimes reflect more from what authors know ahead of time about what must be true instead of what they find in their research to have happened.

In making this comparative judgment between history writing that illuminates, to at least some degree, developments as they actually happened and historical writing that depends, at least to considerable degree, on preconceived conclusions brought by historians to their tasks, one further parallel can be noted between history of political thought and history of religious ideas. Of course, all history writing is perspectival to some degree, and even the most doctrinaire historians can be helpful if their research is broad and deep. Yet a clear difference remains between attention to the past aimed primarily at getting the history straight and attention to the past aimed at illustrating a truth about the human condition.

Skinner and Pocock view themselves as standing between materialists (often Marxists) who treat political ideas as if they could be reduced to the struggle for social hegemony and political philosophers (sometimes following Leo Strauss) who treat political ideas as timeless contributions of descriptions of ideal states of human affairs. So too might historians of theology who pursue primarily an understanding of convictions over time be viewed as standing between two alternatives. On the one side are the equivalent of materialists who interpret religious ideas as being primarily about something else, often personal or group interests. For these historians, writing about the past presents an opportunity to explain what religious people were really saying when they talked about religious ideas. On the other side are the equivalent of political philosophers who interpret religious ideas as being primarily right or wrong. For these historians, writing about the past presents an opportunity to illustrate how unambiguous theological truth was supported or undercut by the religious ideas at work in a given era.

Historians of religious thought who follow approaches similar to the ones advocated by Skinner and Pocock should not deny that material interests influence thought. Nor should they deny the possibility of unambiguous theological truth. Yet what they can affirm is that *for the purposes of a genuine historical inquiry*—for trying to understand what ideas meant in their times and how those ideas changed over time—it is more important to understand ideas over against other ideas and over against their contexts than to reduce ideas to material interests or to assess ideas according to their ultimate truth or falsity.

To put the matter directly, by following the general principles of Skinner and Pocock, historians of theology can steer between the Scylla of unabashed dogmatic triumphalism (or dogmatic denunciation) and the Charybdis of unabashed materialist reduction. Such historians are in position, as an example, to appreciate Iain Murray's denunciation of Charles Finney's revivalistic theology as spiritually deceptive and also Paul Johnson's account of Finney's revivals in Rochester, New York, as an instance of early capitalist social control.[30] But they will also go on to assert that for an actual history of Finney's theology it will be necessary to read carefully what he wrote and to interpret that reading in light of what it could have meant in Finney's own day. Similarly, such historians may find something edifying in the host of right-wing American populists who point to the American Revolution as a distinctly Christian event, and they will certainly benefit from efforts by a host of secular historians who mostly avoid writing about the religious aspects of the Revolution. Yet they will also want to research diligently the ways that dominant traditions of theological expression and rising traditions of political speech interacted with each other, as they attempt to write a theological history of the era. For the history of theology, following such an approach holds out the prospect not only of history attuned to change over time, but also for better history as such.

THEOLOGICAL POSTSCRIPT

A final question is pertinent for Christian historians who want to use something like the methods of Skinner and Pocock to write the history of theology. That question asks if the methods of Skinner and Pocock do not amount to only a more sophisticated kind of reductionism. It arises from an awareness that in their scheme the principal query is not whether political propositions are true or false, but rather how those ideas reflect and mold other ideas, or reflect and mold projects active in the period under consideration. Skinner is aware of the force of the question, as indicated by his statement from 1998: "To many students of moral and political theory . . . the adoption of such an historical approach appeared to embody a betrayal. The value of our studies was supposed to be that of enabling us to disclose what is of perennial interest in a great sequence of classic texts. The more it was argued that these texts should be viewed as elements in a wider political discourse, whose contents change with changing circumstances, the more it seemed that our studies were being robbed of their point."[31] For Skinner the answer to his own query is that the historical methods he promotes allow individuals in the present "to acquire a self-conscious understanding of a set of concepts that we now employ unselfconsciously"[32]—and so presumably to make individuals into more self-aware and hence better citizens.

A Christian historian who studies the history of theology with something like Skinner's methods could make another kind of response. To study the history of religious ideas in relationship to other ideas and to contextual situations need not be the same as denying their potential truthfulness as accounts of how things really stand between God and humans. Rather, principles of classical Christian theology provide, if not exactly a rationale, then pointers for carrying out historical inquiry in this Skinner-esque fashion.

The first principle is well articulated by the missiologists Andrew Walls and Lamin Sanneh.[33] It is the conviction that differences among Christian traditions can be explained in terms of the incarnation of Jesus Christ. While the Son of God was incarnate in one specific time and place for the redemption of people from all times and places, Walls and Sanneh suggest that Christian faith in the Son of God has constantly been incarnated in different varieties in different cultures and at different times. The best explanation for why Christian traditions differ among themselves is that God is responsible for the diversity of human cultures, God accepts that diversity as a good thing, and God allows the Christian faith to be adapted to the shape of diverse human cultures. As God was incarnate once for all humanity in Bethlehem, so the Christian faith is incarnate repeatedly in the diverse cultures of the world. The historical implication of this reasoning follows. To study closely the connection of Christian ideas to other conceptual clusters and to the contextual situations in which they are experienced is not a naturalistic reductionism but rather an effort to record, understand, and interpret the particular circumstances in which belief in the incarnate Christ has been, so to speak, incarnated itself in particular times and places.

Another theological principle that might legitimate historical consideration of Christian theology is the doctrine of providence. In particular, orthodox theology affirms that God rules over every aspect of life and not just the spheres where explicitly theological explanations prevail. Thus, it is a heresy to fall into Manicheanism, or the fallacy that the world can be divided simply into a portion governed by God and another portion not governed by God. Against such heresy, the Christian doctrine of providence affirms that God governs all—the actions of those who know and worship him as well as the actions of those who have never heard of him, the actions directly related to the history of salvation and the actions not so related, the actions of believers and the actions of unbelievers. Instead, the proper biblical distinction is between God's general providence, which he makes known through general revelation, and God's special work of salvation, which he makes known through special revelation. Christian historians too should embrace the fullness of divine providence—as governing alike the development of agriculture in tenth-century pre-Christian China and the amazing expansion of Christianity in contemporary post-Mao China. With a full-orbed doctrine of providence in place, the study of how ideas relate to other ideas and to contexts offers the same opportunity for exploring divine providence at work as do inquiries aimed at the overtly theological interpretation of historical events.

Finally, historical work that focuses on the this-worldly connections, whether intellectual or contextual, of religious ideas can be defended with reference to the fifth-century Chalcedonian definition concerning the person of Christ. According to that definition, the incarnate Son of God was "one and the same Son, our Lord Jesus Christ: the same perfect in divinity and perfect in humanity, the same truly God and truly man . . . one and the same Christ, Son, Word, Only-begotten, acknowledged in two natures, which undergo no confusion, no change, no division, no separation; at no point was the difference between the natures taken away through the union, but rather the property of both natures is preserved and comes together in a single person and a single subsistent being; he is not parted or divided into two persons, but is one and the same only-begotten Son, God, Word, and Lord Jesus Christ."[34] This definition for Jesus Christ, the central actor in the Christian story, surely provides warrant for thinking that other, lesser realities in human history may share the quality of *concursus,* or of simultaneity, affirmed at Chalcedon.

For historical purposes, a Chalcedonian perspective means that studying the naturally occurring dimensions of Christian ideas over time is a task dignified by how the eternal Son of God took part in the temporal affairs of the created realm. In terms of Chalcedon, a believing historian may expect that important historical developments, especially where obvious spiritual realities are present, will require multiple interpretations, each true unto itself, but none entire unto itself. For *historical* interpretations of Christian ideas over time to be as illuminating as possible—for the *concursus* defined by Chalcedon to be active in historical practice—a promising way forward is research keyed to the interplay of normative languages and the connection of normative languages to their social contexts.

And so from British historians of political thought and British historians of cross-cultural missionary activity, I have found much to assist my efforts, as a Christian, in writing a contextual or social history of theology in America. Free trade may or may not be the best thing in other global domains, but for an American trying to write the history of theology it has been a great boon.

NOTES

1. Mark A. Noll, *America's God, from Jonathan Edwards to Abraham Lincoln* (New York: Oxford University Press, 2002).
2. Quentin Skinner, *Liberty Before Liberalism* (New York: Cambridge University Press, 1998), 101. For extended treatment, see the essays collected in Skinner, *Visions of Politics,* vol. 1, *Regarding Method* (Cambridge: Cambridge University Press, 2002).

3. J. G. A. Pocock, "Introduction," in *Virtue, Commerce, and History* (Cambridge: Cambridge University Press, 1985), 7–10.

4. J. G. A. Pocock, "The Concept of a Language and the *metier d'historien*," in *The Languages of Political Theory in Early-Modern Europe*, ed. Anthony Pagden, 19–38 (Cambridge: Cambridge University Press, 1987), 21; Quentin Skinner, *The Foundations of Modern Political Thought*, vol. 1, *The Renaissance* (Cambridge: Cambridge University Press, 1978), xi.

5. J. G. A. Pocock, *Politics, Language, and Time* (New York: Atheneum, 1971), 22; Pocock, communication to the editor, *William and Mary Quarterly* 45, no. 4 (Oct. 1988): 815 (emphases added). For instructive criticism of this approach, see James Tully, ed., *Meaning and Context: Quentin Skinner and His Critics* (Princeton, N.J.: Princeton University Press, 1988); John Patrick Diggins, *The Lost Soul of American Politics: Virtue, Self-Interest, and the Foundations of Liberalism* (New York: Basic Books, 1984), App. 3, "The Problem of Language," 359–65; and Melvin Richter, "Reconstructing the History of Political Languages: Pocock, Skinner, and the *Geschichtliche Grundbegriffe*," *History and Theory* 29, no. 1 (1990): 38–70.

6. These judgments are expanded *in extenso* in Noll, *America's God*, 253–329.

7. N. W. Taylor, "Concio ad Clerum" (1828), in *Theology in America*, ed. Sydney E. Ahlstrom, 213–49 (Indianapolis: Bobbs-Merrill, 1967), 249, 225n.17, 237, 229.

8. Robert Wuthnow, *Meaning and Moral Order: Explanations in Cultural Analysis* (Berkeley: University of California Press, 1987), 145, 328. Many of Wuthnow's monographs use something like this notion of "ideology" to credit both what people say they believe and the reality of circumstances shaping what they say, for example, Wuthnow, *The Restructuring of American Religion: Society and Faith since World War II* (Princeton, N.J.: Princeton University Press, 1988).

9. The indiscriminate application of Thomas Kuhn's *Structure of Scientific Revolutions* to historical reasoning has been properly criticized, for example, by David Hollinger, "T. S. Kuhn's Theory of Science and Its Implications for History," in *Paradigms and Revolutions: Appraisals and Applications of Thomas Kuhn's Philosophy of Science*, ed. Gary Gulting, 195–222 (Notre Dame, Ind.: University of Notre Dame Press, 1980). Yet Kuhn's account of scientific revolution is still useful for conceptualizing change in American religious ideas from the 1730s to the 1860s. In his terms, "normal science" (in this case Puritanism as representative of a European kind of establishmentarianism) does in fact give way to conceptual strife (populists vs. elites, Calvinists vs. Arminians vs. modified Calvinists, Methodists vs. Baptists), only to be followed by new

conventions of "normal science" (the widespread acceptance of common sense conversionist biblicism in antebellum American Protestantism).

10. Much, however, can nonetheless be gained from such interpretations of key American relationships, for example (politics as religion) Catherine L. Albanese, *Sons of the Fathers: The Civil Religion of the American Revolution* (Philadelphia: Temple University Press, 1976); (religion as politics) Alan Heimert, *Religion and the American Mind from the Great Awakening to the Revolution* (Cambridge, Mass.: Harvard University Press, 1966); and (both religion and politics as expressing more basic psychorhetorical realities) Donald Weber, *Rhetoric and History in Revolutionary New England* (New York: Oxford University Press, 1988).

11. I am pleased to thank Grant Wacker for the metaphor of languages "bleeding" into one another.

12. Mark Pattison, "Tendencies of Religious Thought in England, 1688–1750," in *Essays and Reviews*, 254–324 (London: John W. Parker & Son, 1860), 276.

13. Edmund S. Morgan, ed., *Puritan Political Ideas, 1558–1794* (Indianapolis: Bobbs-Merrill, 1965), xiii–xiv.

14. Edmund S. Morgan, *American Slavery, American Freedom: The Ordeal of Colonial Virginia* (New York: Norton, 1975).

15. Edmund S. Morgan, *Inventing the People: The Rise of Popular Sovereignty in England and America* (New York: Norton, 1988).

16. Bernard Bailyn, *The Ideological Origins of the American Revolution* (Cambridge, Mass.: Harvard University Press, 1967), 230–319.

17. John M. Murrin, "Religion and Politics in America from the First Settlements to the Civil War," in *Religion and American Politics*, ed. Mark A. Noll, 19–43 (New York: Oxford University Press, 1990), 27–28.

18. Nathan O. Hatch, *The Democratization of American Christianity* (New Haven, Conn.: Yale University Press, 1989), 34–35.

19. Boyd Hilton, *The Age of Atonement: The Influence of Evangelicalism on Social and Economic Thought, 1785–1865* (Oxford: Clarendon, 1988), 8, 297.

20. D. W. Bebbington, "Religion and Society in the Nineteenth Century," *The Historical Journal* 32, no. 4 (1989): 997–1004, at 1002 (comment on providence, 1003).

21. The next paragraphs expand Noll, *America's God*, 312–13.

22. Daniel Walker Howe, *The Political Culture of the American Whigs* (Chicago: University of Chicago Press, 1979), 158–61 (quotations, 158).

23. On the republican, or "commonwealth," values, see ibid., 8, 32, 48, 51, 63, 67, 75, 87, 91, 126, 171–73, 187, 203, 217, 231, 248, 256, 261, 290; and on the use of Scottish moral philosophy, 27–28, 32, 48, 67, 160.

24. Ibid., 159-60.

25. Helpful interrogation of Howe's conclusion is found in Douglas A. Sweeney, *Nathaniel Taylor, New Haven Theology, and the Legacy of Jonathan Edwards* (New York: Oxford University Press, 2003), 102.

26. Richard Carwardine, *Evangelicals and Politics in Antebellum America* (New Haven, Conn.: Yale University Press, 1993), 122-23.

27. Allen C. Guelzo, *Abraham Lincoln: Redeemer President* (Grand Rapids, Mich.: Eerdmans, 1999), 63, 72, 138-40, 176, 456-63.

28. Carwardine, *Evangelicals and Politics,* 123.

29. Marguerite Van Die, *Religion, Family, and Community in Victorian Canada: The Colbys of Carrollcraft* (Montreal: McGill-Queen's University Press, 2005).

30. Iain H. Murray, *Revival and Revivalism: The Making and Marring of American Evangelicalism, 1750-1858* (Edinburgh: Banner of Truth, 1994); Paul E. Johnson, *A Shopkeeper's Millennium: Society and Revivals in Rochester, New York, 1815-1837* (New York: Hill & Wang, 1978).

31. Skinner, *Liberty Before Liberalism,* 106.

32. Ibid., 110.

33. See Lamin O. Sanneh, *Translating the Message: The Missionary Impact on Culture* (Maryknoll, N.Y.: Orbis, 1989); Andrew F. Walls, *The Missionary Movement in Christian History: Studies in the Transmission of Faith* (Maryknoll, N.Y.: Orbis, 1996); Andrew F. Walls, *The Cross-Cultural Process in Christian History: Studies in the Transmission and Appropriation of Faith* (Maryknoll, N.Y.: Orbis, 2002); and Lamin O. Sanneh, *Whose Religion Is Christianity? The Gospel Beyond the West* (Grand Rapids, Mich.: Eerdmans, 2003).

34. Jaroslav Pelikan and Valerie Hotchkiss, eds., *Creeds and Confessions of Faith in the Christian Tradition* (New Haven, Conn.: Yale University Press, 2003), vol. 1, 181.

10 Intellectual History and Religion in Modern Britain

ALISTER CHAPMAN

All of the preceding chapters in this volume have dealt with societies in which religious observance was commonplace, and while some may choose to explain such observance in nonreligious terms, it is difficult to ignore. This chapter, by contrast, focuses on a society where regular religious observance has become a minority interest and where it is common to think that religion has little importance for public life and debate. Radical Islam has now put religion back on the political agenda, but for many historians of twentieth-century Britain the ruling assumption seems to be that religion can be all but ignored. And with some reason: few would contest that organized religion is less influential in Britain today than it was a century ago.

Yet diminished importance does not mean no importance; marginality does not equal irrelevance. The ongoing importance of religion in the United Kingdom since 1900 is seen in everything from the social consequences of increased religious diversity (driven largely by immigration), to the confessional dimension of Northern Irish politics, to the inspiration provided by Christian belief for politicians such as Clement Attlee and Tony Blair, to the cultural effects of continued churchgoing among a substantial minority of the population. Whatever the reasons for the willingness of many historians to ignore religion in Britain after 1900, there is therefore a need for further study to illumine the nature of religion's ongoing social significance in British society.

This chapter suggests that intellectual history can provide methodological pointers towards a better understanding of religious belief and practice in modern Britain. More specifically, intellectual history can help historians to analyze sympathetically the intellectual worlds of recent believers while also shedding light on more general cultural change. The chapter has two parts. The first will provide reflections on the difficulties facing historians wanting to study religion in apparently secular societies. The second will outline what intellectual history has to offer. The focus here is on Christianity in modern Britain, but the argument has relevance to other religions and to other countries in Europe.[1]

IN THE SHADOW OF SECULARIZATION THEORY

The dominant paradigm for understanding the religious experience of modern Europe is secularization.[2] Put simply, secularization theory argues that modernization brings with it a decline in the social significance of religion.[3] In the last thirty years, the theory has been the focus of a great deal of revisionist effort from social historians such as Jeffrey Cox, Simon Green, Hugh McLeod, Jeremy Morris, Mark Smith, and Sarah Williams, who have argued that the process was not as inevitable, nor as total, nor as early as had been maintained.[4] But this revisionist work is less pertinent for historians of late-twentieth-century Britain, for the arguments usually relate to the ongoing social significance of religion in the late nineteenth and early twentieth centuries. Indeed, Callum Brown, a prominent critic of secularization theory, has argued that Christian Britain died only in the 1960s.[5] The theory may be under attack, but the reality of the contemporary secularity of European society is rarely contested. Historians and sociologists continue to debate the matter from their differing disciplinary perspectives, but most would agree with Brown that while "[t]he *theory* of secularisation may be a myth ... *secularisation* is not."[6]

Taking on the Goliath of secularization theory, this great interpretative champion, is not part of the rubric of this chapter. Nor is pointing out chinks in its armor, which many have done before.[7] But it is important to recognize the ways in which the theory's success has created a significant problem for historians interested in Europe's recent religious past. The problem stems from the fact that secularization is the dominant master narrative by which educated people understand religion in European society. Indeed, as Jeffrey Cox has pointed out, it is really the only master narrative: it stands virtually unchallenged as an explanatory paradigm for religion in the modern world.[8] The problem is that when people encounter expressions of religious belief in twentieth- or even nineteenth-century Europe, it is easy for them to assume that such expressions reflect either disingenuousness or the last gasps of a soon to be extinct worldview. Despite the fact that sociologists such as Steve Bruce do not claim that secularization is inevitable and irreversible, that is how the concept is commonly understood.[9] Charles Taylor has written of many people's unrecognized assumptions that "religion must decline . . . because it is false . . . because it is increasingly irrelevant . . . and because religion is based on authority," and noted that such assumptions are especially common in academia.[10] Such assumptions militate against patient analysis: understanding is not required when teleology will do.[11] As Jeremy Morris put it: "The problem with secularisation arguments, on the whole, then, is not so much that they are wrong, but incomplete: they cannot describe with sufficient sensitivity what is actually going on within religious communities themselves, nor the complex way in which those communities interrelate with other social groups."[12]

The secularization paradigm has set the agenda for the bulk of research on twentieth-century British religion.[13] A good example is the attention paid to sectarian forms of religion. Some advocates of secularization theory have posited that as religion becomes more marginal, it will increasingly be expressed in sectarian forms. Thus new religious movements (NRMs) have received a good deal of attention from sociologists, as have the more historic sects such as the Jehovah's Witnesses.[14] Introductions to books by social historians such as Green, McLeod, and Smith, all of whom have significant quibbles with secularization theory, show the extent to which their work revolves around questions raised by the theory. The same is true for those writing about religion in the second half of the twentieth century. Here, a common approach has been to argue that secularization is not as pervasive as had been thought by defining religion in a noninstitutional and even a noncreedal sense and then arguing that people in the modern world are still religious, albeit in a slightly different way. Whether it is Grace Davie arguing that most Britons still believe even if they don't go to church, or Maurice Cowling suggesting that historians antipathetic to religion are religiously committed to their secularism, the argument is that religion is still significant, even if its significance is expressed in unorthodox or nontraditional ways.[15] And Callum Brown, despite his rejection of the sort of social scientific determinism associated with secularization theory, has continued to focus on the topic of religious decline.[16]

Most of these approaches to the religious history of Britain since 1945, however, either marginalize the lives of active participants in religious communities or analyze religious life in ways that such participants would find almost unrecognizable. In trying to carve out creative interpretations of religion in the modern world, they eschew or distort more mainstream religious belief and practice. Such belief and practice continue to diminish, but Britain's churches remain among the country's most popular voluntary societies, with some recent surveys putting the figure for weekly attendance at 6 percent or even higher.[17] (Even here, secularization serves to obscure the significance of ongoing religious devotion, as Cox has pointed out: instead of saying that 30 percent of Spaniards practice their faith, for example, it is common to say that "only" 30 percent of Spaniards practice their faith.)[18] And to understand Christianity's significance in recent Britain, historians need to pay patient attention to the ideas and deeds of those who have peopled these churches. If the churches are judged by their own vast ambitions, they will be adjudged to have failed, and the task will then obviously be to account for that failure.[19] But the fact that they continue to attract the allegiance of a significant minority of the population suggests an ongoing social significance that requires study apart from any narrative of decline. Belief and allegiance are more than just leftovers.[20]

To be sure, some are still interested in the lives and beliefs of people and communities in the religious mainstream. The "insider" tradition of religious history is still alive and well, with numerous books published each year by religious people, about religious people, for religious people.[21] Moreover, these people would certainly recognize themselves in what is written. But although these books present people's religious beliefs on their own terms, they usually make little attempt to relate these believers to broader cultural or intellectual changes and receive little attention outside of faith communities as a result.

All of these approaches have contributed to our understanding of the history of religion in modern Britain. Social history certainly has a great deal to offer, and a recent article by Matthew Grimley on religion and Englishness shows the promise of cultural history.[22] What is clear is that there is a growing desire to move the study of religion in modern Britain out of the shadow of secularization theory and into fresh light.[23] The rest of this chapter will suggest that further study of the intellectual aspects of Britain's recent religious past could do much to improve our understanding of this field.[24] In common with other chapters in this volume, it will argue that the work of Quentin Skinner provides particularly useful resources for historians wanting to counter both the reductionism common in a field where secularization theory holds sway and the tendency to ignore religion in twentieth-century Britain. Intellectual history can so do inasmuch as it both encourages interpretive sympathy and requires the sort of contextual study that facilitates discussion of wider social significance. Too often, those who have interpretive sympathy (most commonly those in the insider tradition) have little interest in questions of wider significance, while those who are interested in wider significance paint with such broad strokes that they fail to understand the religious people of the past on their own terms. Intellectual history offers a way out of this disjuncture.

RESOURCES FROM INTELLECTUAL HISTORY

The idea of using intellectual history to illumine the recent religious history of Britain may seem strange. A list of major religious thinkers in the twentieth century and a list of major intellectuals for the same period would not have many names in common. The classic work on religion and the intellectual history of modern Europe is Owen Chadwick's *The Secularization of the European Mind in the Nineteenth Century,* and that title sums up what is generally and on the whole rightly regarded as the trajectory of elite thought in Europe since the eighteenth century.[25]

Earlier chapters have already made clear, however, that intellectual historians are interested in more than the canonically "great" thinkers of any given era.[26] Intellectual history provides useful tools for historians wanting to understand anyone who has left written marks in history. Indeed, for the later twentieth century written remains are not even required: audio and visual recordings of sermons, interviews, and the like will do.

Intellectual history can prove useful to historians of modern British religion because of the encouragement it gives to take people's beliefs seriously on their own terms. There is a tendency to discuss religion in modern Europe simply with reference to culture, class, ethnicity, and politics. Whether it is an emphasis on communal solidarity, political allegiance, or gender roles, the influence of Durkheim lives on as belief itself is sidelined.[27] Cox has aptly summarized the problem: "There is something about the theory of secularisation that leads repeatedly to a stripping away of the legitimacy of the religious point of view of individuals in the modern world.... [I]nvoking the theory does an injustice to individuals, who should be allowed to define their own point of view."[28] Resisting temptations of this nature lies at the heart of Quentin Skinner's approach to intellectual history. On his view, good historical practice requires us to present others' ideas fairly, no matter what we may make of them ourselves. For Skinner, the historical task is "to be conceived as that of trying so far as is possible to think as our ancestors thought and to see things their way.... [W]e should recover the concepts they possessed, the distinctions they drew and the chains of reasoning they followed in their attempts to make sense of their world."[29] As it relates to his own work, Skinner is primarily concerned with challenging ahistorical accounts of key political philosophers, but the resultant distortion that he sees as characterizing the work of Leo Strauss and others is comparable to the distorted picture of religious belief given in much historical writing. In both cases, it is easy for the personal and contemporary concerns of the historian to manipulate the alterity present in the sources.

The importance of making the attempt to see things their way has been stressed throughout this volume, and it is vital for people studying religion in modern Europe. It is easy to explain away religious belief in twentieth-century Europe because the period is supposed to be secular. Admitting religious motivations in seventeenth-century Scotland is one thing, but religious motivations in twentieth-century Scotland are quite another. Yet surely interpretative sympathy should hold for all times and places. The condescension of posterity is just as bad whether the twentieth or the thirteenth century is in view. Probing the ways in which religious practice relates to political convictions or social position will provide useful insights, but statements of religious conviction must be understood first as religious-intellectual phenomena. It is a different sort of challenge from that encountered by Skinner and others who write on the early modern period and before, where understanding people's beliefs in witches and the divine right of kings are among the problematic issues. But sympathetically understanding any credal or supernatural views after Hume may be even more difficult.

It would be wrong to conclude from this that Skinner is interested merely in some independent, ethereal, intellectual realm, for Skinner sees a close link between ideas and action. Skinner has been strongly influenced by the speech-act philosophy of J. L. Austin and John Searle, and in his work on renaissance and early-modern political thought he has emphasized the importance of assessing what authors were attempting to achieve through what they wrote, what they were trying to "do with words."[30] This is an obvious corollary of the resolve to see things their way, with the focus here on the particular intentions, as opposed to beliefs, of a particular author. In his collection of articles on method, Skinner stresses that what he is most interested in recovering, and defending against critics influenced by postmodern scepticism, is the authorial intention present within texts: what we can learn about their purpose from the words they used.[31] Skinner even extends his defence of the recoverability of intention to authors' intentions for entire works.[32] In short, Skinner is interested about the power of language in society as well as the language itself.

This concern with intention offers the historian of religion another antidote to reductionism. It exhorts her to the careful study of religious texts so as to understand what their authors were attempting to achieve through writing. Texts are used as a means of understanding their authors' purposes in society. For example, careful examination of a Christian leader's writing on social involvement can give us a more sophisticated understanding of his or her reasons for involvement than mere observation of what he or she did.[33] Given the premise of secularization, such observation is likely to produce overly simple and patronizing conclusions about the person's lamentable reactionism or trendiness.[34] Social context is vital for intellectual history but the focus on individual intention means that it does not predominate—which may be an advantage in the attempt to put some space between historical inquiry and the strictures of social scientific analysis.

Skinner has gone further and argued that his approach to texts can be used to analyze intention in people's actions off the written page.[35] R. G. Collingwood may have been going too far when he suggested that all history is the history of ideas, but it is important to note the ways in which intellectual history may take us beyond close textual analysis to the examination of much broader fields of agency.[36] Significantly, this may offer a way forward for historians interested in the many religious communities where ritual is more central than creeds.

A contrast can be drawn between Skinner's confidence and postmodern approaches to history and textual interpretation, approaches that are much more skeptical about recovering authorial intention. For poststructuralist sceptics such as Jacques Derrida authorial intention in anything but the blandest sense is unrecoverable. Michel Foucault is interested in past agents' words and deeds, but he is more concerned about what they reveal about the dynamics of power in society than in what doctors, gaolers, and others understood themselves to be doing. Skinner is well aware of the challenges presented to speech-act theory by these approaches, and has dealt with them at length.[37] But other historians have been happier to adopt these more skeptical approaches. Callum Brown has welcomed the growing influence of postmodern thinking, which he believes promises ways forward for religious history by challenging the dominance of the social scientific study of religion in general and of secularization theory in particular.[38] Brown has shown the possibilities offered by such an approach in a book on Christianity and cultural discourse in Britain in which he argued that the Christian element of such discourse disappeared in the 1960s and caused *The Death of Christian Britain* (to use the title of the book). Brown is interested in personal testimony and is a noted exponent of oral history, but his emphasis on broad, social discourse and his reliance on poststructuralist philosophy pushes his analysis back toward the sort of reductionistic generalization which he is trying to avoid. The title tells its own story: speaking of the "death" of Christian Britain is too strong and too simple. Brown offers a different prescription for historians of religion in modern Europe, one which may prove attractive to social historians trying to get a handle on the overall story of religious decline, but skepticism about the recoverability of authorial intent is not conducive to the sympathetic reimagining of believers' worlds.[39] What is missing in Brown's work is attention to the particularities of the religious experience found in the extraordinary array of communities of faith in modern Britain.[40] The brush strokes are still too broad.

Intellectual history thus provides a philosophically astute model for examining people's beliefs and intentions, a model that provides safeguards against both social scientific reductionism and linguistic indeterminism. From one perspective, this is where the task of the intellectual historian ends: examining and seeking to understand the thoughts and actions of people in the past. In reality, however, history is always written with the present in mind, and some degree of translation is required if historians are to communicate with their contemporaries. Here again, Skinner provides useful resources. For him, seeing things their way does not mean simply presenting what someone else has said in all its strangeness. Seeing things their way involves delineating someone's thought in such a way that, on its own terms at least, it makes sense. Annabel Brett, one of Skinner's former students, has written that intellectual historians are interested in people's ways of speaking "as ways in which people in the past *made sense* of their world."[41] The golden rule for Skinner is that, "however bizarre the beliefs we are studying may seem to be, we must begin by trying to make the agents who accepted them appear as rational as possible."[42] The idea here is not that the historian will be able to make precise translations of different ways of thinking into ways which make sense to us—a commitment to religious uniformity, for example, is going to be very difficult for most readers to get their heads around.[43] Rather, the historian must strive to make the people concerned appear rational in their contexts, to make beliefs and actions appear plausible, and therefore comprehensible on that level at least. Indeed, it is here that modern religion presents a particularly difficult challenge, for decreasing levels of religious belief make the continued faith of some even more of a conundrum. But the determination to make people's beliefs plausible to others is essential. This is surely one of the attractions of the explanations of sociology and some forms of social history: they offer plausible, nonreligious explanations for behavior that is increasingly seen as deviant. But resorting to such explanations before attempting to present and account for people's beliefs on their own terms is making the historical task easier than it should be.

This task of cross-cultural communication presents particular challenges both to historians with religious commitments and to those with none. For the former, there is a need to acknowledge quite how strange their beliefs seem to others. It is easier to write a sympathetic account of someone with whom one by and large agrees, but the job of making such a history comprehensible to others is likely to be much harder. For the historian with little or no religious commitment, the challenge is the reverse: to avoid giving a narrative whose comprehensibility within the academic guild owes too much to oversimplification of the peculiarities of people who believe. The need is for histories that are simultaneously accounts that the people in question would recognize and stories that others can understand.

But given the reigning assumption that religion is of little importance in the recent past, will anyone be interested in such histories? A partial answer to this question lies in the recognition that the only way in which one can portray others' beliefs sympathetically and ascertain their intent with any degree of accuracy is by extremely careful attention to their context. What did other people believe? How did contemporaries see the world? What were the debates these people were entering? What threatened them? What did they want to see changed in their society? What were their peers and interlocutors pressing for? It is impossible to see things their way, to understand people's beliefs or actions without answering these questions. It is impossible to see things their way in isolation. The language in which believing people expressed themselves was shaped by everything from parliamentary debate to popular music lyrics. Insider history, then, does not really work. One can't understand, say, the social thought of Alec Vidler without reference to contemporary nonreligious thought. One can't understand intellectual trends among British Muslims without taking wider debates about immigration and education into account. And it is by paying attention to such contexts that religious history can contribute to historians' understanding of these broader intellectual, social, and political currents. Boyd Hilton's work on the relationship between evangelical and economic thought in nineteenth-century Britain is an excellent example of this.[44] Intellectual history as applied to subjects with a definite religious aspect will, if done properly, have much to say to historians working in other fields. And because of this, it offers a promising path towards understanding the nature of religion's ongoing social significance in modern Europe.

Intellectual history is certainly not the only way forward to a more satisfactory history of religion in modern Britain. Questions remain about how well methods from this subdiscipline will allow historians to explore popular religion, and the study of individuals to which intellectual history lends itself means that it may not be attractive to people who are eager for comprehensive interpretations of religion in modern Britain. But a sharper focus should be welcome after years of secularization overreach. Such focused studies may not sell as well as books that have a grand, explanatory story to tell, but intellectual history will continue to encourage its practitioners to be good hosts to their subjects, dealing with them and their writings with care and sympathy.

NOTES

I would like to thank Mark Smith and John Coffey for their comments on this chapter.

1. For the contention that Europe has its own distinctive religious experience, see G. Davie, *Europe: The Exceptional Case; Parameters of Faith in the Modern World* (London: Darton, Longman & Todd, 2002).

2. For two excellent recent summaries of the field, see C. G. Brown, "The Secularisation Decade: What the 1960s Have Done to the Study of Religious History," and J. Cox, "Master Narratives of Long-term Religious Change," in *The Decline of Christendom in Western Europe, 1750–2000*, ed. H. McLeod and W. Ustorf, 29–46 and 201–17 (Cambridge: Cambridge University Press, 2003).

3. For a good summary of the secularization theory, see S. Bruce, *God is Dead: Secularization in the West* (Oxford: Blackwell, 2002).

4. See especially: J. Cox, *The English Churches in a Secular Society: Lambeth, 1870–1930* (Oxford: Oxford University Press, 1982); S. J. D. Green, *Religion in the Age of Decline: Organisation and Experience in Industrial Yorkshire, 1870–1920* (Cambridge: Cambridge University Press, 1996); H. McLeod, *Religion and Society in England, 1850–1914* (Houndmills: Macmillan, 1996); H. McLeod, *Secularisation in Western Europe, 1848–1914* (New York: St. Martin's Press, 2000); J. N. Morris, *Religion and Urban Change: Croydon, 1840–1914* (London: Royal Historical Society, 1992); M. Smith, *Religion in Industrial Society: Oldham and Saddleworth, 1740–1865* (Oxford: Clarendon, 1994); S. C. Williams, *Religious Belief and Popular Culture in Southwark, c.1880–1939* (Oxford: Oxford University Press, 1999).

5. C. G. Brown, *The Death of Christian Britain: Understanding Secularization, 1800–2000* (London: Routledge, 2001). For criticism of the theory by Brown see ibid., esp. 10–14, and C. G. Brown, "A Revisionist Approach to Religious Change," in *Religion and Modernization: Sociologists and Historians Debate the Secularization Thesis,* ed. S. Bruce, 31–58 (Oxford: Clarendon, 1992).

6. Brown, "The Secularisation Decade," 41.

7. See the books listed in note 4, as well as C. Taylor, *A Secular Age* (Cambridge, Mass.: Belknap, 2007).

8. Cox, "Master Narratives," 207–8. See also the comments of David Hempton in *Methodism: Empire of the Spirit* (New Haven, Conn.: Yale University Press, 2005), 189. For one attempt to provide an alternative paradigm, see R. Stark and W. S. Bainbridge, *A Theory of Religion* (New York: Peter Lang, 1987).

9. See Bruce, *God is Dead,* 37–43.

10. Taylor, *A Secular Age,* 428–29.

11. Cox makes a similar point in "Master Narratives," 205.

12. J. Morris, "The Strange Death of Christian Britain: Another Look at the Secularization Debate," *The Historical Journal* 46, no. 4 (2003): 963–76, at 975.

13. The same point has been made in the introduction to *Redefining Christian Britain: Post-1945 Perspectives,* ed. J. Garnett, M. Grimley, A. Harries, W. Whyte, and S. Williams (London: SCM Press, 2007), 2–8.

14. For a useful introduction to this field, see "Sects and New Religious Movements," *Bulletin of the John Rylands University Library of Manchester* 70, no. 3 (1988): 3–240.

15. G. Davie, *Religion in Britain since 1945: Believing Without Belonging* (Oxford: Blackwell, 1994); and M. Cowling, *Religion and Public Doctrine in Modern England,* vol. 3, *Accommodations* (Cambridge: Cambridge University

Press, 2001), especially xx. For a helpful typology of some of these new approaches to religion in the modern West, see Green, *Religion*, 8–16.

16. Brown, *The Death of Christian Britain*.

17. See Tearfund, *Churchgoing in the UK: A Research Report from Tearfund on Church Attendance in the UK* (2007), available at http://www.tearfund.org/webdocs/Website/News/Final%20churchgoing%20report.pdf; and P. W. Brierley, *Pulling out of the Nosedive: A Contemporary Picture of Churchgoing; What the 2005 English Church Census Reveals* (London: Christian Research, 2006).

18. Cox, "Master Narratives," 207.

19. On the danger of judging churches by their own lofty standards, see Cox, *The English Churches*, 265.

20. For an example of a general history that treats religion in twentieth-century Britain in this way, see P. Clarke, *Hope and Glory: Britain, 1900–2000*, 2nd ed. (London: Penguin, 2004), 159–66, especially 160.

21. For further comment on such an approach to religious history, see G. Wacker, "Understanding the Past, Using the Past: Reflections on Two Approaches to History," in *Religious Advocacy and American History*, ed. B. Kuklick and D. G. Hart, 159–78 (Grand Rapids, Mich.: Eerdmans, 1997), 169–70.

22. M. Grimley, "The Religion of Englishness: Puritanism, Providentialism, and 'National Character,' 1918–1945," *Journal of British Studies* 46, no. 4 (2007): 884–906.

23. See *Redefining Christian Britain*, ed. Garnett et al.

24. Compare the comments of Hugh McLeod on religion in Victorian Britain, where he states the need to make greater use of the history of ideas in McLeod, "Varieties of Victorian Belief," *Journal of Modern History* 64, no. 2 (1992): 321–37, at 337. The editors of *Redefining Christian Britain*, ed. Garnett et al., make the same point in their introduction, 2.

25. O. Chadwick, *The Secularization of the European Mind in the Nineteenth Century* (Cambridge: Cambridge University Press, 1975).

26. Cf. A. Brett, "What is Intellectual History Now?" in *What is History Now?* ed. D. Cannadine, 113–31 (Houndmills: Palgrave Macmillan, 2002), 114–15, 118.

27. Thomas Kselman has made the important point that Durkheim's positivistic followers were often much more reductionistic than Durkheim himself. See T. Kselman, "Introduction," in *Belief in History: Innovative Approaches to European and American Religion* ed. T. Kselman, 1–15 (Notre Dame, Ind.: University of Notre Dame Press, 1991), 3–4.

28. Cox, "Master Narratives," 204–5.

29. Q. Skinner, *Visions of Politics*, vol. 1, *Regarding Method* (Cambridge: Cambridge University Press, 2002), 47.

30. Ibid., 90–102.

31. Ibid., 97–101.

32. Ibid., 83.

33. For an example of this approach, see chapter 7 of A. C. S. Chapman, "John R. W. Stott and English Evangelicalism, 1938–84" (PhD diss., University of Cambridge, 2004).

34. See for example D. C. Anderson, ed., *The Kindness that Kills: The Churches' Simplistic Response to Complex Social Issues* (London: SPCK, 1984).

35. Skinner, *Visions of Politics,* vol. 1, 83, 134–36.

36. See the discussion in Brett, "What is Intellectual History Now?" 115.

37. Skinner, *Visions of Politics,* vol. 1, 90–127.

38. Brown, "The Secularisation Decade," 38–41. See also Brown, *The Death of Christian Britain,* 10–14.

39. For a critique of Brown, *The Death of Christian Britain,* which accuses Brown of over-simplification, see Morris, "The Strange Death," 968–76.

40. I am indebted to Mark Smith for his comments on this point.

41. Brett, "What is Intellectual History Now?" 127. Italics in the original.

42. Skinner, *Visions of Politics,* vol. 1, 40.

43. Ibid., 47.

44. B. Hilton, *The Age of Atonement: The Influence of Evangelicalism on Social and Economic Thought, 1785–1863* (Oxford: Clarendon, 1988).

11 Response: The History of Ideas and the Study of Religion

DAVID W. BEBBINGTON

The character of this chapter is largely determined by its role as a response to the others contained in this volume. Responding is a dangerous business. It requires trespassing on alien territory, and so carries the risk of misrepresenting subjects where specialist expertise is properly needed. Perhaps all that can be done is to beg for understanding, offering the standard excuse of the historian that most topics are "not my area." Responding also entails being derivative, and so of submitting material that is secondhand and unoriginal. The defence on this score probably has to be that repetition of a telling point can be a worthwhile exercise. And any response, since it necessarily has to be as much a survey as an argument, risks falling into the trap of making unguarded assertions. The wisest justification here is possibly that some commentary, however inadequately supported by carefully crafted reasoning, is better than none. The reader might like to bear these cautions in mind while exploring in this chapter some of the central issues raised, implicitly as well as explicitly, in the book as a whole.

How, contributors to the volume have asked, should we apply the techniques of the history of ideas to the study of religion? It will be useful to divide this synoptic discussion of that question into three sections. First there is a catalogue of general issues surrounding the examination of religious ideas in the past. Next there is engagement, from the standpoint of students of religion, with the thought of Quentin Skinner about the application of the method he recommends for the history of ideas to their subject matter. Finally there is an attempt to consider how the history of religious ideas can fruitfully move beyond the Skinnerian model.

GENERAL ISSUES

The general issues encountered in the history of religious ideas may begin with the problem of skepticism. There is a radical epistemological critique of any claim to possess knowledge about the ideas of our ancestors. The French Pyrrhonists of the late seventeenth and early eighteenth centuries were already questioning whether history, by contrast with the emerging natural sciences, could gain any assured information about the past. In our own day postmodernist theorists pose a similar challenge. The past is inaccessible, they urge, because we do not live in it. We may write what we like to call history if we choose, but the result will be no more than historical fiction. History, according to the French cultural theorist Roland Barthes, is "an inscription on the past pretending to be a likeness of it."[1] Keith Jenkins is one of those who adopts this point of view, contending that history is a species of ideology, a construct arising from historians' personalities rather than from any evidence.[2] Brad Gregory, however, has suggested in this volume that this epistemological approach undermines not only historical knowledge but all knowledge. If we cannot understand the ideas of agents in the past, we cannot understand those of our contemporaries, and that claim is either trivial or false.[3] Postmodernist premises, furthermore, are highly questionable, going back to the supposition shared by Friedrich Nietzsche and Ferdinand de Saussure that there is an unpassable gulf between language and reality. The words we use, on their account, do not capture anything of the external world. There is much room for doubt, however, about whether language is so utterly impotent, since it suffices human beings for everyday life. If there is some sense in which language grasps the realities of the contemporary world, there is, in principle, no reason to doubt that it can also gain some knowledge of ideas in the past. The problem of skepticism as a barrier to the historical enterprise of studying religious ideas may be set aside.

A second problem is that of reductionism. Historians have been adept at treating religious ideas as though they were really something else. The sacred, on this interpretation, is a mask for the secular. Christopher Hill, for example, argued, particularly in his earlier oeuvre, that Puritanism represented the rising bourgeoisie of the seventeenth century. Puritan literature could therefore be quarried for passages that revealed the alignment of the movement with progressive economic interests.[4] Although Hill was remarkably successful in discovering such extracts, he was definitely aiming to study Puritan ideas as an expression of something conceived to be deeper. His Marxist views induced him to see the intellectual dimension of religion as a product of the fundamental economic processes that determined the course of history. It is not only Marxists, however, who have classified religious ideas as something that needs to be reduced to something else. Anna Sapir Abulafia points out in her contribution to this book that according to Gavin Langmuir the Jewish-Christian debates of the middle ages expressed a form of nonrational thinking about preserving identity. On this reading, the medieval debates were not, as the participants supposed, about the truth claims of the two faiths, but about irrationalities that were a consequence of suppressing rational doubts. That interpretation, however, is to misrepresent a society that was marked by striking advances in the power attributed to reason.[5] Such reductionism is in any case problematic. Quentin Skinner has argued that an account of the words of historical agents should be subject to the test of acceptability to the people concerned. Only if the agents are content that their intentions have not been misrepresented can the account stand. That is part of what is meant by the obligation "to see things their way."[6] An objection to that case might be that an outsider can sometimes appreciate the significance of an agent's words better, for example, by knowing about the next stage of a debate. The onlooker sees more of the game. Howard Hotson's response to that contention, however, is that the historian must always start with the point of view of the agent, even if subsequently other approaches allow a further interpretation to be added.[7] That principle should be sufficient to guarantee that what people in the past conceived as religious discourse is not misrepresented as something entirely different.

Thirdly, there is the problem of prejudice. Unlike the two previous considerations, this is a difficulty of practice rather than of principle. Writers of history can be blinded by their polemical purposes. Prejudice has often presented formidable obstacles to authentic retrieval of the religious ideas of the past. Denominational preferences have traditionally shaped Christian history, even when the aim, as in Gottfried Arnold's *Impartial History of Churches and Heretics* (1699–1700), was to adopt an undenominational stance. His book was anything but impartial, a celebration of exponents of personal piety at the expense of their opponents. Similarly Richard Muller's chapter in this volume illustrates how Catholic and Protestant annalists alike were so eager to stress the importance of the year 1517 that they exaggerated the intellectual break it represented, distorting the historiography of the period.[8] Yet bias is by no means insurmountable, for it can be superseded by conscientious scrutiny of the available evidence. In the case of the interpretation of 1517, more recent work has shown that there were greater continuities between the medieval period and the subsequent age of Reformation than earlier confessional historians were willing to concede. Bias, which may sometimes actually enhance a historian's perception by fostering empathy, is in any case not an immutable phenomenon. Just as others can draw attention to evidence that has previously been neglected, the point of view of particular historians can be modified over time in the light of their own fresh discoveries. Although there are problems for the understanding of religious ideas arising from the presuppositions of their investigators, they do not pose absolute barriers to understanding.

A fourth reason for dismissing the venture of exploring the thought of religious folk in the past is the apparent triviality of the exercise. This consideration might not loom large in the minds of committed practitioners of the discipline, but for many others it is probably the most serious objection to the history of religious ideas. The pursuit is often treated as mere antiquarianism, without relevance to the contemporary world. It is highly significant that over the past forty years the number of established chairs of ecclesiastical history in Britain has dwindled from ten to three—and at the time of writing, two of those were being kept vacant so that the university concerned, rather like the crown in the Middle Ages enjoying the revenues of vacant sees, could save money. The academy clearly does not rank church history among its priorities. Nor do many contemporary religious people. Christian bookshops, with a few honorable exceptions, are notably thin in their stock of church history. Theological colleges commonly allocate the history of subdisciplines such as ethics or apologetics to their contemporary practitioners. The notion that specialist skills are required for the appreciation of the significance of past contributions does not seem to occur to those responsible for this state of affairs. But how can Kant be approached without some sense of his Enlightenment context? And how can Justin Martyr be grasped without an awareness of neoplatonism? The charge of triviality, however patently absurd it might appear to historians of religious thought, is one that needs to be strongly rebutted.

Fifthly, there is the problem of the present. It is sometimes held that we are restricted to understanding the past in our own terms. Our inquiries are initiated by questions that are provoked by personal experience, and we cater for readers whose interests are conditioned by passing contemporary fashions. In the end, on this view, historians purvey not an authentic grasp of truth but a subjective view of reality derived from their own day. The remoteness of eras when people fought wars to vindicate the gospel of the prince of peace or supposed a whole people to have become Christian because their king received baptism can indeed baffle a historian holding more recent assumptions. Yet this obstacle to empathy does not, Brad Gregory holds, rule out an understanding of people with religious motivation in the past. The ideas of the sixteenth-century Mennonite Jacob de Roore, though strange in some respects, nevertheless concerned doctrinal preoccupations that are still intelligible. There is sufficient similarity to ideas with which we are familiar, Gregory insists, to allow authentic reproduction of past thought-worlds.[9] The otherness of the past does not prevent its sympathetic reconstruction.

Sixth on the list of general difficulties is the problem of distortion. Willem van Asselt argues that Reformed scholasticism has been seriously misrepresented in the secondary literature. It has been characterized as being at odds with the original Reformers, Luther and Calvin, as regressive in the sense that it harked back to medieval models, as static, antihumanist, and Aristotelian. None of these ways of describing the scholasticism of the Reformed world is valid.[10] Likewise Howard Hotson shows how social scientific models have distorted rather than illuminated millenarianism.[11] In this case the remedy may lie in dropping a theoretical framework that patently underplays or misrepresents the intellectual content of millenarianism, but a wider issue is raised. Are we bound to distort the past in some way? Or as historians in successive generations examine the phenomena of the past, is there a growth of understanding over time? In surveying the representations of sixteenth-century controversies in subsequent ages, Richard Muller points out that the concept of "the Reformation in Germany" is a construct of the era of the modern nation-state.[12] That view is less an advance in understanding than a distortion, yet it was hailed at the time as a significant step forward in scholarship. Some of the more positivist schools of historical theory would lean towards claiming that knowledge arises from an accumulation over time, while antipositivist analysis would see historiography as ineluctably bound up with a particular culture and epoch. Perhaps the truth is that both perceptions are valid. There is, at least potentially, a firmer grasp of the past as each generation enters into the labors of its predecessors; and yet the angle from which each set of historians views a subject will reflect their own preoccupations. There can be progress in appreciation of the significance of religious ideas in the past so long as we remain aware that what we see is likely to be molded by the concerns of our own cultural setting.

Finally there is the problem of spirituality. Whereas each of the previous six considerations, with the partial exception of the second on reductionism, would apply broadly to many types of history, this difficulty is peculiar to the study of religious ideas. In Christianity, as in Judaism, Islam, and related forms of monotheism, believers hold that the source of their ideas about religion is ultimately revelation. Doctrines are not invented by human beings but given by God. There is, in the eyes of adherents of the monotheistic religions, a sense in which their notions fall beyond the province of the historian. Their beliefs are not merely part of the flux of thought but are infused with a spiritual dimension.

Hence the invasion by historians of sacred ground can sometimes be stoutly resisted. To suggest that beliefs have a history may be understood as an attack on their authenticity. Thus the conviction that the teaching of the church has always been the same yielded only gradually during the eighteenth and early nineteenth centuries to a recognition that dogma has developed over time.[13] The diffusion of a greater appreciation of doctrinal development, and therefore of the relativity of human dogmatic formulations, may be seen as part of the vocation of historians of religious ideas, whether believers or not. Yet there is a sense in which the defenders of spiritual religion against its historicizing have a point. Revealed religion entails a claim to a relationship with the divine, a mixture in some terms of faith and obedience. Can the historian claim to understand other people's vertical bonds with their God? It may be that this task is easier for believers than for unbelievers. A person knowing the fear of the Almighty may be in a stronger position to appreciate similar sentiments in past agents. Indeed texts that contain a great deal of the spiritual may be easier to interpret than those that do not. Twenty-first-century Christians may well feel a stronger affinity for the experiential Augustine of the *Confessions* than for the dogmatic Augustine of *Against the Donatists*. An awareness of the significance of the spiritual is not the monopoly of orthodox monotheists, but orthodox monotheism may help.

QUENTIN SKINNER AND THE STUDY OF RELIGION

The general problems that have been touched on so far have a miscellaneous character, but that is not true of the subject of the next section of this paper. A very specific contribution to the study of the history of ideas, probably the most substantial in the last generation, has been made by Quentin Skinner, the inspiration for the theme of "seeing things their way." Skinner's achievement needs to be set against the background of the Cambridge University history curriculum in the middle years of the twentieth century. The history of ideas at Cambridge concentrated on political thought alone, and the discipline bore the stamp of Ernest Barker, professor of political science from 1928 to 1939. Trained at Oxford, Barker treated political thought as the equivalent of "Greats" at the University of Oxford, combining as it did philosophy with history.[14] The central concern was with great texts, from Aristotle down to recent times, and with perennial issues such as sovereignty and consent. Students were expected to ask what the attitude of successive thinkers was to the fundamental questions of politics. Skinner, however, challenged that approach, calling for a more *historical* technique. The issues addressed by political theorists were not perennial, he argued in the 1960s, for each writer was concerned with particular problems thrown up by contemporary terms of debate. The texts, consequently, were not to be viewed in isolation, but seen in their original context. It is possible, Skinner contended, to reconstruct the intentions of political theorists by discovering the place of their utterances in the literary and social setting of their day. By comparing their discourse with that of other contributors to the same debates, the force of their statements could be decoded. Embodied in his article of 1969, "Meaning and Understanding in the History of Ideas," these views revolutionized the way in which the history of political thought was taught in Cambridge and elsewhere.[15] That they can broadly be transferred to the study of theological ideas is evidenced by Mark Noll's contribution to this volume and by his book *America's God* (2002). While repudiating any need to employ Skinnerian language, Noll contends that, as Skinner recommends, theology ought to be understood in its intellectual and (rather less) its material context.[16] The approach of Quentin Skinner has already proved to have merits in the religious sphere.

There are specific advantages accruing to the discipline of the history of religious ideas from the application of Skinnerian method. Skinner himself criticized Arthur O. Lovejoy, the father of the history of ideas in the United States, for his approach of tracing the morphology of doctrines, a practice leading to praise for anybody introducing a concept in a way that anticipated later usage.[17] Richard Muller identifies that technique as a variant of the Whig interpretation of history that was subjected to cogent criticism by Herbert Butterfield in 1931.[18] The weakness of the Whig view is that the historian selects what is important in the past from the standpoint of the concerns of the present. Skinner's approach, by contrast, examines a body of ideas in its own original context, so escaping the undue preoccupation with the interests of the historian's own time that has already been discussed as a potential pitfall. The crime of "presentism" is avoided, or at least minimized. Historians of religious ideas have frequently fallen into that trap. In this volume Jim Bradley points out that discussion of the English Enlightenment has been retarded by the sympathy for the views of the theological liberals that has often marked writers about the period.[19] Likewise Alister Chapman contends that the religious experience of modern Europe has been misinterpreted teleologically as leading irreversibly towards the secular.[20] In both cases a more just interpretation would lay greater stress on the language of contemporaries, treating people in their own terms rather than looking at them from a standpoint alien to their own. That is to appropriate the Skinnerian revolution in the history of ideas, and so to escape the snare of Whig historiography.

There are nevertheless a number of difficulties surrounding Quentin Skinner's recommendations on method. In the first place, there is the problem of the communal. Skinner equated the meaning of a text with the intentions of the author. Like J. G. A. Pocock, another influential leader in the reformulation of the history of political thought and a man with whom Skinner is often linked, the Cambridge historian urged that the linguistic stock available at a particular point shaped how theorists formulated their questions and answers. Skinner differed from Pocock, however, over the weighting of personal intentions. For Pocock, broad paradigms of thought determined the vocabulary of writers, but for Skinner the intentions of individual authors were crucial.[21] By focusing on authorial intentions, he argued, the historian could recover the original sense of a body of discourse. The problem here is that individuals frequently operate as members of groups. Theology in particular is normally a collegial exercise. Theologians commonly teach together in faculties, so that, for example, Melanchthon was a colleague of Luther and so ought not to be treated as having had aims diametrically different from those of the other Reformer. Skinner's methodological individualism, however, can lead to a downplaying of the communal dimension in the formulation of ideas. In his own work, Skinner tends to ignore shared assumptions. The general conviction of early modern political theorists, John Coffey points out in his paper, was that morality underpins political authority, that morality depends on belief in God, and so that acknowledgement of the Almighty is an essential feature of any well constructed polity. Toleration, even according to John Locke, was not to be accorded to atheists. Yet Skinner ignores the role of the fear of God as an element in political thought.[22] There should be a greater awareness of the place of communal thinking in the history of ideas than Skinner's principles encourage.

There is also the problem of coherence. Skinner urges that historians of ideas should vindicate the rationality of past thinkers. A precept of interpretation, he says, is "to exhibit the utterance in which we are interested as one that it was rational for that particular agent, in those particular circumstances, to have held to be true."[23] Consequently he holds that our reconstruction of political thought should aim to reveal its exponents as consistent writers. It is true that Skinner attacks what he calls the "myth of coherence," the supposition that every text by a given author must be congruent in its teaching with every other. Writers, he points out, need not be self-consistent throughout their oeuvre.[24] Yet the implication of the form of rationality he attributes to past thinkers is that they upheld what he calls "the importance of consistency and coherence."[25] We need to assume, for instance, that they shared with us a belief in the principle of noncontradiction, so that they did not deny one of their own propositions and suppose that they were avoiding absurdity. A problem arises here for the historian of religious ideas, especially when dealing with popular expressions of religiosity. Doctrines held by the rank and file of Christians are not necessarily thought through systematically. A Wesleyan in the eighteenth-century revival might simultaneously believe in the providential ordering of all human affairs and yet insist on the capacity of every human being to embrace salvation freely. Humble Cornish miners writing their testimonies might not have been able to recognize an apparent logical contradiction between divine and human agency, let alone to explain how they reconciled their convictions. Religious beliefs may be fragmentary rather than congruent, predominantly experiential rather than rational. It may be that the requirement of the full Skinnerian approach that statements should have coherence does not well serve the study of religion.

A further difficulty may be labelled the problem of evidence. Skinner contends that historians must scrutinize contextual material to locate a written work in its proper intellectual milieu. Thus Machiavelli's *Prince* can be understood only through examining the teaching of contemporary advice books for rulers in order to establish its similarities and differences from the canons of the genre. There is, however, an assumption here. It is a requirement of the method that there should be a body of adjacent literature to form a judgement on the purpose of a given text. In the case of Machiavelli, there is clearly sufficient evidence, but in other instances that may not be true. Texts have survived from some periods with very little context. The records of the inquisition, for example, enabled Emmanuel Le Roy Ladurie to establish the ideas of fourteenth-century Albigensian peasants in the village of Montaillou, but there are few if any equivalent caches of documentary sources.[26] There are even harder cases. Only a single fragment has survived from the presocratic philosopher Archilocus, the enigmatic remark that "the fox knows many things, but the hedgehog knows one big thing." There is no context in which to interpret the sentiment—which is why these words could be given an arbitrary meaning by Isaiah Berlin when he employed them as a useful epigraph for his study of the historical thought of Tolstoy.[27] Sometimes there is simply insufficient evidence to perform the Skinnerian method in order to elucidate the meaning of a text.

The next problem is one of delimitation. An issue that arises in relation to any given work is the question of how we know the extent of its context. In some cases the task may be relatively easy. In the instance from the previous paragraph, Machiavelli's *Prince*, the context is fairly clear: there was plainly a genre of Renaissance "how-to" books on questions of government to which the *Prince* bears a tangential relationship. In other cases, however, it can be more difficult to define the boundaries of the literature that is relevant to a particular work. Boyd Hilton's *Age of Atonement*, for example, is a wide-ranging study arguing that mainstream British evangelicals in the nineteenth century favored public policies of laissez-faire.[28] The writings of the Scottish theologian Thomas Chalmers on political economy are adduced in favor of the thesis, but works by ministers from the Highlands who followed Chalmers into the Free Church of Scotland are not. Some of them were more inclined to measures of intervention, a policy that apparently does not fit the overall schema.[29] Should they be included in the analysis? Because most of their writings were marginal to contemporary debate, Hilton very reasonably left them out, but it could be argued that they deserve a place in the explication of Chalmers's intentions. The broader problem is that, on Skinner's principles, there is no criterion for determining which works are sufficiently relevant to be analyzed alongside any book under interpretation. The decision about the parameters of what to read in order to understand a text is left surprisingly open.

A final difficulty arises over what may be called the problem of the text. Skinner insists that meaning cannot be read off from a single text in isolation. Since what is written may adopt an oblique rhetorical strategy, what is said must not be confused with what is meant. Thus Daniel Defoe, a master of biting irony, could urge the massacre of Dissenters as the shortest way of dealing with the problem of their separation from the established church, but his actual intention was to recommend toleration. Only if Defoe is read in the context of contemporary writings, so that the ironical mode becomes plain, can the force of his language be appreciated.[30] The problem that arises here is one for certain believers. The Reformation, through wanting to deny any need for ecclesiastical commentary on the Bible, insisted on the principle of the perspicuity of scripture. The Bible may contain obscurities, but on this view it is a self-interpreting document. The meaning of the text can be recovered without any knowledge of the shared conventions of its original setting. No advanced learning is called for in grasping the message of the scriptures. In principle, therefore, a text can be understood without a context. Protestants still adhering to this point of view might therefore find it hard to give their wholehearted allegiance to Skinner's method. It might be thought that the problem ought to be resolved by traditional Protestants dropping their inherited prejudice, but to them it is a matter of religious conviction, not to be surrendered lightly. There may be ways of accommodating their theological opinion to scholarly exploration of the setting in which the scriptures were written (after all, that is the procedure of much biblical scholarship amongst conservative Protestants), but it is worth noting that there is at least a certain tension between Skinnerian hermeneutics and the axiom of perspicuity. Some historians of religious ideas may face a difficulty arising from a clash between their own views and the technique adopted by Skinner.

BEYOND SKINNER

The problems of applying Skinner's approach considered so far are probably resoluble and certainly do not rule out entirely its use in the history of religious ideas, but the remaining section of this paper considers ways in which the discipline can usefully move beyond Skinner's methodological prescriptions. There is, in the first place, the problem of argument. Skinner sees the history of political thought as an account of written debates about public affairs. Wanting to break with the notion that great texts are the repositories of abiding wisdom, he is adamant that his concern is with contested notions. One of the lessons that Skinner draws in the republication of his methodological statements in 2002 is that "the battle is all there is." This principle is applicable, he holds, to all ideas and not just to those within the political sphere. "The only histories of ideas to be written," he claims, "are histories of their uses in argument."[31] A consequence is an emphasis on contentious passages, a concentration on the polemical. Other styles of exposition, however, may be equally fraught with significance. John Coffey dwells in his contribution to this volume on the importance of narrative as well as argument, not least because political theorists sometimes invoke narratives such as the Exodus account of liberation from bondage.[32] Other disciplines treat narrative as the central genre to be studied. Theology in particular has recently stressed that biblical teaching is often transmitted in narrative form, whether Israel's history in the Old Testament or Jesus's parables in the New. Likewise other religious texts do not necessarily consist of argument. While much Christian literature is indeed polemical—whether the apostle Paul's letters against errors at Corinth or Aquinas's treatises *contra Gentiles*—a great deal is not. Devotional writings, which form a large portion of the inherited texts from the Christian centuries, are a case in point. The contemplative works of Teresa of Avila, for example, call for appreciation in a different mode from that brought to the study of argumentation. The range of literature studied by the historian of religious ideas must not be conceived as subordinating its purpose to argument.

Another issue may be called the problem of privilege. Skinner, as a historian of political thought, naturally privileges the political. Although in his theoretical discussion he is also explicitly concerned with ethical, religious, and other similar modes of discourse,[33] in practice he concentrates on political topics. This preoccupation with politics in the history of ideas, which is by no means confined to Skinner, may be regarded as a curious survival. In other branches of history, the traditional dominance of the political, which persisted down to the 1960s, has been largely overturned. Social history has displaced its political equivalent as the prevailing mode of inquiry to such an extent that in nineteenth-century British studies, for example, political history is now commonly conceived as a sub-branch of the social variety. In the history of ideas, however, the history of *political* thought retains its hegemony, still being the chief branch of wider intellectual life studied at Cambridge and in many other universities as part of the history curriculum. There is criticism of this state of affairs from within the tradition. Stefan Collini, with colleagues, has demonstrated that John Stuart Mill and other thinkers usually classified as political theorists had much broader concerns, in which politics were interwoven with a variety of other interests.[34] They ought to be treated more as moralists than as "political thinkers." That perception, however, has led Collini away from the discipline of history, where he began, to that of English, where he now teaches at Cambridge. The primacy of politics in intellectual history that he calls into question can be detrimental in practice. In Skinner's own work, Coffey suggests, far too little attention is paid to the place of theological considerations in early modern texts.[35] The exclusive emphasis on politics actually affects the study of political thought adversely. The time is ripe for the central place of politics in the history of ideas to be rethought.

It may be suggested that there are grounds for proposing that the history of religious ideas should be privileged more than the history of political thought. One reason is that religion commonly generated the chief form of intellectual activity in the past. Dante was fascinated by most dimensions of life including the political, even writing a whole treatise *De Monarchia*. Yet his central intellectual preoccupations, as no reader of the final canto of the *Paradiso* can doubt, were religious. The Cambridge tripos examination has traditionally divided the study of

British history into two halves, the political and constitutional on the one hand and the economic and social on the other. It might be a fairer treatment of most periods in the past if the division were to be between the secular and the sacred. Certainly, so long as the barrier were recognized as permeable, that principle of weighting could apply to the history of ideas. If we really want to see things their way, we too should give pride of place to the religious. Another reason for reaching the same conclusion is that religion is concerned with ultimate issues. The sacred provides a sanction for other beliefs. Coronation ritual, for instance, traditionally conferred significance on kingship. Because religion supplies an overarching framework of meaning, it has normally been the ultimate court of appeal on questions of public policy as much as on matters of private behavior. Anthropologists would assume that religion is the primary ideological glue of society. Historians who engage most with anthropologists, especially historians of sub-Saharan Africa, operate with that assumption firmly in place.[36] There is good reason for those who are concerned with the history of ideas to imitate them.

There are therefore a number of problems surrounding the relationship between the history of ideas and the study of religion. Many of the issues are identical or similar to those raised by the examination of any aspect of the past. All historians face the challenge of skepticism about the availability of the past for scrutiny, the danger of subordinating their writings to personal prejudice and the charge of triviality in their interests. They all suffer from the problems of the inescapability of the present and of the risk of serious distortion of their subjects. The threat of reductionism, however, is probably more acute in the history of religious ideas than elsewhere, and in that field there is also the particular question of whether spiritual empathy is more practicable for believers than for others. Historians of religious ideas will want to learn from Quentin Skinner, recognizing in his method a remedy for a species of Whig history. Yet they will also recognize problems in the Skinnerian formula: a neglect of the communal dimension of ideas, a possible deficiency of evidence for establishing an intellectual milieu, and the absence of a criterion for delimiting the context of a text. Again there may be a particular difficulty for students of religion in assuming the rational coherence of past bodies of ideas and, for a number of them, a tension between their own convictions and the prescriptions of Skinner's method. The practitioners of the intellectual history of religion, furthermore, will wish to give full weight to such modes as narrative and devotion, not attaching disproportionate significance to the study of argument. They may well desire to question the privileging of political thought and to propose, if any subgenre is to be preferred, that the study of religious thought should be the queen of the intellectual sciences. While acknowledging their indebtedness to Skinner, they may want to go beyond him in contending that the history of ideas is supremely about religion.

NOTES

I am grateful to Alison Kennedy and Mark Nixon for their comments on this paper.

1. Barthes quoted by R. J. Evans, *In Defence of History* (London: Granta, 1997), 94.
2. Keith Jenkins, *Re-Thinking History* (London: Routledge, 2003).
3. Brad Gregory, "Can We 'See Things Their Way'? Should We Try?" chap. 2, this volume.
4. See for example Christopher Hill, *Puritanism and Revolution: Studies in the Interpretation of the English Revolution of the Seventeenth Century* (London: Secker & Warburg, 1958).
5. Anna Sapir Abulafia, "'Sie stinken biede,' or How to Use Medieval Christian-Jewish Disputational Material," chap. 4, this volume.
6. Quentin Skinner, *Visions of Politics,* vol. 1, *Regarding Method* (Cambridge: Cambridge University Press, 2002), 77–78, vii.
7. Howard Hotson, "Anti-Semitism, Philo-Semitism, Apocalypticism, and Millenarianism in Early Modern Europe: A Case Study and Some Methodological Reflections," chap. 5, this volume.
8. Richard Muller, "Reflections on Persistent Whiggism and Its Antidotes in the Study of Sixteenth- and Seventeenth-century Intellectual History," chap. 6, this volume.
9. Gregory, "Can We 'See Things Their Way'?"
10. Willem van Asselt, "Scholasticism Revisited: Methodological Reflections on the Study of Seventeenth-century Reformed Thought," chap. 7, this volume.
11. Hotson, "Anti-Semitism."

12. Muller, "Reflections."

13. W. O. Chadwick, *From Bossuet to Newman: The Idea of Doctrinal Development* (Cambridge: Cambridge University Press, 1957).

14. Sir Ernest Barker, *Age and Youth* (Oxford: Oxford University Press, 1953), 159, 162.

15. Quentin Skinner, "Meaning and Understanding in the History of Ideas," *History and Theory* 8, no. 1 (1969): 3–53. A revised version of the article is printed as chap. 4 in Skinner, *Visions of Politics*, vol. 1.

16. Mark Noll, "British Methodological Pointers for Writing a History of Theology in America," chap. 9, this volume.

17. Skinner, *Visions of Politics*, vol. 1, 62–63.

18. Muller, "Reflections"; Herbert Butterfield, *The Whig Interpretation of History* (London: G. Bell, 1931).

19. James Bradley, "The Changing Shape of Religious Ideas in Enlightened England," chap. 8, this volume.

20. Alister Chapman, "Intellectual History and Religion in Modern Britain," chap. 10, this volume.

21. The contrast between Pocock and Skinner is helpfully drawn out in the critical appraisal by Mark Bevir, "The Errors of Linguistic Contextualism," *History and Theory* 31, no. 3 (1992): 276–98. Bevir's book *The Logic of the History of Ideas* (Cambridge: Cambridge University Press, 1999) is a stimulating critique of the two theorists to which the present analysis is indebted.

22. John Coffey, "Quentin Skinner and the Religious Dimension of Early Modern Political Thought," chap. 3, this volume.

23. Skinner, *Visions of Politics*, vol. 1, 42.

24. Ibid., 67–72.

25. Ibid., 54.

26. Emmanuel Le Roy Ladurie, *Montaillou: Catholics and Cathars in a French Village, 1294–1324* (London: Scolar Press, 1978).

27. Isaiah Berlin, *The Hedgehog and the Fox: An Essay on Tolstoy's View of History* (London: Weidenfeld & Nicolson, 1953).

28. Boyd Hilton, *The Age of Atonement: The Influence of Evangelicalism on Economic and Social Thought, 1785–1865* (Oxford: Clarendon, 1988).

29. Allan W. MacColl, *Land, Faith and the Crofting Community: Christianity and Social Criticism in the Highlands of Scotland, 1843–1893* (Edinburgh: Edinburgh University Press, 2006).

30. Skinner, *Visions of Politics*, vol. 1, 80.

31. Ibid., 7, 86.

32. Coffey, "Quentin Skinner and the Religious Dimension."

33. Skinner, *Visions of Politics*, vol. 1, 59.

34. Stefan Collini et al., *That Noble Science of Politics: A Study in Nineteenth-Century Intellectual History* (Cambridge: Cambridge University Press, 1983); Stefan Collini, *Public Moralists: Political Thought and Intellectual Life in Britain* (Oxford: Clarendon, 1991).

35. Coffey, "Quentin Skinner and the Religious Dimension."

36. For example, J. D. Y. Peel, *Religious Encounter and the Making of the Yoruba* (Bloomington: Indiana University Press, 2000).

Contributors

ANNA SAPIR ABULAFIA is vice president and college lecturer in history at Lucy Cavendish College, University of Cambridge. She is the author of *Christians and Jews in the Twelfth-Century Renaissance* (Routledge, 1995) and *Christians and Jews in Dispute: Disputational Literature and the Rise of Anti-Judaism in the West, c.1000–1150* (Variorum, 1998), and has edited *Religious Violence between Christians and Jews: Medieval Roots, Modern Perspectives* (Palgrave, 2002).

WILLEM J. VAN ASSELT is associate professor of church history in the department of theology, Utrecht University, and professor of historical theology at the Evangelical Theological Faculty, Louvain. His publications include *The Federal Theology of Johannes Cocceius (1603–1669)* (Brill, 2001), and he coedited *Reformation and Scholasticism: An Ecumenical Enterprise* (Baker Academic, 2001) with Eef Dekker.

DAVID W. BEBBINGTON is professor of history at the University of Stirling. His recent publications include *The Mind of Gladstone: Religion, Homer and Politics* (Oxford University Press, 2004) and *The Dominance of Evangelicalism: The Age of Spurgeon and Moody* (InterVarsity Press, 2005).

JAMES E. BRADLEY is the Geoffrey W. Bromiley Professor of Church History at Fuller Seminary. His publications include "Toleration and Movements of Christian Reunion, 1660–1789," in *The Cambridge History of Christianity*, volume 7 (Cambridge University Press, 2006), and *Religion and Politics in Enlightenment Europe*, coedited with Dale Van Kley (University of Notre Dame Press, 2001).

ALISTER CHAPMAN is assistant professor of history at Westmont College. His publications include "Secularisation and the Ministry of John R. W. Stott at All Souls, Langham Place, 1950-1970," *The Journal of Ecclesiastical History* 56, no. 3 (2005): 496-513, and a forthcoming book on John Stott.

JOHN COFFEY is professor of early modern history at the University of Leicester. He is the author of three books, including *John Goodwin and the Puritan Revolution: Religion and Intellectual Change in Seventeenth-Century England* (Boydell, 2006), and has coedited *The Cambridge Companion to Puritanism* (Cambridge University Press, 2008) with Paul C. H. Lim.

BRAD S. GREGORY is the Dorothy G. Griffin Associate Professor of Early Modern European History at the University of Notre Dame. He is the author of *Salvation at Stake: Christian Martyrdom in Early Modern Europe* (Harvard University Press, 1999) and the editor of *The Forgotten Writings of the Mennonite Martyrs* (E. J. Brill, 2002).

HOWARD HOTSON is professor of early modern intellectual history at Oxford University and a fellow of St Anne's College, Oxford. His publications include *Johann Heinrich Alsted (1588-1638): Between Renaissance, Reformation and Universal Reform* (Oxford University Press, 2000) and *Commonplace Learning: Ramism and its German Ramifications, 1543-1630* (Oxford University Press, 2007).

RICHARD A. MULLER is the P. J. Zondervan Professor of Historical Theology at Calvin Theological Seminary. His publications include *The Unaccommodated Calvin* (Oxford University Press, 2000), *After Calvin: Studies in the Development of a Theological Tradition* (Oxford University Press, 2003), and *Post-Reformation Reformed Dogmatics* (4 vols., Baker Academic, 2003).

MARK A. NOLL is the Francis A. McAnaney Professor of History at the University of Notre Dame. His recent publications include *The Civil War as a Theological Crisis* (University of North Carolina Press, 2006) and *God and Race in American Politics: A Short History* (Princeton University Press, 2008).

Index

Abelard, Peter, 83
Act of Toleration (1689), 185, 193
Addison, Joseph, 179
Agricola, Rudolph, 163
Alcázar, Luis de, 103
Alfonsi, Peter, 84
Alsted, Johann Heinrich, 105–10, 114, 120, 139, 148–49
Altenstaig, Johannes, 166
Althusius, Johannes, 52
Ames, William, 164
Amyraut, Moise, 113
Anabaptists, 25, 41
Anglicanism, 180–81, 182, 183, 184, 191, 192, 197n.31
Anselm of Canterbury, 77, 78–80, 87
anthropology, 6, 254
Antichrist, 96–105
  as a Jew, 96–98, 101–4
  as Pope, 98–100
Antiochus Epiphanes, 97
antiquarianism, 39–40
anti-Semitism, 13, 83, 86, 87, 93–122
apocalypticism, 91–122
Aquinas, Thomas, 145, 146, 166
Archilocus, 250
Arianism, 176, 182, 183, 184–85, 187
Ariew, Roger, 139
Aristotle, 43n.2, 163, 166
Arminianism, 160–61, 188

Arminius, Jacobus, 145
Arnold, Gottfried, 243
Attlee, Clement, 226
Augustine, 84, 103–5, 107, 125n.11, 145, 177, 179, 246
Austin, J. L., 2, 232

Bacon, Francis, 140
Bailyn, Bernard, 212
Baius, Michael, 145
Bañez, Domingo, 145
Baptists, 185, 187, 192
Barker, Ernest, 246
Barrow, Isaac, 177
Barth, Karl, 14
Barthes, Roland, 16, 241
Batalerius, Jacobus, 103
Baxter, Richard, 164
Bayly, Chris, 9
Bebbington, David, 180, 214
Bellarmine, Robert Cardinal, 102, 145, 160, 161, 165, 171n.14
ben Israel, Menasseh, 114
Berger, Peter, 6
Berlin, Isaiah, 55–56, 250
Berrington, Joseph, 181
Besold, Christoph, 108–10, 111, 120
Black, Jeremy, 181
Blackburne, Francis, 178, 184
Blair, Tony, 226

Blasphemy Act (1698), 187
Bradwardine, Thomas, 145
Brantley, Richard, 180
Bremen, 164
Brett, Annabel, 234
Brocardo, Jacopo, 108–10, 120
Brown, Callum, 227, 229, 233–34
Bruce, Steve, 228
Bucer, Martin, 164
Buchanan, George, 50, 52, 53
Bullinger, Heinrich, 138, 141, 147, 164
Bunyan, John, 17, 149
Burckhardt, Jacob, 162
Burgersdijk, Franco, 139, 148
Burgess, Cornelius, 60
Burnet, Gilbert, 177
Burton, Henry, 65
Burton, William, 108–9
Butterfield, Sir Herbert, 135–36, 247

Calamy, Edmund, 61, 186
Calvin, John, 14, 135, 137–38, 141, 143, 147, 155, 159
    relationship to Calvinism, 138–39, 163–65
Calvinism, 52, 147, 188, 216
    and millenarianism, 109
Cambridge, University of, 47, 176, 178, 246, 253
Canada, 216–17
Cano, Melchior, 165
Cellarius, Martinus, 111
Cerinthus, 107
Chadwick, Owen, 230
Chalcedon, Council of, 221–22
Chalmers, Thomas, 213–14, 250
Chamberlain, Jeffrey, 177
Champion, Justin, 178
Chapin, Chester, 179
Charles I, 55, 58, 66, 103
Christian-Jewish disputations, 76–87
Clark, J. C. D., 182–83, 197nn.31–32
Clark, Stuart, 49

Clarke, Samuel, 178, 184
Cohn, Norman, 92–93, 116, 118, 119
Collingwood, R. G., 29, 155, 233
Collini, Stefan, 253
Comenius, Jan Amos, 114
common sense philosophy, 206–8
confessional history, 14–15, 145–46, 243
Congregationalists, 185, 187, 206
Cornish, Joseph, 187–88
Cowling, Maurice, 229
Cox, Jeffrey, 227
Cragg, G. R., 176
Crispin, Gilbert, 77, 78–79, 82–83, 84
Cromwell, Oliver, 62, 66
Crouzet, Denis, 7
Cunaeus, Petrus, 111

D'Ailly, Pierre, 166
Daneau, Lambert, 146–47
Dante, Alighieri, 253
Darwin, Charles, 10
Davie, Donald, 179
Davie, Grace, 229
Davis, Natalie, 7
Defoe, Daniel, 179
Deism, 176, 178, 195n.5
Dekker, Eef, 165
de Reijk, L. M., 157–58
De Roore, Jacob, 24–43
    biography, 25–26
Derrida, Jacques, 16, 233
Descartes, René, 137, 139, 147
Devereux, Robert, 61
dictionaries, 136, 138, 166
Diderot, Denis, 8
Dissenters. *See* Nonconformists
Ditchfield, Grayson, 184
Dobricius, Johannes, 111
Doddridge, Philip, 179
Dominicans, 160
Dreyer, Frederick, 180
Dunn, John, 1, 7, 54, 70n.29

Durandus of Sancto Porciano, 146–47
Durkheim, Emile, 3, 11, 12, 26, 31, 32, 43n.6, 231, 238n.27

Edict of Nantes, 112
Edinburgh, 181
Edward VI, 60
Edwards, Jonathan, 206, 208
Eire, Carlos, 52–53
Elizabeth I, 60
Emerson, Roger, 177
England, 93–94, 148, 149
    Civil War, explanations of, 55–68
Enlightenment, 8–9, 11, 175–94, 192, 194n.1, 198n.32
    religious nature of, 179–81
Eössi, Andreas, 118
evangelicals, 179, 212–14, 216–17
Exodus, 64–67

Fairfax, Sir Thomas, 61
Felgenhauer, Paul, 111
Fell, John, 188
Fermo, Seraphino da, 111
Ferus, Johannes, 111
Feuerbach, Ludwig, 11, 26
Fielding, Henry, 179
Figgis, J. N., 50
Finney, Charles, 219
Fisher, Jack, 53–54
Fleming, Caleb, 188
Force, James, 178
Foucault, Michel, 233
Fowler, Edward, 177
France, 112, 162
Freemasons, 195n.5
French Revolution, 181
Freud, Sigmund, 11, 26

Gadamer, Hans-Georg, 38
Galilei, Galileo, 140
Gardiner, S. R., 57
Gascoigne, John, 175, 178

Gay, Peter, 8
Geertz, Clifford, 6, 31
Georgian literature, 178
Germany, 148, 162
Gibbons, Thomas, 193
Ginzburg, Carlo, 17
Glanvill, Joseph, 177
Goldie, Mark, 8, 50, 54
Goldsmith, Oliver, 179
Goodwin, Thomas, 62–64
Gordon, John, 197n.31
Gottschalk of Orbais, 145
Goudriaan, Aza, 165
Gray, John, 10
Great Britain, 226–36, 243
Green, Simon, 227, 228
Greene, Donald, 179
Gregory of Rimini, 145, 166
Griffin Jr., Martin, 177
Grimley, Matthew, 230
Grotius, Hugo, 103
Guelzo, Allen, 216
Guerrini, Anita, 181

Hall, Basil, 163
Hall, Robert, 179, 193
Hammond, Henry, 103
Hardenburg, Albert, 139
Harlan, David, 16
Hartlib, Samuel, 114
Hatch, Nathan, 212
Hebraic Political Studies, 54–55
Heereboord, Adrianus, 139
Heidegger, Johann, 164
Heidelberg, 118
Heine, Heinrich, 75–76
Helmstedt, University of, 103–4
Henry of Ghent, 166
Herborn Academy, 164
heterodoxy, 187, 190, 194
    link to political radicalism, 181–83
Hey, John, 178
Hill, Christopher, 57, 67, 242

Hilton, Boyd, 212–14, 217, 236, 250
Hitchin, Edward, 188
Hoadly, Benjamin, 178, 186, 188, 200n.49
Hobbes, Thomas, 8, 49, 51, 54–55, 58
Hobsbawm, Eric, 6
Hole, Robert, 181
Holland, 94
Holocaust, 92
Hoppen, Theodore, 9
Horne, George, 197n.31
Horsley, Samuel, 180–81
Hotson, Howard, 148–49
Howe, Daniel Walker, 214–16
Huguenot, 53, 112–13, 114
humanism, relationship to scholasticism, 162–63
Hume, David, 183, 232
Hus, Jan, 141
hymns, 85
Hyperius, Andreas, 138

incarnation of Jesus Christ
   in Christian disputes with Jews, 78–80
   implications for history, 220–22
Ireland, 214
Islam, 10, 226, 236, 245
Israel, Jonathan, 8

Jansen, Cornelius, 145
Jansenists, 145
Jenkins, Joseph, 191
Jenkins, Keith, 241
Jessey, Henry, 110–12, 114
Jesuits, 160
Joachim of Fiore, 80–81, 84
John Paul II, 6
Johnson, Paul, 219
Johnson, Samuel, 179
Jones, William, 197n.31
Journal of the History of Ideas, 4

Judaism, 76–87, 245
Jurieu, Pierre, 112–13
Justin Martyr, 244

Kant, Immanuel, 244
Keckermann, Bartholomäus, 139
Kidd, Colin, 198n.37
Kimhi, Joseph, 80
Kippis, Andrew, 185–86
Kristeller, Paul Oskar, 155, 162
Kuhn, Thomas, 223n.9

Labadie, Jean de, 112
LaCapra, Dominick, 16
Ladurie, Emmanuel Le Roy, 250
Langmuir, Gavin, 12, 85–87, 242
La Peyrère, Isaac, 114, 118
Lapide, Cornelius à, 101
Lasco, John, 164
Laski, Jan, 138
Latitudinarians, 176–78, 183
Laud, William, 103
Le Clerc, Jean, 103
Leibniz, Wilhelm, 103
Levellers, 65–66
liberty, 48, 52, 55–56, 62–65, 67, 182, 187–88, 193, 212
Lincoln, Abraham, 216
local history, 189–90, 194
Locke, John, 7, 9, 52, 54, 66, 175, 180, 186, 188, 200n.49
Lombard, Peter, 144
Lovejoy, Arthur, 2, 13, 247
Low Countries, 25–26, 148
Luther, Martin, 14–15, 99, 100, 101, 135, 154, 159, 248
Lutheran historiography, 14–15

Machiavelli, Nicoló, 49, 51, 249–50
Maimonides, Moses, 103
Malcolm, Noel, 54
Malvenda, Tomaso, 101, 102

Marshall, Paul, 52–53
Marshall, Stephen, 60–61
Marx, Karl, 3, 10, 11, 26, 31
Marxism, 218, 242
Mather, F. C., 180
May, Henry F., 5
McAdoo, H. R., 177
McLaren, Anne, 53
McLeod, Hugh, 227, 228
Mede, Joseph, 109, 111, 120
Melanchthon, Philipp, 15, 23n.41, 99, 139, 163, 248
Mennnonites, 25
Methodism, 217
Mill, John Stuart, 253
millenarianism, 119
    definitions, 104–5
    Norman Cohn's interpretation of, 92–94
    and philo-Semitism, 106–18, 119–22
Miller, Perry, 5
Milton, John, 63
Molina, Tirso de, 145, 165
Montaigne, Michel de, 140
More, Sir Thomas, 51
Morgan, Edmund S., 211–12
Morrill, John, 57, 59
Morris, Jeremy, 227, 228
Muller, Richard, 156, 157–58, 159
Murray, Iain, 219
Murrin, John, 212
Musculus, Wolfgang, 138, 145, 147

Nazism, 92
Newton, Sir Isaac, 9, 175, 178, 180
Nietzsche, 241
Noll, Mark, 55
Nonconformists, 175, 179, 184–94
    legal prosecutions, 191–93
    ordination of Dissenting ministers, 191

Oberman, Heiko, 142–43, 156, 159, 164
Occam's Razor, 35
Odo de Cambrai, 79–80, 84
Outram, Dorinda, 8
Owen, John, 164, 166
Oxford, 181

Paine, Thomas, 10
Paley, William, 178
Parker, Henry, 57–59
Pascal, Blaise, 145
Patrick, Simon, 177
Pattison, Mark, 211
Péchi, Simon, 118
Peirce, James, 184
Pelagians, 145
periodization, 141
Peter of Blois, 83, 84
Peter the Venerable, 83, 84
Pettit, Philip, 55
Pfizenmaier, Thomas, 178
philo-Semitism, 13, 94–122, 123n.7
Pietism, 15, 113
Pitcairne, Gregory, 181
Platonism, 176
Pocock, J. G. A., 1, 7, 46, 54, 175, 182–83, 204–11, 218–19, 248
Poland, 148
Pole, Reginald, 100
Popkin, Richard, 94
Porter, Roy, 181
Powell, William, 185
Powicke, F. J., 185
Presbyterians, 63, 185, 187
Price, Richard, 182
Priestley, Joseph, 115–16, 182
Protestantism, 159–60, 243
Protestant scholasticism, 141, 154–69
    definition, 158–59
Protocols of the Elders of Zion, 92, 98

Puritanism, 149, 206, 208, 242
    and the origins of English Civil
        War, 59–68
Pyrrhonism, 241

Quakers, 193

Rabelais, François, 140
race, 212
Raemond, Florimond de, 101
reductionism, 11–16, 31–35, 42,
    44n.12, 228–29, 242
Reedy, Gerard, 177
Reformation, 134–36, 154
Reformed scholasticism. *See*
    Protestant scholasticism
Renaissance, 146
Renkewitz, Heinz, 115
republicanism, 54–55, 66, 206–8
rhetoric, 142, 148
Richardson, Samuel, 179
Rivers, Isabel, 177
Roman Catholicism, 143, 145–46, 157,
    159–61, 180–81, 217, 243
Royal Society, 175
Rummel, Erika, 163
Rupp, Gordon, 177
Russell, Conrad, 58, 93

Sanneh, Lamin, 220–21
Saumur, 164
Saussure, Ferdinand de, 241
Schilling, Heinz, 168
Schneider, Hans, 115
Schoeps, Hans Joachim, 94, 111
scholasticism, 137, 144, 146, 154–55
    definition, 157–58
    during Reformation era, 163
Scholtz, Gregory, 179
Scotland, 94, 149, 206, 232
Scott, Jonathan, 55
Scotus, Duns, 157

Searle, John, 232
secularization, 3, 9, 10, 176, 189, 194
    theory of, 227–30
Semmel, Bernard, 180
Serrarius, Petrus, 111–12
Seymour, Sir Francis, 61
Sheehan, Jonathan, 55
Skepticism, 28–31, 241
Skinner, Quentin, 1–3, 11, 16, 20n.6,
    24–25, 46–68, 168, 219–20, 242,
    246–51, 252, 253
    career, 46–47
    *Foundations of Modern Political
        Thought* (1978), 3, 50, 69n.14
    historical method, 2, 16, 136–37,
        149–50, 155–56, 203–4, 231–34,
        245–51
    and the origins of the English
        Civil War, 55–67
Smith, Mark, 200n.50, 227, 228
Smart, Christopher, 179
Socinianism, 160–61, 176, 182, 183,
    185, 187, 188
sola scriptura, 159
speech-act theory, 2
Spellman, William, 177–78
Spener, Philipp Jakob, 113
Spinoza, Benedict, 8
spirituality, 245
Spurr, John, 177
Steele, Sir Richard, 179
Steinmetz, David, 156, 164
Stennett, Samuel, 187, 188
Stephen, Leslie, 176, 179, 181, 183
Stephens, John, 184
Sterne, Lawrence, 179
Stillingfleet, Edward, 177
Strasburg, Thomas of, 166
Strauss, Leo, 2, 13, 218, 231
Stubbe, Henry, 67
Suárez, Francisco, 101, 102, 139,
    147–48, 165

subscription controversy in England, 184–94
Sumner, John Bird, 213
Swift, Jonathan, 179
Switzerland, 148
Symmons, Edward, 61

Talmud, 83
Taylor, Charles, 48–49, 228
Taylor, Nathaniel W., 205–9
Tennison, Thomas, 177
Teresa of Avila, 252
Thirty-nine Articles, 188
Thomas, Keith, 5, 6, 57–59
Thompson, E. P., 6, 11, 37
Tillotson, John, 177
Timpler, Clemens, 139
toleration, 182, 189
Toulmin, Joshua, 188
Transylvania, 94, 118
Trent, Council of, 143, 145, 146, 160
Trueman, Carl, 156
Tuck, Richard, 8, 54
Turretin, Francis, 164, 166

Unitarianism, 116, 117, 176, 182, 183, 187, 193
Urdank, Albion, 200n.50
Utrecht, 164

Valla, Lorenzo, 163
Van den Berg, Johannes, 94
Van der Wall, Ernestine, 111
Van Die, Marguerite, 216–17
Vehe-Glirius, Matthias, 118
Verbeek, Theo, 139
Vermigli, Peter, 138, 145, 147, 164
Vidler, Alec, 236
Viret, Pierre, 138

Voetius, Gisbert, 166
Voltaire, 9
von der Hardt, Hermann, 103–4
von Hochenau, Ernst Christoph Hochmann, 114
von Lützemberg, Dionysius, 103
von Rosenroth, Christian Knorr, 113
von Zinzendorf, Nicolaus Ludwig, 114
Vos, Antonie, 156–57

Wacker, Grant, 224n.11
Waldenses, 141
Walls, Andrew, 220
Walter of Châtillon, 85
Walwyn, William 65
Walzer, Michael, 50, 60, 67
Warburton, William, 183
Ward, W. R., 180
Waterland, Daniel, 183
Waterman, Anthony, 178
Watson, Thomas, 178
Watts, Isaac, 179
Weber, Max, 3, 26, 193
Wesley, John, 180
Whichcote, Benjamin, 177
Whig interpretation of history, 135, 139, 247–48
Whigs, American, 215–16
Wilberforce, William, 213
Wilkins, John, 177
Williams, Sarah, 227
Wilton, Samuel, 191, 199n.41
Wooten, David, 52–53
Wuthnow, Robert, 209–10
Wyclif, John, 141

Yale University, 205
Young, Brian, 178, 179, 183

www.ingramcontent.com/pod-product-compliance
Lightning Source LLC
Chambersburg PA
CBHW070236240426
43673CB00044B/1808